Process-Centric Architecture for Enterprise Software Systems

Infosys® Press

In an initiative to promote authorship across the globe, Infosys Press and CRC Press have entered into a collaboration to develop titles on leading edge topics in IT.

Infosys Press seeks to develop and publish a series of pragmatic books on software engineering and information technologies, both current and emerging. Leveraging Infosys' extensive global experience helping clients to implement those technologies successfully, each book contains critical lessons learned and shows how to apply them in a real-world, enterprise setting. This open-ended and broad-ranging series aims to brings readers practical insight, specific guidance, and unique, informative examples not readily available elsewhere.

PUBLISHED IN THE SERIES

Process-Centric Architecture for Enterprise Software Systems
Parameswaran Seshan

IN PREPARATION FOR THE SERIES

Scrum Software Development
Jagdish Bhandarkar and J. Srinivas

Software Vulnerabilities Exposed
Sanjay Rawat, Ashutosh Saxena, and Ponnapalli K B Hari Gopal

Web-Based Outsourcing
Vivek Sharma, Rajasekaran K.S., and Varun Sharma

Process-Centric Architecture for Enterprise Software Systems

Parameswaran Seshan

Infosys® Press

CRC Press is an imprint of the
Taylor & Francis Group, an **informa** business
AN AUERBACH BOOK

CRC Press
Taylor & Francis Group
6000 Broken Sound Parkway NW, Suite 300
Boca Raton, FL 33487-2742

First issued in paperback 2018

ISBN-13: 978-1-4398-1628-8 (hbk)
ISBN-13: 978-1-138-37421-8 (pbk)

Library of Congress Cataloging-in-Publication Data

Seshan, Parameswaran.
Process-centric architecture for enterprise software systems / Parameswaran Seshan.
p. cm. -- (Infosys Press)
Includes bibliographical references and index.
ISBN 978-1-4398-1628-8 (alk. paper)
1. Computer architecture. 2. Information technology--Management. I. Title. II. Series.

QA76.9.A73S45176 2010
004.2'2--dc22 2010001082

Visit the Taylor & Francis Web site at
http://www.taylorandfrancis.com

and the CRC Press Web site at
http://www.crcpress.com

To my lovely children, Bhavya and Vivek, who are giving me abundant joy in my life

Contents

Preface

Information technology systems in enterprises are in the midst of an evolution that impacts both business and technology. Business process management (BPM) is increasingly getting adopted in enterprises the world over; software architects (and programmers) are starting to leverage BPM-based software systems, and process-centric architectures (PCA) are becoming more popular in the field. PCA is an emerging trend in architecting enterprise systems.

This book is written with cognizance of the need of the technical and business personnel to obtain a good understanding of the importance and the concept of process-centric architecture in the context of IT systems in enterprises. Since it is an emerging trend in an evolving field, architects and programmers need to learn to architect their applications and systems based on process-centric architectures. This book will provide readers with a solid foundation on PCA concepts, and help them in their specific situations to architect and design their own IT systems and applications based on this architectural style. It also introduces readers to an IT system architectural style and approach that is centered on the business processes of the enterprise.

This book is primarily a product of my experience that includes

- Research in the BPM area, especially in BPM systems (BPMSs)
- Architecting and developing a BPMS from ground up
- Architecting and implementing IT systems and applications based on this architecture concept

Apart from my experience, I have also benefited from the time spent in the library reading various books in related areas. Each of the books has provided a different perspective, making the resultant picture more comprehensive. Much of the insights that I have been able to derive and the learning that I have obtained from my experience as well as reading have gone into this book.

The book, in brief, introduces and explains the concept of PCA, which is an architectural style and approach for designing the architecture of IT systems in an enterprise, where the architecture is centered on the business processes of the enterprise. It also lays down principles and describes techniques involved in architecting enterprise systems based on PCA. It shows how to design such an IT system architecture by referring to a practical case study and by using examples.

The highlights of this book are

- Concepts of process-centric architectural style
- PCA approach to architecting enterprise IT systems
- Business process–driven applications and integration
- Services-oriented architecture in the context of process-centric architecture
- Standards, technologies, and infrastructure behind PCA
- Case study showing how to architect and design an enterprise application based on PCA

The book is divided into two parts. Part I (Chapters 1 through 7) provides a conceptual understanding of PCA. Part II (Chapters 8 through 12) focuses on how to architect enterprise IT systems based on this approach. In this part, case studies and examples are provided to explain the approach.

The book is primarily meant for

- Software architects
- Enterprise architects
- IT architects
- IT programmers
- BS/BE/ME/MS computer science/IT students
- IT managers with a focus on technology
- Faculty who teach software architecture as a course in academic institutions and internal trainers at corporate houses
- Solution architects with a focus on new technologies

Even though this book is technically oriented, it will be useful for business managers and business analysts, who will benefit most from the first four chapters. All product names and trademarks owned by the respective owners are acknowledged.

Acknowledgments

My heartfelt thanks go to Subrahmanya S.V. (Infosys Technologies Ltd.) for motivating me to write this book and for the encouragement, support, and guidance he provided in this effort—this book would not have been possible without him.

I would like to express my gratitude to a number of people who have been helpful in bringing this book to life. I am indebted to my family—my wife Uma, my lovely children Bhavya and Vivek, and my parents Sesha Iyer and Raji (aka Subbalakshmi)—for standing by me and supporting me through the writing of this book. Their encouragement and endurance saw me through this book. Uma, Bhavya, and Vivek were patient with the long hours, which were rightfully their time, that I spent away from them on the computer and the late nights toiling away with book writing. This long project has been hard on them. I sincerely thank them for their sacrifice.

I thank Dr. V.P. Kochikar (Infosys Technologies Ltd.) for being kind enough to review the manuscript and for providing valuable comments. I am grateful to N.S. Nagaraja (former employee, Infosys Technologies Ltd.) for initiating me into the world of BPM, for giving me an opportunity to architect and build a BPMS, and for giving me the freedom to pursue research in the area. The learning from these experiences has been immensely helpful. I am thankful to Srinivas Thonse (former employee, Infosys Technologies Ltd.) for the discussions on research perspectives in BPM and for the advice provided on BPM-related work. I express my thanks to Khushnood Naqvi (former employee, Infosys Technologies Ltd.) for the stimulating discussions we have had on process execution infrastructure, on BPMS, and on programming in general. I would like to thank Siva K.R. (former employee, Infosys Technologies Ltd.) for giving me an opportunity to implement BPMS in banking application products. My thanks also to Sachindran K. (Infosys Technologies Ltd.) for presenting me with real-life business process implementation issues, which kept prodding me to think deeply about BPMS architectures.

I would like to express my gratitude to Paul Harmon (Business Process Trends) for his insightful and balanced views on BPM (available at the BPTrends Web site, http://www.bptrends.com). Reading his publications has helped me take a realistic view with respect to BPM. I thank Howard Smith and Peter Fingar for their powerful book on BPM, which convinced me and made me visualize the power of process-thinking and the BPM philosophy for software systems for enterprises.

I am thankful to Christian Stefansen (PhD, University of Copenhagen, Denmark), a wonderful researcher, for his views, thoughts, and inputs that triggered my deep thinking into workflows and expressiveness of languages in the context of workflows. I thank Sriram Rajamani (Microsoft Research) for the valuable research mindset and the research rigor that he helped bring into the workflow research we were pursuing together.

I thank Vishwanath Shenoy (Infosys Technologies Ltd.) for the discussions centered on business process requirements while we were working together on the development of a solutions-workbench tool. I thank Dr. T.S. Mohan (Infosys Technologies Ltd.) for providing useful comments on my work in this area. I would like to thank all my colleagues in the E-Comm Research Labs at Infosys Technologies Ltd. for their valuable help during the writing of the book.

I would like to express my gratitude to Pradeep Kumar (American President Lines Ltd., Oakland, California [APL Ltd.]) and Kathy Dimitruck (also from APL Ltd.) for giving me the freedom to explore different technologies and for allowing my relentless technical pursuits during my days at APL. I thank Giora Panigel and K. Ramesh Babu of APL for the stimulating technical discussions related to distributed computing and IT architecture while I was at APL.

Thanks to Mohandas Pai and Srikantan Moorthy of Infosys Technologies Ltd. for the encouragement and support of this initiative. At Taylor & Francis, John Wyzalek, Deepa Jagdish, Amy Blalock, Joette Lynch, Vedavalli Karunagaran and team have helped make this book happen. I am grateful to them for all the help and support provided, and for their patience.

Parameswaran Seshan

Author

Parameswaran Seshan works as a principal (education and research) with Infosys Technologies Ltd., Bangalore, India. At Infosys, he is part of E-Comm Research Labs. He has more than 14 years of experience in the information technology (IT) industry as a researcher, educator, architect, and programmer. Before joining Infosys in 2001, he worked as an advisory systems analyst with American President Lines Ltd. (APL), Oakland, California. He has also worked as a software engineer with Case Consult (I) Pvt. Ltd., Thiruvananthapuram, India. His work in the IT industry has involved research, teaching, programming, architecture, and design. He received his BTech in computer science and engineering from the University of Calicut, India, in 1995.

At Infosys, Parameswaran has been conducting research in the area of process-centric architecture, business process management (BPM), software architecture, and new computing models/paradigms. He has also been teaching architecture and high-end technology courses there. He was the lead architect for the home-grown business process management system (BPMS) from Infosys and was also actively involved in its design and development. He has architected, designed, programmed, and supported a number of IT systems over the course of his career as a software professional.

Parameswaran is an active researcher. He has published papers at international conferences and other forums. He has worked on research projects in collaboration with Microsoft Research, India, and with researchers from the University of Copenhagen and the University of Melbourne in the areas of BPM and agent-oriented software engineering.

Parameswaran has designed, developed, and supported IT systems involving various technologies at APL, and has programmed system tools to automate operations. He has also led a team in software development and support projects at APL, and has programmed system tools based on REXX to automate the conversion of programs from one programming environment to another at Case Consult.

Parameswaran's areas of research include software architecture, process-centric architecture, new computing models, intelligent software agents, and intelligent systems.

THE PROCESS-CENTRIC ARCHITECTURE PARADIGM

I

Chapter 1

Introduction

1.1 Objectives

- To get an overview of IT system architecture
- To understand what business processes are, at a high level

1.2 Enterprise Software Systems

Enterprise software systems are software-intensive systems in an enterprise. They support business functionalities for the enterprise by performing business functions, and their scope is wider than a specific business function. They are also called information technology (IT) systems in the enterprise. We will be using these two terms (IT systems and enterprise software systems) interchangeably throughout the book and they should be taken to mean the same. These systems can be in-house developed ones or packaged software. The word enterprise as used here is regardless of the size of the enterprise—the word applies equally to small, medium, and large organizations.

An IT system comprises of applications, system software (including middleware), data, and hardware. Examples of IT systems in enterprises include transaction processing systems, supply chain management systems, manufacturing support systems, management information systems, customer relationship management systems, customer information management, billing, finance systems (or accounting systems), core banking systems, human resources (HR) management systems, trading systems, office systems, decision support systems, online shopping, enterprise resource planning systems, online payment processing, and knowledge management systems. The term "IT system" has a bigger scope than the term "application"—using the term we take a full system view of specific software such as a customer relationship system.

An IT system may comprise more than one application in its scope. Applications are software that support a specific business work or a user of the software. They refer to the usage of computer by users and the use of computer for various needs of the enterprise. Applications provide business functionality and their focus is only on making use of the capabilities of the computer to perform a function for users. Examples are travel expense management, IT helpdesk, word processors, web browsers, etc. Applications are written on top of system software.

Data refers to all the business data associated with the various business functions performed by the applications. Data is a separate entity since it has a separate existence and varied use beyond the application that created it. Examples of data are customer data, product data, employee data, sales data, etc.

Hardware is the physical aspect of the system or IT. Computing machines such as computers, servers, and mainframes, and networks and equipments such as routers, storage disks, etc., are all part of the hardware for the IT system.

1.3 Architecture for Systems

Architecture is a term that is growing in relevance in the computer software world. It has been a well-established concept in the civil engineering world though. While there is no common agreement on its definition, as of today, the following definition from IEEE 1471 has been adopted by many—"Architecture is the fundamental organization of a system embodied in its components, their relationships to each other and to the environment and the principles guiding its design and evolution." Here, the system can be an information technology (IT) system, an enterprise, a division of an enterprise, and so on. In this book, we use the term "IT systems" to inclusively refer to software and information technology systems.

1.3.1 IT Architecture

IT architecture is a term that has an enterprise-wide or a department-wide scope and is associated with the organization. IT architecture is the architecture of IT in an organization. It is also referred to as the *enterprise IT architecture*, in the case of an enterprise scope. It is the structure of the enterprise organized purely in terms of the various IT systems in the enterprise, how those IT systems relate to each other, and how they relate to the business aspects of the enterprise. All the IT systems in the enterprise structurally fit into the IT architecture of the enterprise. IT architecture includes the structure of the data in the organization, both logical and physical, the infrastructure capabilities (such as hardware, middleware, networking, communications) that are required to support the various systems across the enterprise in a common and horizontal way.

1.3.2 IT System Architecture

IT system architecture is the architecture of an IT system. It is the organization of the IT system as functionality components, infrastructure components, and data components, their interactions with each other to realize the business objectives of the system, and reflects the principles and design decisions made on the system as a whole. It thus includes the data, infrastructure capability, and functionality parts of the system. It defines the structure of the IT system as comprised of its components, how they interact with each other, and the external properties they exhibit, and enables inferencing on the quality exhibited by the IT system as a whole in its behavior. It determines and specifies how multiple applications that are part of the IT system are to work together—how they would interact with each other.

IT system architecture is the key to realizing the functional requirements and *quality attributes** of the system—it primarily determines whether and how well the system meets its stated business functionality and quality goals. "Quality attributes" are properties of the system such as usability, modifiability, maintainability, interoperability, performance, reliability, and availability. The stakeholders† of the system have different concerns related to the IT system, and these become the properties that the system needs to guarantee. Properties here can be functional and quality based. The need of the system to meet or satisfy these properties primarily influences the design of the architecture of the IT system.

The architecture of a system is described in multiple views, each one from a different perspective. The views considered would need to cover the business perspective and the technical perspective of the IT system to make it more complete.

1.3.3 Architectural Styles and Patterns

An architect creating the architecture for an IT system is often faced with design problems to address, forces to handle, or constraints acting upon the system; for example, "how to ensure the system's performance (time-efficiency)" or "how to enable it to become scalable" are some architectural design problems. There are patterns in the solutions to typical architectural design problems and they have collectively become *architectural patterns*. The idea is to reuse the solutions that have been applied in similar or other architectural design contexts and apply them to solve the current architectural design problem at hand. Patterns are template

* "Quality attributes" are also referred to as nonfunctional requirements of the system by some.

† Various people interested in the IT system would be people such as customers, end users, system developers, maintenance engineers, salespeople, project managers, operators, and operation managers.

solutions to repeating problems occurring in a different space. Patterns are not full architectures of any system, but they are used in creating architectures for a system by applying the pattern to the context of the system. For example, pipes and filters is an architectural pattern that solves the problem of partitioning a big task to be performed by a system into smaller tasks that are performed in a sequence—it solves a partitioning problem. Publish and subscribe is another example of an architectural pattern—it solves a communication problem, that is, the communication between components of a system.

Architectural styles are slightly different from patterns. An architectural style is a predefined set of components or a set of elements of architecture with a set of architectural design decisions, which can be applied to a scenario. This is created by extracting a set of common elements and behavior from architectures that are already available. The design decisions that come with a style, influence or constrain further design decisions in the architecture of the system.

An example of an architectural style is client–server architecture style where the entire system is organized as client and server components. Yet another one is the *layered architecture style*—here the system is primarily divided into layers that depend on each other for specific functional needs. Each layer would make use of services provided by one or more layers to complete its responsibility. Thus, when applying the layered architecture style, all system elements would become part of some layer or the other in the architecture and thereby their responsibilities get associated with the responsibilities defined for the layer.

While patterns necessarily solve a generic problem, styles need not. A style is more of a central organizing concept in the architecture. Also, according to some, a pattern is described strictly as far as its constraints on the architectural components go and is widespread in the software world, and an architectural pattern addresses some aspect (problem) that is more concrete. A style is more leniently described: though there can be constraints, the constraints are at an overall level and more abstract—the structuring of the architecture is given more importance. It is less concrete than a pattern in what it addresses (the scenario or the context for the style). The architecture style dominates the overall architecture of the IT system among all the patterns used in the architecture.

When creating architecture for an IT system,* *reference architectures* are sometimes used. Reference architecture is typically created by using an architectural style or a pattern and mapping a set of components from a *reference model* to it. Here, a reference model is a model with functionality components in a specific business context. Its focus is business. On the other hand, the architecture style or pattern is not specific to the business domain. The resulting reference architecture is the architecture of a system for the specific business context. An example of a reference architecture is the IBM insurance application architecture—it is a reference architecture that applies to the insurance domain.

* This is true for any software system and not just for systems in the enterprise.

A common way to create architecture for a new system is by using relevant reference architecture and modifying it to suit the specificities of the problem at hand. Patterns, styles, and reference architectures all help avoid reinventing the wheel.

1.4 Introduction to Business Processes

Business process is an ordered set of activities performed to achieve a business objective. Here, the activity is either a system or manual activity and the business process is usually a mix of both. System activities are automatically performed by IT systems and manual activities are carried out by humans or, in other words, users. The users typically have interactions with an IT system through its user interface (UI).

Some examples of business processes* are loans processing, purchase order processing, customer account-opening process in a bank, credit card transaction processing, order-to-cash processing, and insurance claims processing.

Business processes are the core assets of any enterprise. They define the enterprise and determine how well the enterprise performs in the market. The business processes of an enterprise are unique to the enterprise and they differentiate the enterprise from its competition.

They capture the way the enterprise works and how it goes about its business of providing products and services to its customers.

Typically in an enterprise, there are some roles that are directly concerned with the business processes. *Business manager* and *business analyst* are such roles. A business manager (also called process manager) is a role that is primarily concerned with the business processes that are in operation. This role monitors what is going on with the process at any point of time and takes actions to address issues related to the operation of the process, such as reassigning tasks to different users to manage load, taking decisions to scale up the process execution to meet extra load, handling exceptions in the process, forceful termination of processes if required, and resolving bottlenecks. A business analyst or a process analyst is an analyst role that is primarily concerned with design of business processes and how well the business processes have been performing or meeting their respective objectives. These roles take a long-term perspective and focus on how to improve the processes in the future by changing them or redesigning them.

Processes typically cut across departments in the organization. The enterprise is constantly subjected to change induced by the business environment, forcing its business processes to change as a response, and that too quickly. The pace of change has only been increasing. When responding to a change, the business analyst or manager would want to change the flow or order of activities, change conditions governing the process flow, remove activities, and so on. All these fundamentally

* In this book, the term "business process" is interchangeably used with the term "process." Unless explicitly stated otherwise, "process" is to be taken to mean the business process.

indicate changes in the business process. Thus business processes in an enterprise do not remain static; they need to be adaptable.

1.5 Activities in Business Processes

A business process is composed of a set of activities. Here, an activity refers to a specific logical operation to be performed as part of the process. Each activity is a step in the process. When the process is running, activities are performed in the sequence specified in the process definition. Upon the process execution reaching an activity, the action associated with the activity is performed, and upon the activity's completion, the process progresses to the next step. Some examples of activities are "approve the loan request," "validate the loan application." Completion of an activity results in a change of the state of the process. For example, upon the completion of the "approve loan request" activity, which is part of loan process, the process assumes approved status if the result of performing the activity is approval. If the result of the activity is a reject, then the process state becomes rejected.

Thus, an activity ideally achieves a logically complete action in the process or the primary object that the process (say a loan application) is acting upon. In this sense, activities are atomic in nature, at the lowest level of granularity of the process.

Activities themselves could consist of a set of tasks, where each task is a step while performing the activity. Thus, each activity could be expressed as a task flow where the tasks of the activity are ordered based on the logical sequence. Task flow for a specific activity in a process is a detailed graphical representation of that single activity. It details out the flow involved among the steps within the activity. A task flow is executed by a single user, and this granularity is what primarily contributes to its atomicity property. The user here could be either a human or a system. An example is the "place-order" activity in a purchase order process. Place-order activity can be expressed as the following ordered set of tasks:

1. Select the option to place order.
2. Select a product from the list of products.
3. Enter the quantity.
4. Validate the quantity entered.
5. Validation failed?
   Yes:
6. Enter corrected quantity.
   No:
7. Confirm order.

A graphical representation of this task flow is given in Figure 1.1.

An activity in a process can be said to have been performed (or normally completed) if and only if the tasks in the activity are completed in the correct

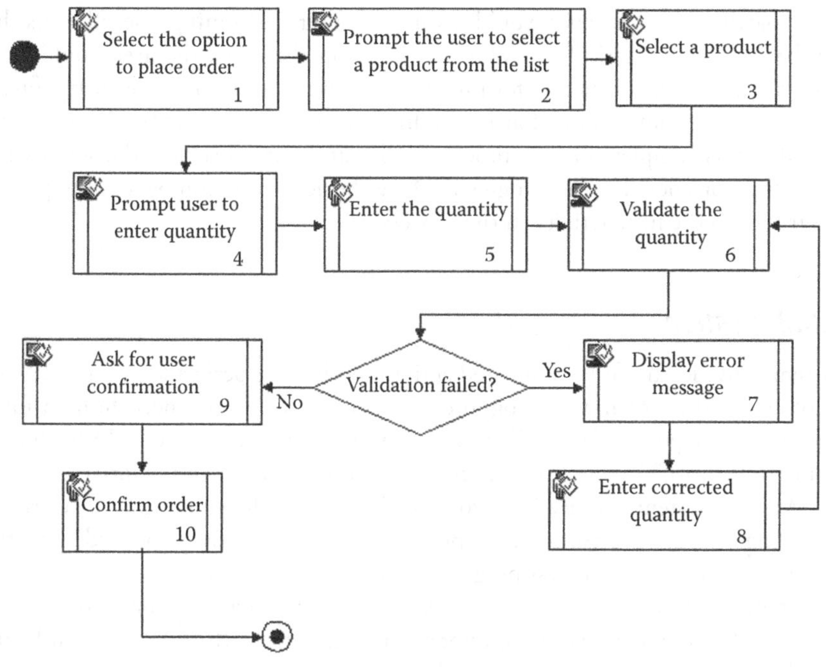

Figure 1.1 Task flow for the place-order activity.

logical sequence (from the start of the task flow to the end) by the user to which the activity is assigned to.

1.6 Types of Activities

Depending on whether they are automatic or not, activities of processes can be categorized either as manual activities or system activities.

1.6.1 Manual

Manual activities are performed by human beings. Examples include "approve the order," "verify the insurance claim," and "review the application." These activities need manual intervention. Some of the manual activities might involve no system interaction at all and the rest would involve some amount of system interaction through a UI.

Manual activities are also referred to as user activities, since in today's world many of them involve the person performing the activity using a UI application. The person becomes a user from that application's perspective.

Typically, a user activity would involve the user performing a set of tasks that can be defined as a task flow. While carrying out the tasks, the user would move from one screen to another performing the task in the respective screen, and finally when the user completes action in the final screen of the activity, the activity is considered as completed in the process. Till that point is reached, the activity status is still considered as "in progress." Once the activity is completed, the process progresses to the next activity in the process flow.

1.6.2 System

System activities are fully automated activities. They are performed by a system or, in other words, a computer program. These activities do not need human intervention at any point of time. Examples are "Validate credit card," "Debit money from credit card," "Send e-mail notification to customer," and "Notify customer by SMS." A system activity is performed directly by the computing platform by executing the specific computer application that is directly associated with this activity, as soon as the process progression reaches this activity.

Another name for system activity is automated activity. Automated activities are typically activities that are mundane and repetitive, which are efficiently and speedily carried out by a computer rather than by a human being. This also allows people to do more creative and challenging work.

As an example, if we consider credit card validation activity, this involves checking of various details of the customer's credit card for authenticity and matching details with that of the credit card services provider. This is best done by a system, where it takes the customer's credit card information and connects to a credit card validation service provider's system through application programming interface (API) and gets the credit card authenticated.

1.7 Importance of Business Processes to Enterprise

Any enterprise would have a set of business processes that it performs. Those processes exist in reality irrespective of whether they have been

- Explicitly designed or just happened in the course of the company's business
- Documented in any form
- Modeled in any approach
- Described in any format

In such cases where the business processes have not been documented in the enterprise, their presence can still be felt—from the way a specific product from the company is built and offered to the customers or from the way a service is delivered by the enterprise to the customers. In many cases, the people that are involved in the particular process would know partial flows of the processes. That is, each person that is part of the process would know at least the following:

- What is the business function that he or she needs to perform.
- How he or she would get to know when he or she is required to carry out that specific work.
- To whom he or she needs to hand off the work item after completing that specific work.

The thing to note in such cases is that though each person knows the respective part (his or her specific job or part) of the process, typically few people would be aware of the entire process with its entire flow. Also, commonly, this process knowledge (whether in part or in full) remains largely in people's heads alone.

Business processes in any enterprise can be typically classified into *core* and *non-core.*

Core processes make up the core competency of the business, and these are processes that directly lead to products and services offered by the enterprise. Core processes for a company are specific to the company or the industry that the company is part of. Let us take the example of a typical cargo transportation company. Its core processes would be those processes such as cargo management, container management, fleet management, and pickup and delivery.

Non-core processes are processes that support the core processes. They indirectly contribute to the business of the enterprise. The processes such as finance accounting, billing and payments, and human resources are non-core processes to this cargo transportation company or enterprise; they are rather enabler processes. Non-core* processes are typically not specific to any industry or company; they are rather generic and apply to most enterprises. They are necessary to carry on the business of the enterprise though they do not directly lead to a product or service.

Innovation activities such as research, generating new products, and strategies come under the category of core processes because they are unique to the company. They are important for the business' future growth and, in many cases, its survival itself.

How well the business processes of an enterprise run and what activities the processes perform determines the success of the enterprise in the market. Efficient business processes provide competitive differentiation to the enterprise from the others competing in the same area.

Processes are thus the blueprint of how the enterprise conducts its business and makes available its products and services to its customers.

When it comes to how the business processes are actually enabled in the enterprise, IT plays a significant role. The IT systems that exist in the enterprise

* Non-core processes are also called background processes.

support the business processes of the enterprise—a business process is realized* by the underlying applications that are part of the IT system.

1.7.1 Processes Are Unique

Factors that make processes unique in an enterprise are many. Some of the factors are as follows.

1.7.1.1 Work Culture

If we take a set of companies involved in the same business and thus are competitors, we can see that each company has its own way of going about the business. This derives to a good extent from the work culture of the company, which has evolved over the period of its existence. As the business grows bigger, this culture only gets reinforced when more employees get added since they adapt to the prevailing culture as the culture is seen as an established one. Most often, the culture reveals itself to the employees by statements such as "This is how things get done here...," "This is how things happen here...," and "We have always done it this way...," and the processes are not explicitly documented and made available to people.

1.7.1.2 Change

As the business continues to exist in the market place, it is constantly challenged to change. These forces include market forces, business environment, competition, and technology advances. The result of this is the change in the way it serves its customers, which means changes in the business processes of the company, both core and non-core. Each company addresses these challenges and brings about changes in its ways of working in its own unique way. This makes the processes again unique for the enterprise.

1.7.1.3 Employees/People

People that work for the organization play an important part in making the processes unique. They bring with them their own individual strengths, specialties, and working styles. This directly contributes to the way and the order in which the business tasks are performed.

1.7.1.4 Systems

Though systems have been traditionally developed with the intention of serving the business, advances in technologies, availability of heavy computation options, and reducing costs of computing resources also influence how the business processes of

* Also means "made to manifest by," "implemented by," etc.

companies evolve. The importance that the enterprise gives to usage of technology, extent of automation, and leveraging of new technologies to serve customers better or improve productivity, varies from company to company, and thus manifests in the company's business processes making the business processes unique to the company.

1.7.1.5 Vision and Mission

Each enterprise's vision and mission differs from others. They lay out the direction for the business processes of the organization, contributing to their uniqueness.

Unique processes are the core assets of the enterprise. Thus, it is important to take a process-oriented view when looking at an enterprise for improvements. If a company wants to stay competitive, it needs to keep its processes in the best shape. This is what the discipline of business process management (BPM) is focused on.

1.7.2 Processes Are Organization Wide

Typically, business processes cut across departments in the organization. Processes are end-to-end rather than being specific to one group. They involve participants from multiple departments working together as determined by the flow of the process to achieve the business objective, whether a product or a service to the customer.

Processes, when connected together, also make the value chains in the enterprise or the value chains that span enterprises. Value chains describe how the enterprise brings together its processes to offer value-added products or services to the end customers.

1.8 Process-Centric Architecture—A Quick Introduction

1.8.1 Background

IT systems in the enterprise essentially support the business of the enterprise. This means they support the business processes of the enterprise by both enabling the business users to carry out business functions or tasks, and also performing specific business functionalities by themselves. And toward enabling this better and better, architectures for the systems have been evolving over the decades. Their architectures have moved from monolithic to *n*-tier ones. Still, IT systems have been found to be not as well-aligned to business as they should have been—the business–IT system gap still exists. The systems still appear to be inflexible to support, effectively and quickly, the changes that frequently occur in the business processes. This has remained a perennial problem that software architects (or IT architects) have been trying to address.

Architectural styles or approaches for IT systems, such as component-based architecture (e.g., EJB™* in JEE™ and business tier), and business rules-based architecture have the objective of making the IT systems more agile and they have introduced higher abstractions in the system architecture. The former abstracted out the business logic of the application into a dedicated business tier in the architecture, while the latter abstracted out the business rules logic from the application into the rules engine (or a business rules management system, BRMS). This made the business logic and rules separately manageable from the other logic in the application. While they were in the right direction, systems still exhibited inflexibility—the IT systems were not reflecting the real business process of the enterprise faithfully. Other recent styles such as services-oriented architecture (SOA) continued take the bottom-up approach to architecture by creating reusable services (from business components) that could be used to support different business needs. While the concept of the services is valuable, the approach is more strongly technique-driven (and technique-focused) than business-driven, and thus by itself is not sufficient to bridge the business–IT gap in systems.

1.8.2 Concept

Process-centric architecture (PCA) is an architecture style that directly addresses this problem by moving the abstraction level further up to the process logic and the process tier. It provides an architecture for IT systems where the entire IT system is conceptualized and centrally organized by the concept of the business process that is supported by the system and the business process component is the central component in the system.

Instead of the conventional architectural approaches for IT systems, where the IT system was always just a derivative of the business process, in PCA the business process becomes the driving force of the IT system in architecture as well as in the implemented system. In the previous software design approaches, the system was built bottom-up to meet the business specifications, and the business process as captured by IT personnel† was coded (tightly/rigidly) into the IT system. Unlike this, in PCA the business process definition specified by the business analyst or manager directly becomes part of the architecture of the system and is a component of the system itself. And this component directs the entire behavior of the system at run-time. This makes the IT system more flexible to the frequent changes in business processes and it allows those changes to be directly made into the system by just changing the business process definition rather than requiring programmers to change code (in most cases). PCA owes its origins primarily to the ideas

* The concept of Enterprise Java Beans in the Java Enterprise Edition is based on business components being explicitly designed and defined as part of an overall component-based architecture for the system.

† This is used throughout the book to broadly refer to system analysts, programmers, software architects, IT architects, system engineers, system maintainers, and so on.

and outputs from research work in process-thinking and BPM. Process-thinking brought in the formalism for business processes. BPM contributed the approach for handling business processes and the rigor for that approach to make them effective.

1.8.3 Benefits

Here is a brief look at the benefits of PCA:

- Better business–IT alignment. The gap between the business process and the IT system gets reduced.
- Better control for the business over the IT system and the supported business process.
- Reuse of business processes, their steps, and business components of the architecture across the enterprise.
- Enables a central store of business processes for the enterprise.
- Facilitates effective process management.
- Mergers and acquisitions (M&A)-related integrations are enabled.
- Much improved flexibility to the IT systems.
- Leads to agile IT.
- Interoperability of IT systems is enhanced.
- Better maintainability of IT systems.
- Scalability of the IT system is improved.

A more detailed list of benefits is given in Chapter 7.

1.8.4 The Book

The book explains PCA in detail. It draws upon the author's research in the area and his experience in architecting and implementing IT systems based on this concept. It also picks from the author's experience in architecting and developing technology infrastructure in the area, especially a business process management system (BPMS). As part of this, the book has drawn from the insights and learnings that have come from the author's deep experience in architecting, designing, and building a BPMS process execution platform from scratch based on standards and process formalisms. The experience leveraged in the book also includes the author's experience with deploying the BPMS and implementing business processes on it for customers.

1.9 Exercise Questions

1. What are some of the architectural patterns that you have come across?
2. What are the unique aspects of some processes in your enterprise? Where do you think that uniqueness has come from?

Chapter 2

Evolution of IT Architecture

2.1 Objectives

- To look at how architecture for IT systems have evolved
- To learn the need for applications to support business processes effectively
- To understand the issues with integration and the best way to support integration
- To appreciate the functions of workflows, EAI, business rules, ERP packages, and their natural convergence

2.2 Historical Perspective on Enterprise Computing Architectures

Architecture for enterprise IT systems has been evolving over the last five decades or so. It would be worth now to take a chronological look at this evolution since this has some significance on the current state of IT system architectures in the enterprise.

Prior to the 1960s, there was hardly any automation. Computers had just arrived in the scene and they were really not looked at for doing business work then. Computing has been continuously evolving, addressing more and more complex business needs along the way (Figure 2.1). Here is an attempt to look at this evolution decade by decade.*

* Here, for the sake of classification, some amount of development overlap over some consecutive decades has been ignored and the development is mentioned approximately under the decade where it has had relatively more impact.

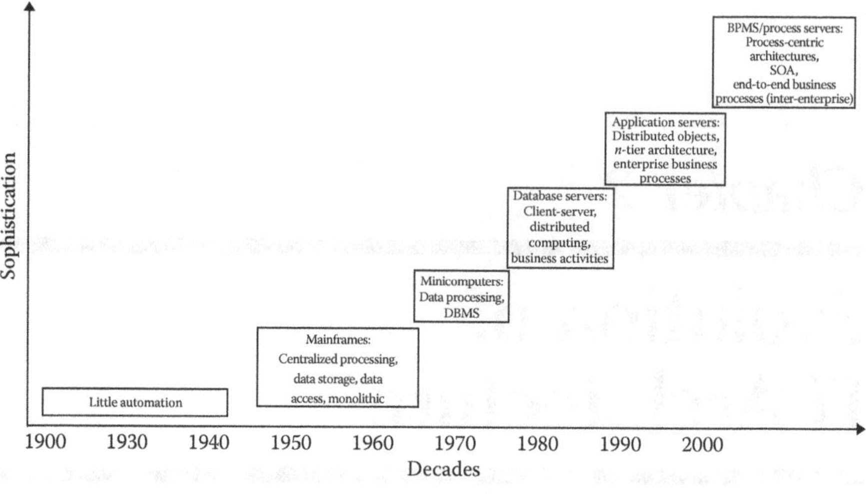

Figure 2.1 Evolution of architecture.

2.2.1 The 1960s

In the 1960s, with the increasing velocity and complexity of business, business enterprises had a need to deploy increasing automation in business processes, and companies such as IBM stepped in to meet this need. Computers were bought by big corporations to help in their business operations and to serve more of their business needs. The mainframe computer with its associated system software was the computing platform. Architecture of the applications was influenced greatly by this. They were architected as monolithic applications made up of huge-sized programs written in languages such as Assembler and COBOL. Structured programming started becoming popular, though it was not uncommon to see unstructured programming in the enterprise applications.

Data storage and retrieval was the primary business purpose of the software developed to run in the computers. These applications' primary responsibility was to store business data of the enterprise in files and enable the users to retrieve the data in a way easier than the old manual ways. Later in the decade, when databases took birth (such as hierarchical and network database systems), it made data access more fast. It separated data management concerns out from the application software and put them into the database management system (DBMS). Some of the popular databases used at the time were information management system (IMS™) and integrated data management system (IDMS™).

Being monolithic in nature, the architecture made the user interface, business logic, and data access parts all to be contained in a single application, and the application ran entirely in mainframe. The scope of the applications was generally intradepartmental and the applications were owned and mainly used by the IT department.

2.2.2 The 1970s

During this decade, mainframe systems continued to be popular with businesses; however, in the latter half, minicomputers came into being and began to enter the business computing space. Applications were still being architected as monolithic ones with users using dumb terminals to connect to the application running on the mainframe or mini. All the processing got done by the program running on the central computer (i.e., mainframe or mini). The objective of the application was mainly to do data processing, where the program would store business data in a DBMS, retrieve it later and process it, and display the processed results either as reports or in a screen for the user. The entire set of applications was segregated based on the function being supported and owned by the respective functional group and its IT personnel.* During this time, relational database management systems (RDBMS) started getting adopted for data storage and retrieval needs due to the user-friendly (i.e., programmer at that time) abstraction it was providing for data access, namely, structured query language (SQL).

Each application was typically serving the data processing needs of a particular department (function) such as finance. And, it would be a few big programs that made up the application, where the focus was on the data processing algorithm. Depending on the nature of duration of the program's execution, it was designed to run as a batch job or an online task with *character user interface* (CUI)-based screens. Batch processing allows the application to be executed in the background, by the underlying system software, without any user's interaction in between. Such applications run as jobs that are either submitted by a user to the system or by the system automatically based on a schedule or based on the dependency on another job's execution. Batch jobs typically run for hours or days. While architecting such applications, the typical approach was to look at the entire function that an application needs to do, say, reporting on the sales that happened in the last quarter, and break the algorithm down into steps. Thus, the steps in this sales report would be

1. Fetch all sales data from all the database structures (whether they are network records or record-sets, or relational tables) and write the records into a file A, where each record in file represents one sales transaction for a product.
2. Sort the records in the file based on a field (say, product number) and write to a new file B.
3. Scan all the records in the file B, one by one, to check for errors and missing data and write corrected data to file C.
4. Compute report data from file C (involves aggregation, numerical computation, etc.) and write it into file D.
5. Generate report from file D (involves formatting) and put in report file E.
6. Print the report file E at the required location.

---

* Includes programmers and IT managers.

Each step above of the application would be a program and each step becomes a step in the batch job.

In the case of an online application, say entering sales data, the design used to be having an online program that would present fields in a CUI screen for the user's input (by specifying their exact positions and lengths in the screen) and accept the user's inputs, edit the input data, and add/update the database records with the data. It would also display to the user already stored data from the database for viewing.

We can see that the architecture of such an application (batch or online) is tightly coupled to the business data processing algorithm. There was very little modularization within the applications. Here too, being monolithic in nature, the architecture made the user interface, business logic, and data access part all to be contained in a single application, and the application ran in mainframe or mini entirely. The scope of the applications was only a department (such as sales) and that department's designated function of selling of products/services. And, the members of that department used to be the users of the system.

These IT systems were dependent on the underlying software* provided by the mainframe, which were proprietary. The network that connected various nodes in the enterprise including mainframes, user terminals, system operators, databases, offline storage systems, and output devices such as printers, was based on proprietary network protocols such as Systems Network Architecture (SNA). All these characteristics made IT systems closed in nature. It also led to an indirect (direct in some cases) lock-in to a specific computing platform that later came to be seen as restricting the options for the enterprise IT.

2.2.3 The 1980s

Mini systems running the UNIX® operating system became popular with businesses. One of the factors that influenced this was the standardization efforts for UNIX that made it more open. Also, personal computers (PC) arrived with the basic notion of dedicated use of computer by just one user. The concept of *servers* that would serve specific type of requests from multiple users connected to the network gained fold. Relational databases became the dominant DBMS type and SQL the accepted data query abstraction. Database servers were the early servers to get established. They abstracted out all database management work from the applications and owned exclusive responsibility to serve any of those requests coming from any application program or from database administrators. Some examples are Oracle®, Sybase®, and Informix®.

---

* Essentially, system software such as S/360™, S/370™, MVS™, JES/JCL, IMS, TSO, and CICS™.

Graphical user interfaces (GUI) made the applications more user-friendly, especially to business managers and end users. Apple with Mac® computers and Microsoft with Windows® operating system drove this development.

This was the time when the thinking on *open** systems started. Open standards such as transmission control protocol/Internet protocol (TCP/IP) for networking, UNIX standards for UNIX operating systems standardization, and SQL for data access in RDBMS became available that the enterprises adopted, leading to efforts to realize the power and potential of computer networks in the enterprise. The enterprise network based on TCP/IP enabled the IT systems in the enterprise to be more open and allow IT architectures that could split the application into parts that are front-end (i.e., the user end) focused and ones that are back-end processing (i.e., server side) focused, where the two parts communicated over the TCP/IP network.

These led to the *client–server* architecture becoming the predominant IT system architecture, where the application essentially had two elements, the *client* (front-end or user side) that took care of the processing related to user interface (UI) presentation, formatting, input validations (editing), customizations, business logic, etc., and the *server* (back-end) that was always up and waiting to receive requests from multiple clients and serve those requests by doing processing on the server machine. The server used to take care of the data, access to it, and its management. In some cases, some part of the business logic used to be an element running in the server machine. Servers in this architecture were databases (RDBMS) running on UNIX servers and the clients were application elements running on PCs. Running them on PCs is what enabled the clients to do their processing. Clients that were GUI programs were typically developed and run using specialized software or tools such as SQLWindows®, FoxBASE/FoxPro, and PowerBuilder®.† These specialized run-time GUI environments (and development environments) provided the support to programmers for developing GUI-based user-friendly UI screens, connecting to database servers, and handling presentation requirements.

As far as the extent of automation is concerned, the IT systems grew up beyond doing just data processing to help with performance of business activities that used to be previously carried out manually. This meant automation of specific activities wherever feasible, including conversion of paper-based forms to online entry/verification screens, business validations of data inputted, automation of numerical

* Software or hardware that has characteristics such as conformance to standards, open (clear and transparent) specifications, and that enables interoperability. These are characteristics opposite to that of proprietary.

† PowerBuilder actually entered the scene in 1990 and became popular in the first half of the 1990s.

calculations and complex business computations with business data, and generation (and printing) of periodic business reports.

The scope of the IT systems grew larger to also address interdepartmental interactions such as transfer of business data from one department in the enterprise to another—say from booking to finance (receivables) in the case of a transportation company. Applications were still designed and developed based on the functional view, that is, by making the application specifically programmed to perform only the function of that department. Business personnel (users) of respective departments were not the only users of the IT systems any more. The top levels of management, typically the set of senior business managers, also became business users of the systems. However, the ownership of the systems was retained with the respective functional department.

As we can see, over all these decades, data continued to remain the right abstraction level to manage for the systems. All the automation that happened was a way to enable the definition and overall management (end-to-end life cycle management) of business data by the system. This used to be done manually earlier.

2.2.4 The 1990s

The following computing trends dominated this decade:

Networking of computers and computing resources became widespread, thanks to the success of TCP/IP. A special type of TCP/IP-based network, the Internet, became hugely popular, changing the way applications got architected. Paper-based communication between people was passé and e-mails took up this role efficiently. Applications such as spreadsheets and document creators/editors entered the business world to improve speed, reduce manual work, minimize errors, etc. Digitization of paper documents, that is, the switch to electronic documents from paper documents, was an important trend. Groupware applications (e.g., Lotus Notes™) helped users share notes and digital documents among themselves for better collaboration and faster updates. The JAVA™ programming language (and its run-time environment) arrived in this decade leading to the popularity of object-oriented programming systems (OOPS) that became a dominant programming paradigm.

The architecture of IT systems evolved toward more and more separation of concerns among the *components* of the applications. The evolution was also to distribution of the system into multiple distributed components that were physically separated from each other at run-time (i.e., executed in physically separate run-time environments) and which communicated with each other remotely during execution. Client–server based two-tier architecture got extended into an *n-tier* (multi-tier) one, where higher abstractions created new tiers. More and more applications became web applications that let users access the application features seamlessly by using just an *Internet browser* as the client. The protocol that the client (browser) and the server had to understand and use for communication was just the standard

HTTP* (and HTML† for the content). These were three-tier architectures based on the Internet, where the client made up the first tier, the *web server* (server on the Internet) that serves the application made the second tier, and the database server became the third tier. The entire communication in this architecture is based on the *request–response* model, where there is a user initiating a request that leads to a response from the application and each transaction is a chain of such request–response interactions.

Distributed computing architectures became established where it involved one or more applications interacting with each other remotely, though they may have been implemented in disparate technologies, say one application in JAVA and the other in C++. In this architecture style, the application would be architected as a set of business components, on the business logic side. These business components may run physically separate or otherwise involve a remote invocation (call) mechanism in the former case.

Common object request broker architecture (CORBA®) was developed by object management group (OMG) as a standard for intercomponent interaction and distributed computing, regardless of the underlying implementation technologies of the components, be it C++, Mainframe, JAVA, or others. This was a good attempt and a clean approach by OMG to enable standardized application interactions. CORBA's focus was enabling application components to remotely call each other in a standard way, overcoming barriers posed by disparate technologies. To this end, CORBA provided a mechanism for application programming interfaces (APIs) of individual applications/components to be defined in the CORBA standard way (through IDL™, expanded as Interface Definition Language), so that any other application could invoke the API remotely. The remote invocation was enabled by providing a run-time CORBA invocation layer, the ORB layer (middle layer), over which the intercomponent communication would take place. These CORBA API definitions would be transformed (mapped) into/from the API definition in the specific implementation technology's parlance so that when the remote call happens, the call is converted at both the ends (caller component and called component) into a call specific to the component implementation technology platform. CORBA is essentially based on remote procedure call (RPC) mechanisms where a remote component could be invoked by another component as if it were a local (meaning, in same run-time environment) call.‡

* Short for hypertext transfer protocol that became the ubiquitous protocol for transferring data and communication in the World Wide Web (WWW).

† Stands for hypertext markup language that is popularly used to describe the content transferred over the WWW. The web servers typically serve HTTP pages/documents in response to the request received from the client (Internet browser).

‡ All the remote aspects of the call, including the network communication, the location address, accessibility, and transformation of data, would be entirely abstracted out of the application components (both sides) by the remote layer.

The popularity of model-view-controller (MVC) pattern-based architecture meant an architecture where the IT system was separated into top-level components based on their specific concerns. Here, the *view* component is responsible for the presentation and formatting aspects, the *model* component takes care of all the business logic and business data, and the *controller* component is concerned with the control flow (routing) involved in each request–response interaction.

Initially, the web server ran all MVC components in itself except the database part. At the next level, the model was moved out of the web tier (the web server) and further split into business components that would offer specific business computing functionalities. This provided more levels of abstractions for the business logic. The common infrastructure requirements for all the business logic (model) such as transaction handling, messaging, security, remote invocation, availability, resource pooling for performance, and component life cycle management was abstracted into a separate component. All this introduced another important evolution in enterprise-distributed computing architecture, the concept of *application servers.* The business components that got abstracted out from the web tier were placed in a separate tier, namely the application server. The application server implemented the infrastructure component requirements mentioned above providing those services to all the business components. In the JAVA world, this architecture got standardized with the release of the J2EE™ (JAVA Enterprise Edition)* and EJB (Enterprise JAVA Beans) specifications (standards in other words) by Sun Micro systems. It is mandatory for all system vendors providing application servers for JAVA to implement these specifications in full.

More and more of business came under the broadening automation umbrella to improve business efficiency. Business rules and business processes within the enterprise were supported by the IT systems. Many of the business rules (complex ones included) such as insurance claim checks for approval; rules for computation of complex pricing, say for cargo transportation around the world; and airline seat allocation rules were programmed in the IT system so that their performance becomes consistent and efficient. IT systems now covered the enterprise business processes by performing tasks automatically behind the scenes and supporting the activities of the process through one or more application by involving the execution of business components in the application server.

The scope of the systems was no longer the enterprise alone; it went beyond that to handle inter-enterprise business functions too. Business models such as business-to-business (B2B) and business-to-customer (B2C) began to be supported by systems through approaches such as dedicated business exchanges (say, payment gateways and exchanges), data exchange, and electronic data interchange (EDI). IT systems were now being also used by the business partners of the enterprise, customers (directly), and, in a limited way, by suppliers. The customers typically accessed the system facilities through the Internet. Thus, the systems were supporting a wide range of users.

* Now this is commonly referred to as JEE.

2.2.5 The 2000s

In this decade, the IT systems have begun to bring business processes from end-to-end under automation, which means the applications together directly support not just the activities that make up a business process within its enterprise (or a portion of a business process relevant to the enterprise), but also the automation of processes whose steps go beyond the enterprise's boundary by integrating the systems on both sides. Automatically performing credit card validations using a third-party service provider's system by invoking it from within this enterprise's system is an example here. Systems have a much broader impact; they impact all the enterprises that the end-to-end processes cover. Almost all business people are users of the systems in some way or the other. This includes end customers (self-serve model) that directly access the services, business partners that collaborate with the enterprise, end users within the enterprise, managers at different levels of the enterprise, suppliers and vendors, and business/process analysts.

The level of abstraction in the architecture increased to handle the business process logic as distinct entities separately from other business components. This has resulted in a new layer namely process server. Business processes are directly executed and managed by the process server.

Though conceptually very sound, strong, comprehensive, and pretty detailed, CORBA, for various reasons, is generally seen as not that successful in distributed computing architectures. The concept of distributed components, however, caught on and an attempt was made to simplify remote invocation of components by piggy-backing on already popular standards (HTTP and XML*) and the ubiquity of the Internet (web). The business components of IT systems, irrespective of the technology environment of their implementation, could be made to expose their respective functionality over the web. This concept is called *web services*. In this, the business component becomes a web service that could be invoked by any client component (program) using the simple object access protocol (SOAP) for the communication or in other words messaging (message protocol). This communication happens using the transport protocol HTTP over the medium of web. Here, the service invoker (client) and the web service exchange SOAP messages by sending these as content of HTTP packets in the HTTP connection between their respective machines.

SOAP is fully based on XML and is a request–response based message protocol. The invoker constructs a SOAP request message and sends it to the web service. The web service sends back a SOAP response message in response to the invocation. Once the invoker receives this response, the communication ends. Here, we can see that SOAP rides on the stateless connection characteristic of HTTP.†

* Extended markup language—the current standard for describing data or a collection of data where the data items are organized with descriptor tags wrapping them around, based on a defined and standardized structure. HTML is based on XML.

† HTTP is inherently a stateless protocol. Each communication between two nodes ends with the receipt of the http response and the http connection ends right away with this. The next communication will involve opening of a new http connection.

There are two other XML-based standards web services description language (WSDL) and universal description discovery and integration (UDDI) that support web services. WSDL is the standard to describe the details of the web service such as the parameters (and data type) that it expects as input (request) from the invoker, the parameters (and data type) it will provide as output (response) to the invoker at the end of processing, message protocol (e.g., SOAP) that the service uses, the protocol used for transport (e.g., HTTP), and the URI* for locating the web service. UDDI provides a standard way to add to and look up a web service's WSDL from a universal† directory based on quickly searchable key logical data or meta-data.

Web services triggered a new architectural style, service-oriented architecture (SOA) that has as its concept, "making software service-oriented." SOA brings location-transparent‡ service abstraction to software by raising the level of abstraction of components (erstwhile) to business components that offer well-defined services. A service is a self-contained software element that provides well-defined business functionality and an interface that is abstracted out as separate from the implementation of functionality. Each service here is a business functionality, which is logically fulfilled. Credit card validation, "check airline seat availability," and "add customer" are some examples for services. The service interface (i.e., API) for a service is well-published by the service provider for potential consumers to look up quickly and easily.

SOA inherently encourages and enables reuse of software; it views service as the right abstraction for business-level reusable software elements. It does not enforce any physical limitation (boundary) on the location of the service consumer; the potential consumer of a service could be within the boundary of the service-providing enterprise or outside the enterprise. This choice is left to the service provider.

Another principle SOA brings is location- and implementation-transparency for a service. The service interface that is published to the world of potential service consumers is independent of (transparent to) the implementation details of the service (such as the technology platform, programming language, transport protocol, and remote invocation application-level protocol). The service can have multiple implementations, each one potentially in a different technology or language, but the consumers are insulated from this as the service interface remains unchanged and separate from this concrete fact.

For example, the credit card validation service could have been implemented by one service provider as an EJB component in J2EE platform. Another service provider could have implemented the same service as a COBOL program running

---

* Uniform resource identifier uniquely identifies and locates a resource. For example, the uniform resource locator (URL) http://www.infosys.com uniquely identifies and locates the web server of Infosys Technologies Ltd.

† The term universal is relative to the context. It can mean an entire enterprise, an extended enterprise, a conglomeration, or the entire world itself.

‡ Here, "transparent" as used in the software architecture world. It means opaqueness.

in an IBM mainframe. Service interface, however, would state the implementation-independent details such as the functionality method name, its input parameters and output parameters (of course in XML standard). The service consumer (invoker) would depend on this service interface alone for its program that has been implemented in say, .NET™. It would then, at run-time, ideally look up the service in a public directory based on UDDI and get the list of service providers implementing this service. Then it can determine the right one for it among the list to invoke and proceed with the invocation based on the suitable concrete binding details (such as transport protocol, application invocation protocol).

It is advocated to use the WSDL standard to describe the service interface and the UDDI standard for publishing it. Web services is one way of realizing SOA.* And, web services is the most popular approach for SOA implementation as they provide a standardized way of exposing and invoking services.

In this stage of evolution, the architecture of IT systems has moved into one where the business process is at the center of the architectural design of the enterprise systems and is not a subordinate or a consequence of what the IT systems can do together. In a sense, this is a paradigm shift in IT architecture as we will see in more detail in the subsequent chapters. The business process is supported by business services that are designed based on SOA, at the lower level of abstraction below the process tier. In this decade, for automation, we have gone still higher up in the abstraction by taking the business process as the entity to be managed at the system abstraction level akin to business data of the earlier decades, and this is a dramatic change for systems architecture. Automation now refers to overall management (end-to-end life cycle management†) of business processes by systems. These specialized systems are called business process management systems (BPMS). The entity such systems would work with would be a business process similar to what DBMSs did with business data in the previous decades.

2.3 Traditional Ways of Supporting Business

Traditionally, enterprises are organized along various functions such as sales, finance, and billing. Each of them was a department that owned the specific function that it was supposed to do. This led to the creation of IT systems to support those specific functions. Often, during the design of the application, a bigger picture view of how it would fit in with the other systems in the enterprise, including

* Many interpret SOA to be the same as web services (interchangeably so). This is an incorrect interpretation. SOA is the architectural style of designing the architecture of software as composed of a set of services. It is not just web services. Web services are just one of the many approaches to do SOA. CORBA, for example, is another way to realize SOA and services.

† Means full cycle, covering design, definition, deployment, run-time execution, monitoring, analysis, and optimization.

its effects on them, was missing or given a very minimal concern. These applications continued to evolve independently as silos with their own independent database schemas, procedures, technologies, etc. Though the applications got built this way, business processes required these applications to interact with each other, in some fashion, to achieve the business objective of the process.

It has been the case over these decades that enterprises have needed custom-made applications or custom-changed software to meet their business needs because each business is unique and the processes followed by the enterprise are unique to themselves. During the initial decades of automation at least, the various departments within enterprises have given preference to custom-made or tailor-made applications to suite their unique way of functioning. This has resulted in a huge number of *in-house* developed applications. This is more true in large enterprises. On the other hand, these in-house applications were built and run on the computing platform (and environment) the enterprise was already heavily invested in (say mainframe and the associated run-time platforms from one technology vendor), leading to vendor and technology lock-in that is, feature enhancements, new applications to be developed for functionality that has some dependency (even small) on existing applications, had to be done in the same platform. Also, the enterprise had to commit to and depend on that vendor for all new (or enhanced) versions of the platform itself as they were proprietary, only then they could leverage more out of the platform and offer justification.

Each department, with its own set of IT personnel, used to manage and evolve these applications, largely considering the needs of that specific department's function as key rather than considering the overall context of the enterprise or the business requirements at the enterprise level. An enterprise level requirement, if at all it came, was usually seen as just some extra requirement that the department's application should also support and thus was never core to the application. When applications in each department evolved this way, the result was that the IT architecture ended up to be nothing but islands of silo applications running on disparate technologies.

Later (in the last couple of decades mostly), they also started to buy off-the-shelf *application packages* and to customize/configure those to meet their specific needs. Examples are SAP®, PeopleSoft®, and ORACLE applications just to name a few. The idea was that they were getting to use and adopt standardized processes or best practice business processes, especially for their non-core business processes and that for the non-core processes (such as HR, ERP, Finance), given the cost (versus benefit) of building and maintaining a custom one on their own it would not be worth going for in-house applications. Also, the feeling was that, all on their own they would find it hard to come up with software that can support the standard processes and continuously evolve it, as well as the packages could; on the other hand, they could rather focus on building applications to support their core business. That said, vendor lock-in was a characteristic in the case of software packages too since it was the vendor that decided when new versions would be released and what business requirements it would meet.

Thus, a typical enterprise's IT architecture looked more like something that came to happen than being designed for: It had islands of applications that were either developed in-house or packages procured from outside and run in heterogeneous technologies. The package usually brought with it its own database schema and database separate from the existing database(s) in the IT architecture. Redundancy, inconsistency, and errors in business data were common effects of this. If business needs demanded combined functionality or data, then it meant multiple individual applications had to work together to achieve that. Due to the ownership and organization structure, this would make IT and business personnel that owned the respective applications to work together and do it as a software project, spanning months if not years implementing the identified changes in the applications involved.

In a way, this is inevitable in a large enterprise. There would be so many people, a lot of divisions and departments, and each feeling they are in a separate company of their own and end up doing lot of reinventing the wheel, creating the same software that some other division has already created, and not have a process view. Process view and process roles are more important than just function-based roles.

Thus, traditional IT systems were data focused—the most important entities for them were data and information. Data being central to them, the architectural design used to start by considering the information needs of the people involved in the business.

2.4 Workflows

Another significant set of software that entered IT in the enterprises, in the last two decades, is the genre of *workflow* systems. Their intent was to support workflows, that is, work that involved multiple people performing different activities on a business entity (say, a document) to take its processing to completion.

An example here would be the processing of a loan application. Here, the loan application would first be received by a front desk clerk at the bank and then transferred to the officer in the loan department. The loan officer, after checking the details in the application, enters the data into the loan system, maybe puts notes in it and sends it to another officer who would verify the eligibility of the applicant. This officer updates the system with the eligibility data and hands off the application to a finance officer who is in charge of verifying the credit history (and assessing the risk) of the applicant. The application is then handed off back to the loan officer who now takes a decision on the loan application based on the information available. If some criterion, say loan amount greater than US$20,000, requires the loan department manager to approve the loan, the application is forwarded to the manager. Once the manager approves, the loan officer completes the application processing by ordering the system to generate the loan sanction letter. This is then mailed to the applicant.

Some of these software mainly helped with sharing of documents, collaboration, and communication among employees/personnel (i.e., groups): groupware like Lotus Notes, e-mail, etc. are examples of this type. The rest focused on automating the flow of work from one person to another thereby automating manual hand-offs, sending notifications to the persons concerned on their work items, and sharing of the business document (say, the filled-up application); they also allowed updates to document details and made the status of the work visible to everyone concerned, which was previously a hard thing in the manual world. They were called *workflow management systems* (WFMS) and enabled automation of paper-based processes to an extent. Some of them also supported scanning of paper documents into digitized documents and enabled automated document routing in the workflow. Filenet®, Staffware®, DSP, etc., are examples of WFMS.

2.5 Packages

We discussed how packages developed by independent software vendors entered the enterprise IT space, providing pre-built software for business. Application packages typically support specific business processes, addressing them in a standardized way. While some of them namely, enterprise resource planning (ERP) packages typically support processes of HR, supply chain management (SCM), and inventory, others packages support a specific business function in total, such as sales, and customer relationship management (CRM). These packages picked up standard practices in the respective business functions from across the world, including reference models, and incorporated those into the package so that enterprises (customer) could buy it as standard business software.

Though packages provided ready-made business functionality, it took substantial effort deploying (or implementing) them in the enterprise. Implementation invariably included customizing the package (program changes, new programming, configuration, etc.) to suit the specific needs of the enterprise (to suit the way the business is done in the enterprise), making it a long drawn out software project in itself. Packages appeared to be not flexible enough to easily incorporate the enterprise's unique process needs into them as they offered a canned business function with own database, schema, limited interfaces, technology platform, and so forth. They were not primarily designed up front with coexistence (fitting in the enterprise's IT ecosystem with existing applications) as a key philosophy (goal).

Implementation projects for medium-to-large enterprises often ran for years overrunning cost/time estimates, with many, on hindsight, considering it as overspending for the business benefits brought in. In quite a few cases, the adoption of packages led to changes in the existing business itself, where the business managers ended up changing their processes to that of the standard business process offered by the package or around the functionalities it could provide.

2.6 Integration

Enterprises have always had the need to integrate the various applications in their IT ecosystem. This is due to various reasons. The company's business keeps expanding, making it serve newer markets and more customer bases. Its business environment and competition forces it to stay competitive by launching newer products and services, cutting costs, reducing cycle times, and providing better quality to the customer. It might get involved in mergers and acquisitions (M&A) with other companies, creating a bigger enterprise in the process. Other enterprises might partner with the company to deliver more value to customers in a virtual extended enterprise mode. Technology changes rapidly with the arrival of new technologies and platforms or evolution of existing ones. All of this would result in modifications in the existing applications including addition of new capabilities to support new business requirements, creation of new applications to support new business features and functionalities, rationalization of applications* to minimize redundancy of functionalities, reusing existing applications from merging entities (in M&A scenario), applications being changed or reengineered to use a different technology, and supporting evolution of existing business function using a new application on a modern technology that runs on top of the existing old application. That means applications would be required to talk to other applications, and new applications that serve bigger business goals could get developed by combining two or more existing applications.

Though there has been strong business and technical needs for it, integration of IT systems has been a hard task for enterprises as IT systems have evolved into islands of automation in the enterprise, as we saw previously. Each one got created as a silo and continued to evolve like one due to focus on functional thinking behind their creation and evolution of technology, leading to applications both getting built and run in disparate technologies. In a typical large enterprise that has existed for some time, we would come across older mainframe-based applications running on proprietary technologies, monolithic applications running on flavors of UNIX, applications relying on communication based on SNA network protocol, applications relying on communication based on TCP/IP network protocol, packaged applications in different platforms, traditional client–server applications (such as PowerBuilder–Oracle), web applications, JAVA-based applications, and so on, just to name a few.

Each of these applications (though some may be legacy) would be considered important to the enterprise in some way as it serves a business function and precious money would have already been invested on it. In many cases, this business function is all that is visible to the enterprise that indicates to it the application's presence; its

* The merged enterprise would end up inheriting IT systems from both the merging entities. Post M&A, it is likely that some applications are redundant (or duplicate), performing same or similar business functionalities.

documentation (design or others) would typically be unavailable, its original programmers would often no longer be present in the enterprise. And these applications cannot be gotten rid off. Application packages were well integrated within themselves, but were not found easily integrable with other software, whether in-house applications or other packages. The more they were customized by the enterprise, the more difficult integration became as it made the package even more complex.

When it came to integrating the various IT systems, integration was viewed as just an interoperability problem. The problem of integration sounded more technical. The efforts made were primarily to make one application somehow talk to another. Technically, systems could not natively communicate with other. For example, a SNA network-based application such as a mainframe COBOL program, cannot communicate with a COBOL application running on UNIX that is based on TCP/IP network since the data packets in the respective networks speak different languages. A COBOL/IDMS application running in mainframe could not communicate with another COBOL/IDMS program even though it is running in the same mainframe, if their database records were in different IDMS schemas (i.e., IDMS partition) through IDMS is in the same mainframe. Another impediment was the proprietary ways in which character encoding* was done in different technology platforms. IBM mainframe-based systems used EBCDIC for encoding characters as bits whereas ASCII was the encoding used by systems on minis and personal computers, though ASCII later emerged as more popular. This means, systems integration by transferring just data between applications had to deal with the problem of encoding.

Broadly, there were four approaches followed for integration. One was where the integration was data driven. Here, one application would transfer data directly to another. This usually used to be done offline using batch processes/programs. Another approach was *messaging* driven integration where applications send messages to each other. An example is using a product such as IBM MQseries™. Yet another was API invocation (function-call)-based. Custom integration mechanisms involving remote method calls with lower level method parameter transformations over a common backbone (custom) to which all the applications exposed themselves to, were also not uncommon. Both these were point-to-point integration solutions. Enterprise Application Integration (EAI) tools appeared in the scene to solve this interoperability problem, taking primarily a hub-spoke approach.

Figure 2.2 shows typical hub-spoke architecture used for integration, where nine applications are integrated using an EAI tool as the broker sitting in the middle. Each application is connected to the hub by exactly one connector and this connector is expected to be light.

EAI tool took upon the role of *information broker* in the architecture by mediating in between the applications that needed to interact with each other. They

* It refers to representing characters (alphabets of natural language, numbers, symbols, etc.) of text as a set of bits. Each character is converted to a predefined pattern of bits based on the definition given by an encoding mechanism.

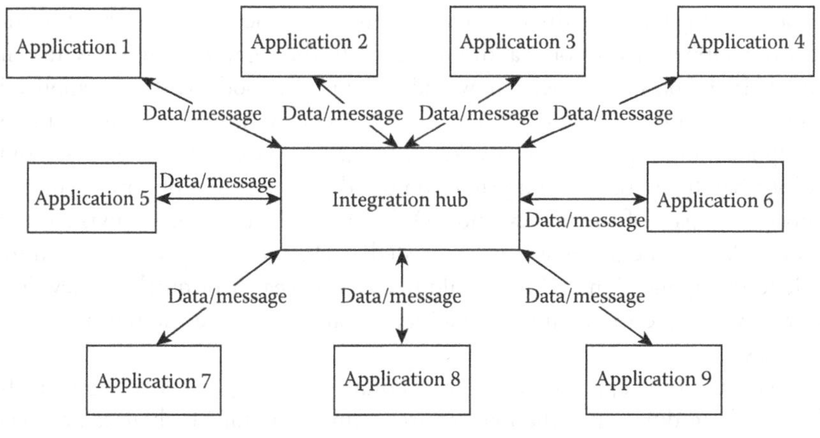

Figure 2.2 EAI tool-based integration—hub-spoke architecture.

generally took care of the data transformations/message transformations, data validations, transport, routing, delivery of messages, and the accessibility (from outside the application) aspects of applications that are interfacing with each other. Examples of such tools are TIBCO®, SeeBeyond®, Vitria™, and Biztalk®.

There are many fallouts to these integration approaches. Business data gets duplicated leading to ambiguity and errors in data. A customer details record, for example, may be available in more than one application in the application's own database. It may be present in an ERP package, in the finance system, and in the sales application. But, for a single customer, each one may have conflicting or ambiguous information and it would be hard to make out which one is the correct one. The approaches result in tight coupling and increased dependencies between applications. Systems become more inflexible to change. Post integration, if an application needs to be changed for some requirement, it needs to be looked at as a bigger system now, with the systems it integrates with also needing to be considered—they are likely to be impacted as well. The automation appears as skewed automation since the systems lack the coexistence philosophy in architecture thinking. Though they get integrated for enabling a business process, the systems and the architecture lack transparency* for this business process they jointly support. Whenever the process changes, the tightly done integration also needs to change and it becomes complicated.

2.7 Business–IT Gap

The conventional architecting approaches resulted in the process logic and business rules being hardwired and embedded in the application code. The systems, especially the earlier ones, were architected with a strong business function view that

* Here, "transparent" is used in the traditional sense, meaning clearly visible.

did not directly serve the direct support of business processes; support for business processes happened with only additional code in the application for flow and integration. If the business process flow had to be understood clearly, the application programs required to be looked into closely. The code would tell which function (i.e., application) is going to be invoked next (i.e., the next step in a process). In the case of a batch job, the program step would indicate the order of flow of control in a process (or part of the process mostly). In any case, it remained invisible to the business. When the business process needed to change rapidly, changes had to be made to the application and this could not be done easily or quickly. They do not inherently provide the required flexibility to rapidly change the business process and rules.

Changes to the applications to incorporate business process changes involved efforts of long durations. The longer turnaround time for IT changes has been a major concern for the business for a long time. By the time systems are changed to meet the process change requirements, the business process would have further changed leading to a perennial gap between business requirements (essentially business processes) and IT.

As far as packages are concerned, they supported specific business processes, but entirely within the application. This process was still implicit in the programs of the application and not one available for quick changing. While they did so, they lacked capability to support generic business processes beyond their own processes that span across applications (and functions). And even if some of them did, they were not optimized for handling generic processes. It would mean unreasonable extension of those packages beyond their areas to make them applicable in areas where they just do not naturally fit. Take, for example, a CRM package being extended to make it support an order-to-cash process. As long as the business processes remained buried, and not taken outside of the applications, the application packages would remain inflexible to the enterprise's business processes.

Another aspect of the earlier styles is that, since the process logic is implicit in the application, the process logic becomes hidden from the business (business managers, end users, business analysts, senior management). This gives no direct control to the business over the business processes to modify or manage those as mandated by business requirements. IT systems architected in conventional ways do not naturally lend themselves to the needs of the business to monitor, analyze, and improve business processes. This is a critical need if the enterprise has to stay competitive. Business managers need to be able to measure performance of processes and take corrective actions.

The systems, be they packages or in-house applications, do not support end-to-end enablement of business processes where they have to support a process from the start end step fully to the finish step. The best they could do was to automate to some extent the parts of processes.

WFMS on the other hand supported (limited) some type of business processes; they supported only those processes that had only manual activities. They were found wanting as far as handling typical processes that had system activities too. Some of them enhanced the core application functionality to also support workflow between users.

EAI, workflows, rules addresses specific parts of the problem. EAI tools enabled integration between systems and this helped support business processes that had system activities. Such processes heavily depended on integration capabilities as activities could be part of different applications; however, they had to be part of the process. However, EAI tools were not good for handling manual processes. Business rules management systems (BRMSs) focused only on abstraction of business rules into human-friendly specification, access, and execution. However, they were not meeting business process logic or control flow requirements of processes. All the three types of systems had to converge to address the problem as a whole.

The fact is that IT systems primarily exist to serve the business needs of the enterprise. But, clearly there is a gap between business processes and the IT systems supporting those. How to align IT systems well to the business processes and the business managers has been a concern of the IT architects for long.

2.8 Exercise Questions

1. What are the reasons for the natural convergence of EAI, workflows, and rules?
2. Think of at least three scenarios from your industry where integration of disparate applications has always been an issue.
3. What are the reasons for the gap between enterprise applications and the business processes?
4. Using off-the-shelf packages for supporting specific functions or business processes is always a good idea since it would help the enterprise standardize its operations. Do you agree or disagree with this statement? And why?

Chapter 3

Concept of Process-Centric Architecture

3.1 Objectives

- To appreciate the need for a new architectural approach for enterprise
- To understand the central philosophy behind process-centric architecture
- To know what PCA offers
- To appreciate the power of process definition and execution
- To see what is fundamentally behind this concept; the mathematical foundations that it is rooted on

3.2 The Case for a New Approach

We saw that there are major problems with the conventional architectural approaches. Some of the causes for these are

- The process logic is implicit in the application code making the application less flexible to change.
- The IT systems were not architected with business processes as their core.

Business processes in an enterprise constantly change, consequently changing the business requirements for the IT system. Such changes often mean changes to the process logic of the IT system. All these changes fundamentally indicate changes in the business process that the IT system is supporting. Some of them are

1. Changes to the flow of activities or order of activities, including
   a. Parallelization of activities
   b. Rearrangement
   c. Conditionally splitting the flow
   d. Sequencing parallel flows into one flow
2. Changes to the rules (conditions) that determine the control flow of the process
3. Dropping some activities in the process that are no longer relevant, or useful, or adding value to the objective of the process
4. Adding new activities to the process
5. Replacing some activity with a more effective one (or a set of activities) when the existing activity is seen as dragging the performance of the process

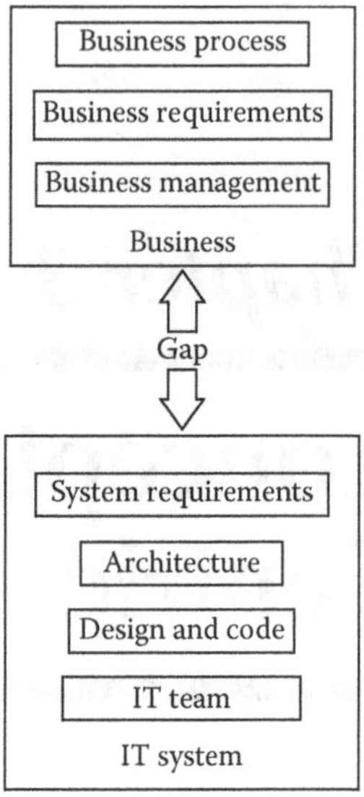

Figure 3.1 Business–IT gap.

There is a clear need for a different type of architecture for business systems. And, we can see that while architecting IT systems, two important aspects, namely, business–IT alignment and IT systems flexibility, need much attention. Figure 3.1 shows the gap that gets created between the business and the IT system.

Given that the business process in an enterprise does not remain static, the IT system supporting it needs to be adaptable to that. An architectural approach that is focused on business processes of the enterprise can help enable these qualities in the system and close the business–IT gap. Such an architecture can enable the IT systems to support end-to-end processes and not just process parts. Process-centric architecture is an architecture that takes care of this well.

3.3 What Is Process-Centric Architecture?

Process-centric architecture (PCA) is an architectural style for software systems in which the software system is organized around the central concept of business process and the business process drives the behavior of the components in the system. The objective of this style is to provide for the IT system, an architecture that suits the support of business processes of an enterprise well.

Figure 3.2 illustrates the PCA architectural style. It divides the system into the following components: the business process components, the business function (logic) components, the user interface (UI) application components, the process database components, and the external processes/systems that communicate with this

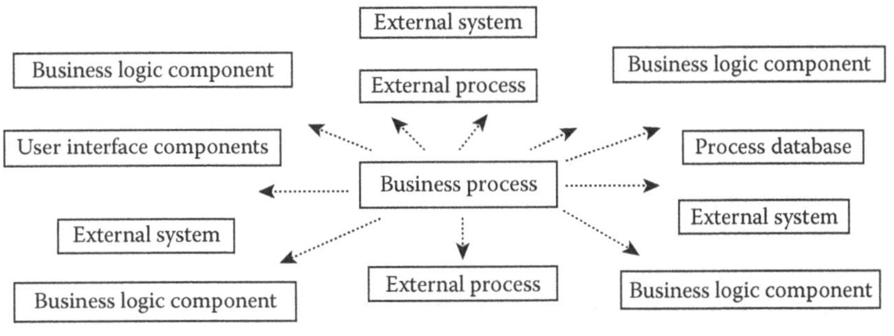

Figure 3.2 PCA illustrated.

system. This style separates the process logic from the business functionalities that the system is supposed to deliver. Each business logic component is responsible for a specific business function of the IT system's business, while the process component is responsible for the process logic and its being carried out. The UIs are responsible for enabling the users to perform their specific actions.

This architectural style is focused on the business process of the enterprise. The architecture ensures that the system faithfully implements the business process. In this architecture, the business process occupies the central position, with the other components organized around it. It is the business process component of the architecture that drives the other components.

Enterprise applications provide the right scenarios to apply this architectural style, since they are so full of business processes. The architectures following this style have clear separation of concerns among the components of the system between the process logic, business logic, business rules, and UI logic.

3.4 Process Logic Abstraction

Figure 3.3 depicts the logic in a typical software system in the enterprise. A typical IT system in the enterprise would have the following types of logic in its program code:

1. User interaction logic that takes care of
   a. The presentation, display to and enabling interaction of user with the system
   b. Screen flow for a particular business function that the user would perform with the help of UI
2. Database logic—that handles the storage, update, and retrieval using the database.
3. Business logic—achieves a specific business functionality or computation that the software is expected to provide. For example, generating a report of past due items, withdrawing money from a banking account, etc.

4. Process logic—this takes care of (or implements) the flow involved in the business process that the system is supporting or part of. This includes taking care of the flow of the processing from one business function to another, flow of control from one application serving a business function to another one serving another business function, executing business functions in parallel, and branching the flow of execution to one or more business functions based on business conditions, so on and so forth.
5. Rule logic—This part of the code implements the business rules that apply in the business context of the system. Example, if the system takes care of insurance claims processing, the business rules related to checking claim eligibility based on the various clauses applicable to the insurance policy become part of the code of the system as rule logic.

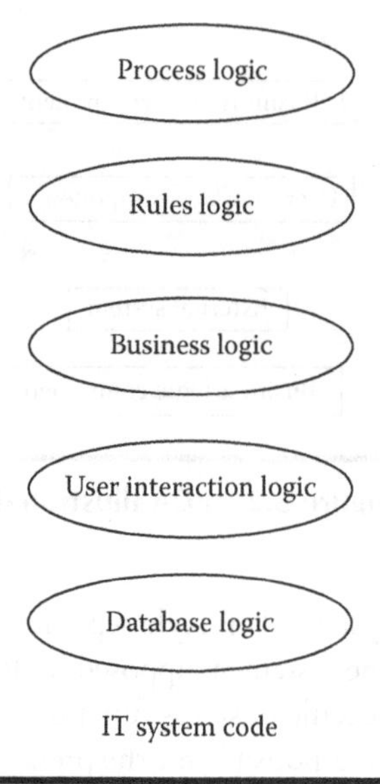

Figure 3.3 Logic in IT system.

As we saw in the previous chapters, IT systems have conventionally been designed and built in such a manner that, all of the above logic ends up getting intertwined in the code of the implemented IT system. Each of the above logic is actually a different concern and mixing them up together does not help make the system more adaptable—they need to be addressed separately. And, that is one of the main reasons for the IT system becoming inflexible to adapt to business changes. Over the last three decades, we have seen the architecture going higher and higher up in abstraction thereby introducing more separation of concerns (which is a key software architecture principle) toward making the systems more flexible. This separation of concerns also resulted in more tiering in the architecture with each tier handling a specific concern.

At first, the database logic was separated out with the introduction of the data tier and 4GLs (e.g., SQL). Then with the model-view-controller (MVC) architecture pattern, the UI logic, the screen flow logic, and the business logic got separated into different tiers advocating *n*-tier architectures for IT systems. With that the

- UI logic became part of the presentation tier.
- Screen flow logic and specific request–response flow logic became the controller tier.
- Entire business logic became part of the business tier. They came to be called business components.
- The data access logic or the database logic was part of the data tier.

A good example of such business component based architecture is Enterprise Java Beans (EJB). It was a realization of good separation of business concerns from the presentation, controller, and data logic. This *n*-tier architecture model brought the IT system changes closer to the business than before and thus even more flexible. Still, the business–IT alignment remained a considerable gap to be addressed because the business component (i.e., the business tier) code, instead of holding only the business logic, buried the business process logic and business rules too in it. This is less desirable since the business process that is most susceptible to change and the most important aspect of the business–IT alignment, manifested as hard-coded business logic, making the system less flexible than it could be and farther from the business than it should be.

Continuing the evolution with abstractions in the architectures, business rules were separated out from the business logic and made part of a separate tier named business rules tier in the architecture. This allowed business rules to be manipulated by business folks without forcing IT system changes or code changes.

The realization, that process logic is distinct from business logic and abstracting out the process logic is an important element of making business–IT alignment better and making systems more adaptable, gained ground. Thus in the next step of evolution (which is where we are at present), the next higher abstraction introduced was to separate the process logic out from the business logic (and business tier) and move it closer to the business than ever before.

Figure 3.4 illustrates the different levels of abstraction made possible by this evolution. The topmost layer is the closest to the business. The bottommost layer is closest and most friendly to the machine (computer). The process layer, the business rules layer, and the UI layer are at the business level of abstraction—the system is specified, designed, and constructed at this level with business-friendly languages and human-friendly languages. With PCA, a good part of system creation is done at this level itself and it is expected to be done mostly by business itself. The topmost in this is the process layer, and its specification has the biggest impact in the creation of the system. Specifications made at these layers in the business level are translated automatically (or manually in some cases) to the next lower level, that is the technical-level abstraction specification. The technical-level abstraction is oriented toward technical people such as software architects, programmers, and systems analysts. Here the specifications for the system are in high-level programming languages and it covers the business logic and data logic. The specifications and the languages used for specifications are closer in orientation to the system than business. Some of them are human friendly though such as 4GLs for example. At this level, the programmer adds code to implement mainly the business logic. In some cases, the business logic might be implemented by the auto-translated code from the business rules specifications itself, which is not modified by the programmer.

The specifications (the programs and code) from the technical level get converted automatically to the specifications for the machine level. This is the lowest level of abstraction and it is machine friendly. It is not comfortable for humans to

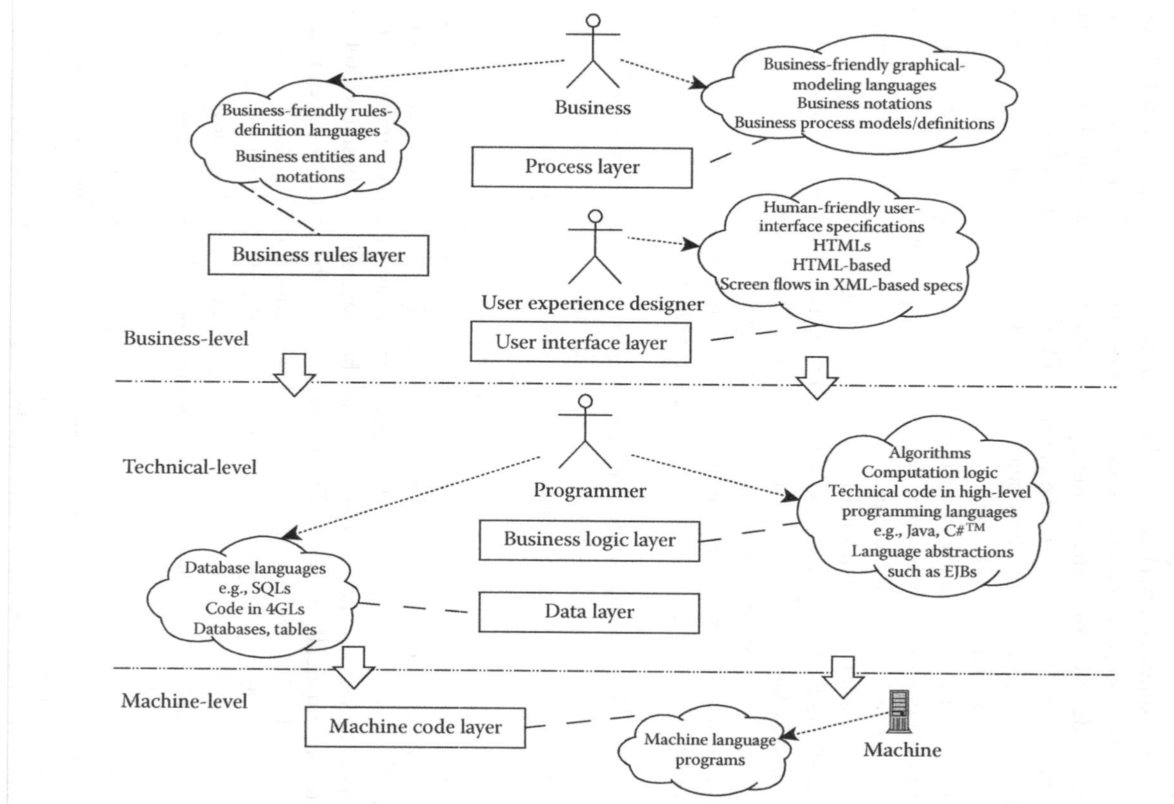

Figure 3.4 Levels of abstraction.

work with. All the specifications at the machine code layer are programs in machine language. With these levels of abstraction in the system, changes to the system are expected to be made more and more at the business level itself, which is the most comfortable to the business and eliminate (or minimize) the need for changing any specification at the technical level or machine levels. This directly and positively impacts flexibility and modifiability of the system.

This introduced a new tier to the *n*-tier architecture, namely the process tier. The promise it brings is the ability for business folks to directly design, describe, and change the business process that the IT system supports. This is the philosophy behind the PCA architectural style. In this sense, PCA makes the system even more flexible than the conventional architectures such as those described above, by raising the abstraction of the IT system to a level closest to the business personnel's level of abstraction. The resulting architecture is also *n*-tier but with the additional distinct tiers of process tier and the business rules tier in the architecture—with the process tier playing the central role in the architecture, orchestrating, and managing other tiers.

With PCA, the process layer now being distinct is also advantageous to the business layer.

- In PCA, the business tier is purely concerned about business logic alone and freed of the process logic and rule logic concerns.
- With this separation, the business tier can scale separately from other tiers to meet increased load on business functionality execution as required.
- The business tier now becomes much more maintainable and manageable, with it getting devoid of the process and rules logic.

3.5 Qualities Addressed

PCA enables the architecture to very naturally address some quality attributes of the system. All the architectures following this style share this feature. These qualities are

- *Portability* and specifically the *adaptability* quality sub-characteristics in that—A system where this style has been applied, can work across operating environments. The environments can be multiple, heterogeneous, and disparate. Business requirements of the system can change due to the changes in the business processes and the system can handle it well. When the process specification is changed, the system effectively adapts its behavior according to that specification. A person tasked with enhancing the system would be more able to extend the system to take care of additional process capabilities or do additional processing, as required by the business. The run-time behavior would happen seamlessly over multiple computing environments, in some cases they would be working in parallel. The architecture focuses on a concept of the system that is not dependent on any implementation environment. Individual components of the architecture that are concerned with business functionality can be replaced with other components serving the functionality and are thus "plug and play mode" supporting ones.

- *Functionality,* including the *suitability, accurateness,* and *interoperability* quality sub-characteristics under that—Business requirements and the IT system are well aligned in this style. The business process specified drives the system directly. The flow of control and data would be accurate to the business process specified. It also aligns the thinking of business and technical folks leading to a holistic business–IT alignment. Enabling the interaction of other systems and components is a strong characteristic of this architecture. This IT system can work with other systems in the course of its support of the business process at a level of interaction and abstraction higher than the common application level.
- *Maintainability* that includes the *flexibility/changeability* and *analyzability* quality sub-characteristics under it—It makes the IT system very flexible to deal with changes in the business. If the system has to be changed, it allows the change to be done with minimal effort. Such changes, in many cases, involve no change in the code (i.e., computer program). The system operation is readable because the core is explicit and realized in a business-friendly specification. It is also well modularized in the form of separating components logically based on their concerns such as process logic, business logic, presentation, and process infrastructure. Support of the IT system becomes easier since errors can be localized within the individual components that have been clearly separated in terms of their respective concerns. A person tasked with maintaining the system would get better ability to analyze quickly and locate the root cause of a problem in the case of error situations. One of the efficient ways de-bugging can be done is to follow the trail provided by the process to the failure point.

This architectural style does not specifically address the following quality attributes: Efficiency (performance), reliability (availability, recoverability), and security. If these need to be met by the system, the architecture needs to be specifically enabled to take care of them, by the architect. For the specific contexts of the IT systems, the architect can apply relevant architectural patterns and either use or introduce other layers in the architecture to support these qualities as well.

3.6 Structure

Figure 3.5 shows the logical view of the architecture in PCA. This architecture is composed of the following components and each has a specific role to play in the system:

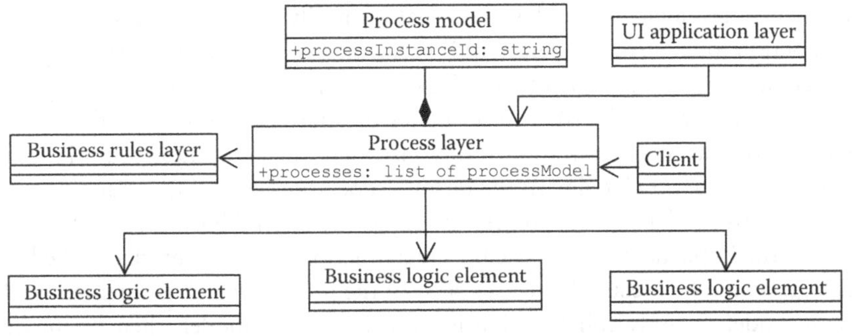

Figure 3.5 Logical view of the architecture.

3.6.1 Business Process Model

This is the core of the architecture. The entire process logic of the IT system is abstracted out into this component. It is responsible for realization of process flow, process context maintenance and availability, interaction with other processes, and any process-level issue handling. It collaborates with all the components of the architecture.

This component acts as the single driver for the IT system's business execution and invokes the components responsible for business functions during the execution of the business process and ensures their participation. It takes part in inter-process communication by interacting with other business processes and also allowing them to initiate interactions with it. This component utilizes the services of the process layer during the process execution. On the other hand, the process model allows the process layer to invoke it to trigger the process execution and to perform other process life-cycle-stage related operations, and to hand-over (to this process) messages or transfer invocations received from other systems or processes. It also interacts with the UI applications and allows them to send messages to it.

3.6.2 Process Layer

The process layer component provides the process infrastructure functionalities in the architecture. It is a container for the process model component and manages the life-cycle of the process. It provides generalized interfaces to the UI applications, and clients of the process model to enable interaction with the process model. It collaborates with the process model, clients of the process, and UI applications for manual activities in the process. This layer's objective is to support the process model with its process execution.

3.6.3 Business Logic Elements

Business logic elements (BLE) provide specific business functionality that each step in the process is required to provide in the IT system. They are concerned with only the business logic of the IT system that primarily include how a specific business function (or a business operation) is performed by the system and strictly does not include any process logic of the IT system. This is the computation logic for the business function. The BLE encapsulates the algorithm of its specific business operation, the business rules applied or considered in the business operation, and full business data associated with the business operation. Then it provides interface to the process model for the process model to invoke the business function and separates the implementation of the business function from the interface. The business logic would be executed in the context of the process, which is supplied by the process model. Its only collaboration is with the process model when the process model invokes it.

3.6.4 UI Application Layer

This element of the architecture has the UI applications that the users use to perform the manual activities in the process. It concerns itself with purely supporting the user to help him or her carry out the function expected of that activity by providing interface screens and relevant information. It is responsible for owning and maintaining the full business data that is input by the user. This element interacts with the process model using the interfaces provided by the process layer. The process model interacts with the UI application in some cases.

3.6.5 Clients

This refers to the external systems and other processes that initiate interactions with this system. They invoke the process model using the services exposed by the process layer. These communications can be messaging-oriented or real-time invocations. They interact with the process model at relevant stages in the process execution including start of the process execution. They communicate with the process layer to get process model details, assigned user activities for process administration functions, etc. Ideally, they represent an IT system entity that is separate from this IT system.

3.6.6 Business Rules Layer

We can abstract out the business rules part of the program logic and put it in a separate component called the business *rules layer*. The business rules layer houses the business rule and manages its entire life cycle. This design allows the rules to be modified separately from the business process and the other components of the IT system, without directly impacting them or their code. The business process interacts with the business rules layer at the appropriate point in the process, which is an activity. During this activity that corresponds to a rule, the process invokes the rules layer to execute the business rule. The rules layer executes the rule and returns the results of the rule execution to the process right away.

While modeling the business process, business rules applicable in the business context could explicitly be specified in a business-friendly manner. Out of these, the rules that influence the business logic within an activity in the process, for example in an insurance claims process, the claim approval activity typically involves a complex set of business rules to be applied to verify the claim made and approve it for subsequent processing. These are the rules that are defined and housed in the rules layer.

3.7 Dynamics

At the IT system's design time, the business process that the IT system is supposed to support is modeled in the design-time component of the system, which is the business process modeler. This process model becomes part of the run-time environment as an executable system component that interacts with other components. The design-time model is also the business specification of the business process including all the control and data flow details and this alone determines the execution flow at the run-time for the IT system.

Let us take the scenario of a sales order processing system that processes sales orders. The business process for the system is the sales order process. At run-time, the execution starts with the customer placing an order for buying a set of items. Let us say this is done by the customer by placing the order over the Internet. This Internet application plays the role of the client of the IT system, and invokes the process layer interface service to launch the execution of the sales order process for this new order.

Figure 3.6 shows a dynamic view of the architecture as per PCA.

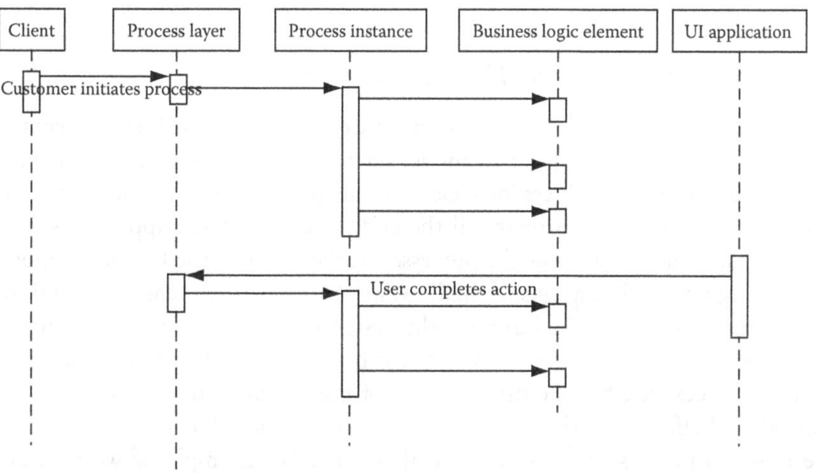

Figure 3.6 Dynamic view of architecture.

The process layer creates a run-time instance of the process model and initiates the process instance's execution by invoking it. The process model component then executes the activities in the sales order process one by one in the order. The first activity, "review the order details," is a manual activity to be performed by the order clerk. So, the process component assigns the activity to a user by invoking the services of the process layer. Then the process model awaits invocation indicating completion of the activity from the UI application that the user uses to perform the activity. The UI application invokes the process layer services to get details of the user activity and after the user performs action for the activity notify the completion of the activity. Then, the process layer invokes the process instance to hand over this notification to it. The process then continues execution on to the next activity where the "inventory is checked." This being a system activity, the process invokes the business logic element corresponding to the activity, by invoking the process layer interface provided for communication with other components, by supplying the service details and invocation mechanism-relevant information. In turn, the process layer actually connects with the BLE and invokes the business service (corresponding to the activity) exposed by the BLE for this operation, taking care of all the communication technical details such as protocols involved. Then the process component executes the subsequent activities ("picking the products," "receive payment," "shipping products to the customer") in the process following the specified order and completes the process.

3.8 Principles

Let us look at the key properties, characteristics, constraints, and principles of this architectural style.

3.8.1 Business Process-Driven System

The entire execution in the IT system is driven by the business process. The execution happens in a top-down mode, starting with the business process at the top and down to the business logic elements at the bottom, with the process steering the control flow all through till the end. In conventional approaches, the IT systems had a big role in how the processes worked or how the business happened. Depending on the limitations of the IT systems or the alignment issues with business, often business worked around the systems. IT systems were designed and created specifically for business. On the other hand, in this new paradigm, the business process itself is the driving force of the system and not a derivative or a coincidental effect from the system or from its run-time behavior. That is, in PCA, the business process itself creates and drives IT. For example, if we take an IT system that supports the travel agency's travel booking process, in PCA the travel booking process model drives the system at run-time. It itself becomes an active, explicit, and changeable component of the system and invokes other components that execute specific business responsibilities, such as creating itinerary, generating a quotation for each itinerary, look up of reservation availabilities, payment, and making reservations related to the entire selected itinerary.

Behavior the IT system exhibits in production is exactly as per the business process specification in the process model. The business process is the single driver when the IT system is architected, designed, and developed and that remains so also at run-time. The business process changes the way the IT components are used in the IT system. All the business components of the IT system including applications become subservient to the business process.

3.8.2 Highly Abstracted Components

This architectural style raises the level of abstraction higher, to the business process level. Previously, as far as business systems were concerned, the highest level of abstraction in the architecture was the business component. In those systems, the business logic was abstracted out from the rest of the application (i.e., separated from the infrastructure logic, presentation logic, data logic, and the controller logic of the IT system) and separately put into the application server* layer as business components that expose low-granular operations (often in a distributed way). The application container takes care of the infrastructure logic that handles concerns such as persistence, transactional integrity, and security in a standard way. The business component was concerned with only the specific business problem. The specific ways in which those business components performed their business operations were encapsulated by the components and only the interface to the component was exposed to the other elements such as the application server layer and controller layer.

Just as we had the business component abstraction, PCA takes the abstraction still higher to the business process level (or concept). Here, the process logic is separated (abstracted out) from the business logic (or application logic in a simple legacy perspective†) and is put in a new architectural layer, the process layer, as the business process component of the architecture. We put this process abstraction at the center of the IT system and the business process as the IT system's key component. The process component will be primarily concerned with the process logic of the system. The abstracted out business process component is housed and managed in a separate layer, namely the process layer where the process-infrastructure needs of the process are served. This style decouples the process logic and the application logic. Thus, process models and the process layer are the most important parts of this architecture. Process is the top-most layer in this architecture because of the abstraction.

---

* Also called application containers.

† We use the term application here for legacy reasons. An IT system based on PCA, can really involve one or more applications in it, since it takes a business process view. Most likely, those applications are preexisting.

In this paradigm, the business component (or the application that it is part of) is no longer burdened with the process logic. It concerns itself with only the specific business functionality it has to deliver and no longer worries about which applications (or business components) it should invoke or vice versa, unlike in the conventional approach where it had to be aware of these. Business logic elements are not aware of the process flow. They do not know to which business logic element the control will go to after they relinquish control. This is unlike the conventional architectures, where they would have been aware. The business components and the application container layer (as in the previous abstraction) that houses them are still useful in the new architecture; however, they are no longer the most important parts of the architecture. They become more of implementation options for the system architecture.

3.8.3 Automated Processes

This is a strong characteristic of the architecture. It automates the execution of the system activities in the process and integrates the applications (or application components) automatically along the way. System activities are activities in the business process that can be automated and where there is no human involvement and the execution of such steps happen without any human control.

In some situations, process automation means digitization of paper-based processes where the employees work with computer-based forms and the computer form details are flown automatically from employee to employee. Of course, value comes from redesigning the process before its automation.

Depending on the triggers for the process and the timing for the activities (schedule or as per the sequence and completion of the prior activities or events), each system activity is automatically executed by the process when the time for the activity comes. The process execution thus becomes system-controlled. With process automation, the system assists the employees throughout the enterprise in performing their actions in the process.

As an example here, let us take the mutual funds redemption process in a financial services company. The moment the customer places a request, through a broker company for redemption of units of the mutual fund that the customer holds, the process gets triggered. This process gets automatically executed in the mutual funds company, following the steps in the process automatically—steps are selling the stake in proportion to the units being redeemed; calculation of the amount taking into account the exit load, applicable charges, taxes, and other obligations; updating the amounts; crediting the customer's account with the amount received as part of the redemption; crediting the tax amount applicable to the tax department systems; and passing on the amount corresponding to broker charges to the broker company. All these steps are automatically executed and the entire redemption process itself is automatically performed with no business user involved. Thus, it is a natural way to build automation in the enterprise, given that automation is about enabling performance of business functionalities automatically with no intervention by a human.

3.8.4 Process Thinking Oriented

Business process is the central concept in the IT system and is central to the architecture. The most important aspect of the IT system is the enterprise business process that the system is to support. As far as the system is concerned, process centrality persists right from the requirements stage all the way into the functioning system in production (through design, development, deployment, operation, and support). Figure 3.7 illustrates the process centrality in the software through its stages.

This is a shift away from the conventional functions thinking to the new process thinking, where functions are only enablers to the process. Process performance and overall optimization is more important than optimizing individual functions. The philosophy is, "Think 'processes' instead of 'functions'"—process thinking is central. Process is the core of the system. An aspect of this thinking is the coherence

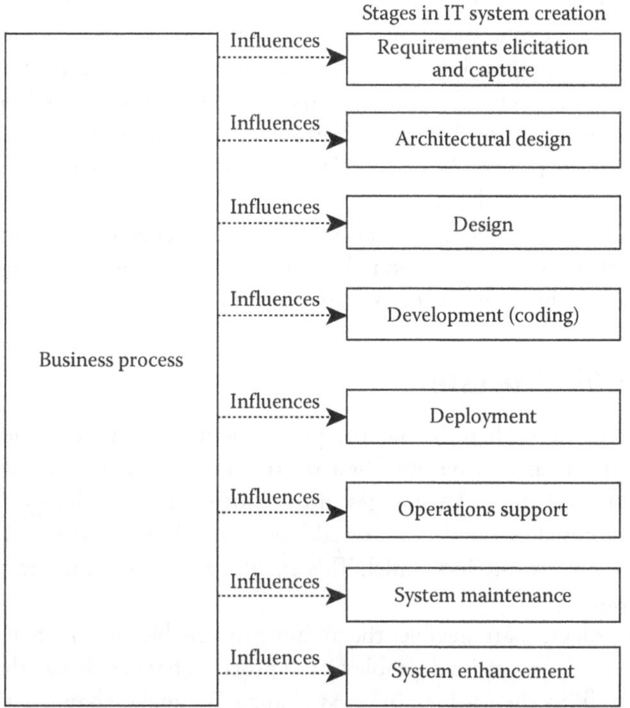

Figure 3.7 Process centrality in the system.

that this enables with the other components of the system especially the business logic components.

The system is designed directly from the business process rather than being designed for it. In this thinking, architecture comes from the strong view of what the process needs and not from what all a system can provide (or support). What a process needs is more important than anything else. In terms of work done by the IT system also, process is the right abstraction for work. That is, processes are the units of operations, handling, and manipulation as far as the system is concerned when it works. Process is the unit-of-work for the system. For the system, the primary entities are the run-time occurrences of the process; a unit of work for the system completed is the completion of one full process execution.

If the system is used for account opening in a bank, the account opening process would be the central concept with which the architecture and the realized system would work. The number of accounts opened would be the primary concern of the system as far as entities are concerned and each account opening occurrence would be considered as a separate unit of work.

3.8.5 Explicit Processes

Here the business process flow is taken out of the software code and made explicit. Business process is explicitly defined and this forms the process component of the system. The entire process logic is available in this process component. In the traditional styles, the process-flow control, rules, and process logic are implicit in the software. The process model in the process-centric architecture would include the flow control for the process, business rules, and the process flow per se. This logic is clearly defined in the model.

Apart from being explicit, the process logic is also defined in a business-friendly format. Both these allow the process to be easily managed. With explicitness, the processes are discoverable from the IT system. Process discovery becomes a trivial task.

3.8.6 Flexible Processes

The key thing to note here is that the process logic is now decoupled from the application and thus can be modified separately without necessarily touching the application code to make changes in the process flow, or change rules associated with the branches (condition), or add new branching, or drop/add activities, or make activities execute in parallel. This enables a rapid response to the changes in the business.

Business processes are flexible; the architecture enables quick changes to business processes. IT system is adaptable to the process changes. It has the capability to adapt quickly to the business process change. To make changes, the business process model is what is manipulated and this automatically results in a change in the behavior of the IT system run-time since the process drives the execution.

In this architecture, change is enabled naturally and this quality is inherent in its design itself. It allows changes to be done at the business level itself. In the real world, what changes is the business process, and the entity that changes is the very entity being modeled and changed easily in this style rather than changes in another entity such as code.

While the conventional approaches meant that any business changes would necessitate an IT system change (program change) in the PCA concept when the business changes, the change is done to the business process definition (i.e., the process logic model) and not to the IT system code. It means no change to the code or minimal changes to the code in the software. We can see this in Figure 3.4—it shows the business process and rules logic as being specified (or coded) in business-friendly languages by the business itself. This is a lot more flexible, less complicated, and business friendly a change than making the IT systems change and that too the business person being enabled to do this process model change himself or herself by virtue of the process speaking his or her language.

3.8.7 Service-Based Activities

In this architecture paradigm, each activity in the process is seen as a *service* provided by a human or a system. In that way, the process is really an orchestration of services. A service is a self-contained software element that provides well-defined business functionality and an interface that is abstracted out and separate from the implementation of functionality. It could also be referred to as a component in some sense, provided the component performs a high-granular (logically complete) business operation at a level appropriate for the process. In the case of a system activity, the service is provided by the application and during execution of the process, the process invokes the exposed interface defined for the service. Such services (i.e., the ones associated with activities) are *stateless* in nature. They just perform a high-granular (from the process perspective) business action and do not recall any past actions performed. It is the process that provides the service the context to operate in so that the action is performed in the context of the specific occurrence of the business process at run-time. Services are offered by humans or systems. These systems are implementations of the services. They need not necessarily be applications within the IT system's physical boundary or even within the enterprise. They could very well be third-party service providers too and they are only loosely coupled to the business process, making them replaceable at any point.

The services here follow the service oriented architecture (SOA) architectural style. At the process component level, they are technology neutral as no assumption is made about the technology underlying the application providing the service. The implementation of the service involves lower level (low granular) business components, layers or tiers, etc., that would together take care of the business logic for the service. Let us take the example of the "check inventory" activity in the sales order processing system. The application (or the system component), say inventory application, that implements this service, would have low-granular business components such as "get the inventory for the type of product," "get inventory details for an inventory," and "check for stock threshold limit," that it uses to realize the check inventory service. The inventory application would thus offer a set of services such as "check inventory" that are exposed to various business processes.

3.8.8 Implementation-Isolated Processes

Isolation is a property of processes in this architecture. The business process model is isolated from its own implementation since there can be different options for the run-time version of the process model component. This means, the manifestations of the process at run-time (called the process instances) can be varied depending on the run-time environment chosen for the system. For example, they can be objects in a particular object-oriented programming environment such as JAVA and .Net, or scripts or programs generated in a structured programming language such as COBOL that become part of the overall code of the application (coexisting with other programs), or chunks of human-friendly specification in formats such as XML that are read and processed by other programs (when the process needs to run) in the application or in the IT system. All of this can happen independent of the process model and without affecting the process model.

Another aspect of isolation is that processes are loosely coupled with the business logic elements, that is, the ones that support specific activities in the process. As shown in Figure 3.8, the elements that support the service for the activity are loosely coupled with the activity. A1 through A5 are activities in the process. C1 is a conditional branch in the process flow. B1, B2, B3, and B4 are business components that implement the service required by activity A4—all of them are service providers implementing the same activity service; however they may have differences in the implementation.

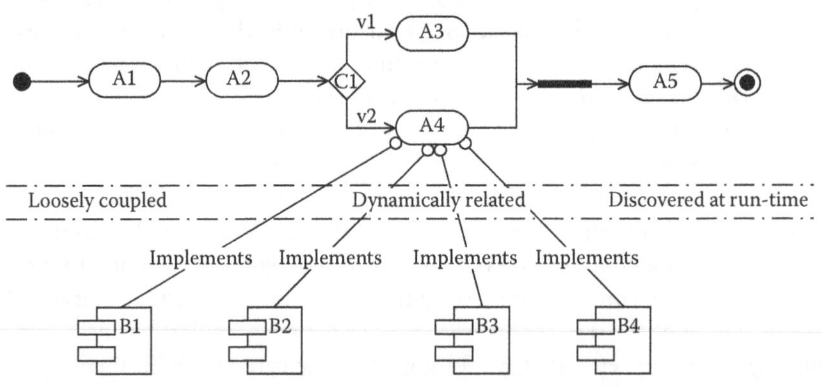

Figure 3.8 Activity and the coupling to the business components.

They can be detached and attached to the process as per the business need. Conceptually, the process is loosely coupled with the providers of the business functions involved in the business process. These providers could be third party service providers too. Thus the business process in the IT system is isolated from the implementations of the activities in the process. The implementation needs to be discovered only at run-time—one of the implementing components or service providers can be selected based on appropriateness to that particular process instance and the activity then gets dynamically connected to that service implementing element.

Process definitions can achieve another level of isolation when they are defined as abstract process models rather than concrete ones. A process defined in abstract form, leaves the implementation for the IT system to complete the essentials and make it a concrete process definition.

3.8.9 Executable Process Specifications

Business processes are not just models on paper, but are executable in a computer as code. The process models have the power of getting executed in a computing environment or platform. Run-time manifestations of the business process model in the IT system are from computer-executable code translated from the process model.

This is a key nature of business processes in this architecture and is the foundation for the architecture's realization. Process definitions are not just in business-friendly form, but are also formal. The definition is formally defined so that it can be translated or converted into computer-executable code. This means the processes can be executed automatically at run-time by the system, faithfully following the flow sequence as defined. The power for the process to direct the system's execution at run-time comes from this nature.

Formal representations have roots in process formalisms such as process algebra, petri-nets, and pi-calculus. Such formalisms give process definitions the rigor required by computing machines, including modeling of concurrent computation.

Executable processes also can exhibit concurrent execution behavior. Concurrent computation is inherent in processes. More than one occurrence of the same business process (say account opening process) can execute at the same time in the IT system. Also, multiple business processes (say account opening process, account closure process, account verification process, etc.) can execute concurrently in the system. Each run-time occurrence of the business process is a physically separate entity for the system. Figure 3.9 shows the concurrent behavior of executable processes possible at a point of time in the run-time system supporting banking processes in a bank. At that point of time, there are 12 process instances that are active and executing at the same time. All are operating on different accounts and each process instance is of a specific process model such as accounting opening, closure, or verification.

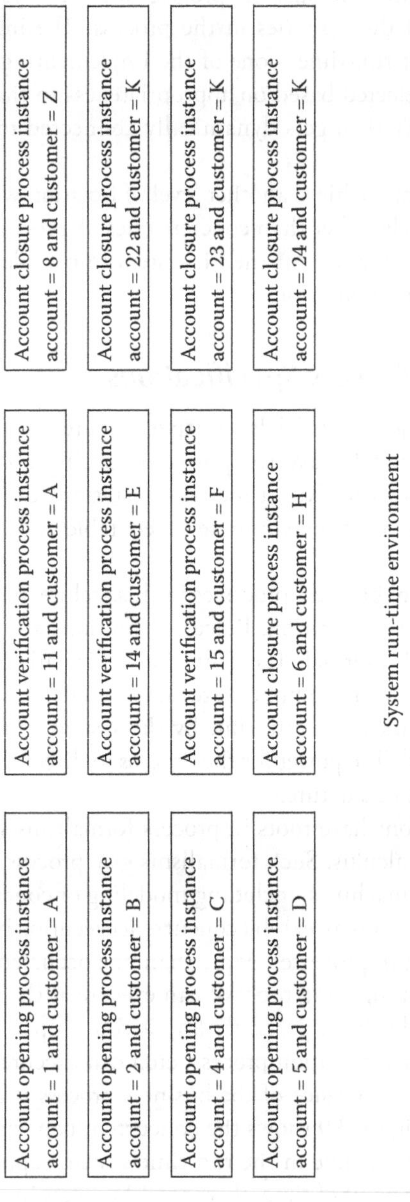

Account opening process instance
account = 1 and customer = A

Account verification process instance
account = 11 and customer = A

Account closure process instance
account = 8 and customer = Z

Account opening process instance
account = 2 and customer = B

Account verification process instance
account = 14 and customer = E

Account closure process instance
account = 22 and customer = K

Account opening process instance
account = 4 and customer = C

Account verification process instance
account = 15 and customer = F

Account closure process instance
account = 23 and customer = K

Account opening process instance
account = 5 and customer = D

Account closure process instance
account = 6 and customer = H

Account closure process instance
account = 24 and customer = K

System run-time environment

Figure 3.9 Concurrent executable processes in the system run-time environment—a snapshot.

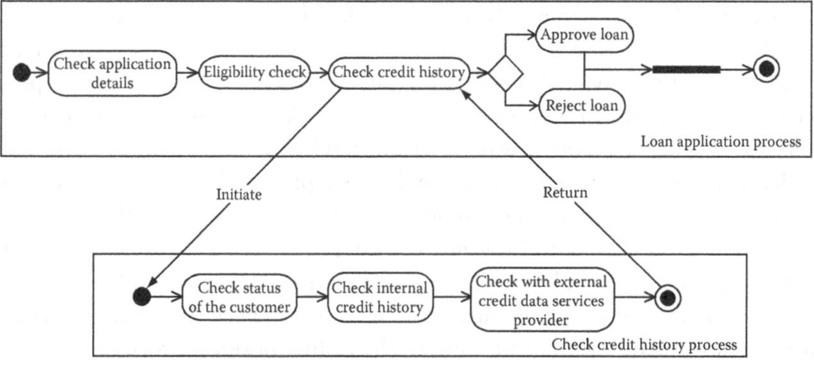

Figure 3.10 Inter-process interactions.

3.8.10 Interacting Processes

This is about interacting processes—processes interact with each other. Two or more processes can be interrelated. They communicate with each other at run-time while they are in execution and this is a dynamic relationship. For example, a loan application process, in the "check credit history" activity, could interact with the credit history process that has a set of activities to check the credit history of the loan applicant. The credit history check process would have steps to check with a credit data services provider, validate the customer's internal credit history, status of the customer, etc. The credit history would communicate back to the loan application process in the activity subsequent to the "check credit history" activity, whether the credit check is successful or not, the latter process would have been awaiting the reply message from the credit history process. Figure 3.10 illustrates inter-process interactions.

3.8.11 Business Controlled System

The IT system here is controlled by the business folks and they are the ones primarily expected to change and control it. When the business changes, the change is primarily done to the business process definition, which takes care of the system and minimizes changes required to the IT system code. This is done by someone from business such as a business analyst or a business manager since the process definition is explicit and in a business-friendly format, one that is closer to his or her language. They would find this a less complex and a more business-friendly approach to change IT systems.

3.8.12 Reusable Processes

Reuse is another concept in this architecture. It is done at the highest level itself. This architecture inherently encourages and enables software reuse at a higher level of abstraction. Processes themselves are reusable; they can be invoked from a step in more than one process, where the reused process completes its process and returns to the process that invoked it. For example, an inventory replenishment process may be used by a sales order process, a periodic stock check process, and a "manage production" process. Another way is reusing services across processes. A particular activity in a process may be part of more than one process. For instance, the "Check inventory" activity (and service) could be reused by any process that has a need to do inventory checking and not just the sales order process. The context of that process might be different however, from that of sales order process. Still the service can work transparent to that because its job is to only check the inventory data and return back the status or quantity info to the calling business process.

3.8.13 Mobile Processes

Mobility is a characteristic of processes. It refers to the behavioral aspect of a business process. Regardless of the executing process's location or the location of other processes with which it communicates, the data they exchange between each other is seen as being transferred in the same way as a data that is internal to the process getting transferred from one data location of the process to another data location in the same process, purely within the confines of the process.* The processes could be executing in physically different environments, and communicating over a network, or the Internet. This means multiple things, some of them are

1. The channels of inter-process communication and channels the process uses for communication with the BLEs (service implementers) are themselves passed around between the communicating processes just like data instead of any static consideration. To the process, the channel would just be as if it is the value of one of its local variables and one that is identified by a name (variable name). Communication is dynamic in nature.
2. The data transferred by a process to another is, as if the data is moved as value to a local variable in the process (i.e., a variable whose scope is only the process). Again, the data destination and source are identified by names.
3. References are used for processes that these can be exported to. Process identifiers are used as unique logical references to processes, and they can be passed around.
4. Structural changes to processes do not affect other processes. These can be looked at in two ways:
   a. Internal mobility for the process happens when irrespective of the changes to what comes from the other communicating process as input to this process, this process is free from any changes to itself. Even if the other process sends a different data to this process, this process is internally not affected.

* Here for the process, we are drawing an analogy to a computer program that has variables and data being moved between the variables as part of value assignment to variables.

   b. For a process, external mobility happens when no matter what changes happen to the internal process (including data-related changes), that is any changes happening internally to this process, there would be no changes to the processes with which this process is communicating. The name that is used to send data to the external process would remain the same.
5. The relationships between processes (executing) are realized through establishment of links between them, and these links are dynamic and they keep changing including they (existing ones) being broken and new ones being established.
6. Communication between processes can be asynchronous in nature. The same holds good for communication of process with the BLEs.
7. Looked at in another way, the environments where processes execute and communicate with each other change in a dynamic manner. It however, does not affect the process execution as process logic happens transparent to the environment.

An analogy that is often used is that of the cellular phone system. Two persons communicating with each other using their respective cell phones do the following: Start the communication (initiate), communicate with each other by sending voice, and end the conversation. Now, each of these two persons could be on the move while the conversation is on, moving out from one base station coverage area (or cell phone tower coverage area) and moving into another. However, their conversation or communication is not disturbed at all. The protocol ensures the mobility. The base station address and the cell tower address in use are handled dynamically to suit mobility. These addresses would be used as just specific values to variables (names) used in the protocol. They do not get hard bound to the process, that is, the cell phone, the protocol and the communication. These values would keep changing automatically as the cell phone users move from one physical point to another.

Another analogy is that of an aircraft entering and exiting air traffic control (ATC) station ranges in the course of its flight from the origin location to the destination location. As soon as the aircraft enters an ATC range, its aircraft communication would make use of that ATC. This is so till the aircraft leaves this ATC zone. At the beginning of the flight it would be the ATC at the origin, then it goes through various ATCs en route and the last one it would be in is the ATC at the destination. One of the ways mobility is realized here is the aircraft picking up and identifying signals transmitted by the ATC stations dynamically along the way, instead of any binding to any of the ATC made in a hard mechanism. The connections to the ATCs are made and then dropped as the flight progresses.

3.8.14 Process-Level Programming

3.8.14.1 New Programming Abstraction

It takes programming of the IT system to a different level, to the level of business. The programming is done at the process level abstraction. Executable process definition formats are used to define the process and this is a higher level of programming. At this level, the entire process logic is described and this itself is a computer program but at an abstraction much higher than that of the traditional high-level programming languages such as Java. The control flow, decision point and branching, process context properties value settings, finite loops, parallelizations, and synchronizations and so on are all defined explicitly in the executable process definition. The process logic makes the major part of programming for the IT system especially from the perspective of the flexibility of the IT system. Process programming being at the business level, is done primarily by the business folks such as process analysts and process managers. That is a major shift in the nature of programming and is a paradigm change.

3.8.14.2 Minimized Coding

When seen from the flexibility of IT system perspective, coding as meant in the traditional sense is minimal here. Only the specific algorithms that define the individual activities in the process are programmed in a high-level programming language (as part of the service implementation for the activity). This potentially makes programming minimal in the applications because the major part of programming (process logic) that impacts IT system flexibility is programmed using process definitions done by business folks. Thus minimal code is programmed in the IT system and that code is related only to the specific business functionality for the activity.

3.8.15 Composable Processes

Processes are composable from other processes. A new process can be composed from other processes by making the existing process an activity of the new process. This contributes to the reuse capability. From the perspective of process design and managing complexity of modeling, process logic segment that occurs (or can occur) multiple times in the process can be taken out and modeled as a subprocess. The main process then includes an activity that invokes the subprocess and that activity appears as many times as the common process logic has to occur, in the process. Thus a process can be composed of subprocesses.

3.8.16 Autonomous Processes

When each process executes in the run-time environment, it is independent in that it drives its own execution and is not controlled by any other process. The executing process has its own identity and physical existence in the system as an entity. Processes are thus autonomous. Each run-time occurrence is technically independent and runs without interference from others except as part of defined interactions it can have with other processes.

3.9 Integration Concept as Handled in PCA

Integration is about making applications (especially if they are disparate) in the enterprise work together. Previously, EAI tools and message brokers addressed this as only system integration where it enables application-to-application (A2A) flow. PCA takes a different approach to the integration of applications. The effective solution to the application integration problem is process-driven integration where the applications or application components are integrated with a business objective that is determined by a higher level component. This is not one that enables just a system-to-system technical interaction handling primarily technology-compatibility issues. The objective of integration is much beyond simply making one application A some how talk to another application B. To execute the business process seamlessly, the integration of the silos of applications in the enterprise is considered very important. The process model integrates the applications here and is the only one that drives the integration.

The business process provides the context for integration and the process specifies how the human roles and the systems (applications) work together to achieve the business objective for the process. It brings in the enterprise context for integration which provides for the services, the semantics, granularity and syntax that is appropriate to meet the needs of the enterprise. The individual applications would perform the respective functions that are required in the system activities of the process. They individually expose these functions as services at a higher-level of granularity appropriate for processes (i.e., activities in the process) and become BLEs in the architecture for the integrated IT system. At run-time, the process component invokes these exposed services corresponding to the system activities. If we take one such application that is integrated this way, unlike previously, other applications would no longer invoke its services or functionality interfaces. Nor will it invoke other applications as it used to earlier because such process logic would have been moved out of the application's code into the process model. The integration now has a well-defined business meaning. Traditional application interoperability issue is handled in a cleaner way by letting the process definition and service invocations become loose-coupled from the application or service implementations.

The applications are also loosely coupled from one another. Unlike a typical EAI tool, the process layer not only integrates applications but also integrates them with the human roles performing manual activities. The business process that runs in the process layer executes automatically spanning services and user activities.

Figure 3.11 shows how integration is realized in PCA. The applications A, B, C, and D are integrated by the process, as part of the process flow specification. The activity services corresponding to the system activities A1, A2, A4, and A5 are provided by the business components B1, B2, B3, and B4, respectively. Unlike in the conventional approaches, A, B, C, and D do not talk to each other

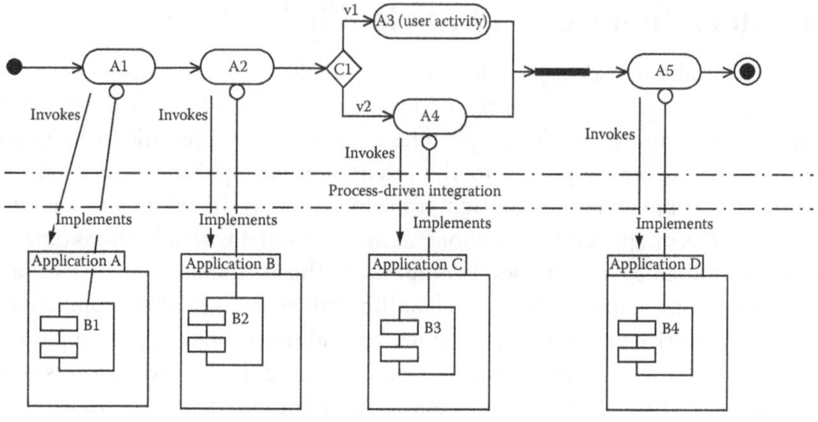

Figure 3.11 Integration realized through PCA.

directly any more, nor are they aware of the next application or the previous application in the flow. Thus they are loosely coupled with the process and with each other.

3.10 Workflow in PCA

Workflows traditionally have meant a work item flowing from one user to another in some order and it gets processed completely at the end of the flow. Workflows involve heavy human involvement in the processing. For example, a customer service call center operation, where a call is received from the customer and the customer's request becomes a new work item that needs to be processed. This item is flown from one user to another involving hand-offs. WFMS is focused on supporting such flows.

PCA treats workflows in a broader way. The flows are seen as business processes that have more human participation. This view allows automated activities also to be included in the process. It not just supports the workflow steps by having those steps as manual activities in the process, but also integrates system activities, thereby supporting a broader flow. The process model drives the human integration by routing the work to each user at the right time in the flow. Each new case or request in the case of a call center process for example, becomes a new occurrence of the process execution at run-time and thus a new work item.

3.11 Holistic View in Architecture

The process-centric architecture concept holistically addresses the portions of enterprise computing that previous technologies attempted to individually (and partially)

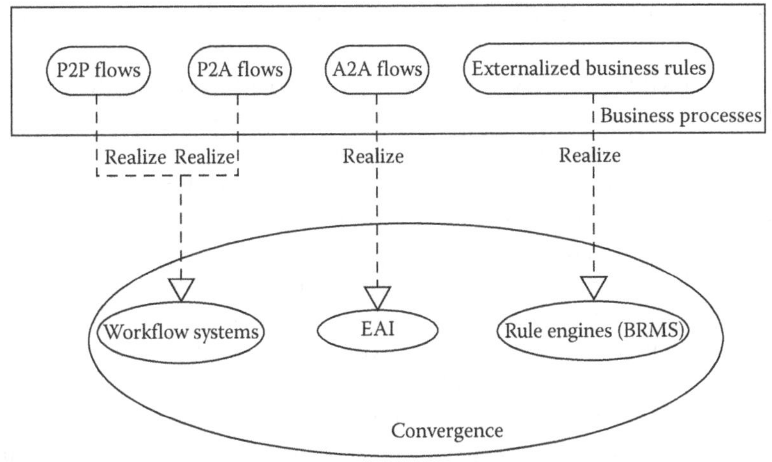

Figure 3.12 Convergence of workflows, EAI, and BRMS.

address. For example, EAI addressed only system integration where it enables A2A process flow parts. WFMS looked essentially at flows involving humans or person-to-person (P2P) flows in other words. Business rule engines addressed the abstraction of business rules at a level specifiable and manageable by business in natural language (that is more business friendly than programming languages) so that they can be changed easily with very minimal change in application code. They were looking at different parts of the business process puzzle. EAI, WFMS, and Rules engines have now converged under the umbrella of BPMS, which is the core layer of IT systems based on PCA. We will see what a BPMS is in detail in the subsequent chapter. It addresses business process support holistically by seeing the business process as a whole consisting of P2P, A2A, and P2A flows, and the rules that govern the activities in the process. Figure 3.12 illustrates the convergence of workflows, EAI, and BRMS into the process layer or process infrastructure in PCA and how they are viewed holistically. PCA moves business processes out of applications (packages or in-house) into the infrastructure layer (a separate one at that) of IT systems where it is managed holistically and in a business-friendly fashion. It therefore represents the next step in enterprise architecture evolution.

3.12 Similar Approaches

PCA might appear similar to software development approaches such as model driven architecture (MDA). PCA has some similarities in the way the business process model defined at the beginning of the architecture work, gets translated further directly into an executable version for the system, similar to the way a higher level model in MDA gets translated to lower level models and finally to the code. However, that is the key similarity between PCA and MDA.

Unlike in MDA, in PCA the business process definition actually becomes an active run-time component in the final implemented IT system. And this component drives the behavior and the execution flows of the IT system.

PCA does not advocate auto-generating the entire code for the IT system, that is, all the code required for all the components that make up the system. When it comes to the other components of the system (the business logic elements, that is), PCA approach is different. The code for the implementation of the BLEs is not always auto-generated, though in some cases it might technically be possible. In quite a number of situations, the BLEs are preexisting services that are getting reused. Integrating existing services or applications into the IT system being designed is addressed and enabled by PCA. Often in PCA, the IT system is not entirely built or rebuilt. The business services that are preexisting are used to support steps in the process without typically rewriting their code. MDA does not appear to explicitly address that—the approach is to build the entire system as new from the architecture by generating code.

Next comes the complexity and manageability of the entire architecting exercise and the implemented system—what really is being modeled, that finally results in the system, is important for this than anything else. Here, PCA focuses on the business process modeling and that is what is being modeled by the business. That (business process) is a concept that the business community is already familiar with; it is their own language and thus less complex to them. Complexity associated with that is more manageable. On the other hand, in MDA, the modeling might involve more complexity as the entire system is modeled and not just the process flows. Even though domain-specific concepts and notations are directly used, it still appears a daunting task to make the modeling complete. Consequently, the system code generated and thus the system itself would be more complete only when this modeling is complete. In practice, it could be very hard to achieve this completeness.

Maintainability of the code for the system is another concern. MDA results in lot of code being generated. In fact, the goal of MDA is to completely auto generate code of the entire system directly from the higher level models created without the programmer having to really change anything. History* shows that such approaches are prone to making the resulting system hard to maintain. The auto-generated code typically becomes hard to maintain because it totally depends on the completeness of the higher level modeling abstractions in fully addressing the needs of the system and reliable faithful translation of that into equivalent code. Such modeling approaches have been found to be far from complete at least as of

* CASE tools are good case studies in this context.

now, so this results in less than 100%* of the code being auto-generated. We have also seen from history that the machine-generated code is typically not optimized for performance, extensibility, and maintainability. One of the reasons is that the auto-code-generation ends up creating extra code that a programmer hand-writing it would judiciously avoid. A programmer also optimizes the program code as he or she writes being conscious of the quality impact such as performance—the programmer can think of various code options for achieving the same business logic and choose to follow or write the code accordingly unlike the machine that would find doing this very hard and would typically generate the same lines of code for the same business logic each time. Bug fixing also becomes a hard exercise. All these make the MDA generated system code more complex to maintain.

If there are existing applications that are to be integrated to the system based on MDA, there could be issues in the generation of interfaces and in linking the new system code to the interface. PCA addresses this with a clean philosophy of loosely coupled interfaces with the business services. The process of code generation in MDA is smooth if the entire requirement is captured and they are captured accurately and documented in the models accurately. PCA follows an iterative approach, the requirements need not be complete and can be evolving.

3.13 PCA in the Context of Other Architectures

In the context of architecting IT systems, it is not uncommon to use multiple architectural styles and patterns in combination. PCA can coexist with other architectural styles and also has influences from some of them and vice versa. Each of these architectures or styles will have a specific scope and focus in the overall system's architecture. As we will see in detail in Chapter 9, PCA and SOA share a complementary relationship with each other when enterprise IT systems are architected.

The layering approach in PCA comes from the layered architecture style—PCA defines a set of layers and their responsibilities. Model-View-Controller (MVC) architecture pattern can be used in combination with PCA for designing the UI application and the UI layer. The UI applications involved in a process-centric architecture can be partitioned into model, view, and controller components with a clear separation of responsibilities. The UI applications can follow a request–response model of interaction within themselves. Basically, the client-server architecture style is the common style applied for UI applications in this context.

PCA is also an instance of an *n*-tier architecture, and each tier in PCA has a direct influence in the physical structuring of the IT system's infrastructure. Some of the tiers in PCA are BPMS, application server, web server, rules engine, and database

* Most of the current MDA approaches and implementations claim up to 80% (of total code) code generation as the best case.

server. The implicit invocation (or event-driven architecture [EDA]) architecture style can be one of the options in the architectural design of the process layer.

3.14 Exercise Questions

1. What is different about PCA as opposed to the earlier technologies of EAI or WFMS or rules engines?
2. Recall two scenarios from your enterprise when P2A flows had to be handled. How where they handled? Now, relook at those scenarios applying PCA concept. What is the difference in the philosophy this time?
3. Can PCA influence the way IT is organized?
4. How is the business–IT gap being addressed by PCA? Does the concept create a solution or preempt the problem itself? What are your thoughts?
5. Do you think its mathematical foundations provide it strength or is it a handicap?

Chapter 4

Business Process Management

4.1 Objectives

- To get introduced to BPM
- To understand the concepts of BPM
- To be aware of the various aspects of BPM
- To understand the business part of BPM
- To be aware of the life cycles of a business process
- To get the big picture of PCA
- To understand what a BPMS is

4.2 What Is BPM?

Business process management (BPM) is about business processes and their management, to put it in simple words. There is a strong philosophy behind BPM, which is that business processes are the *core assets* of enterprises. And, business processes are *central* to any activity or exercise done with the objective of improving business performance. BPM is also expanded by some as *business process modeling.* However, let us stick to the term business process management in this book since we believe this reflects a meaning that is more close to what it really covers.

BPM refers to holistic management of business processes throughout their life cycle with the assistance of systems. It is the set of strategy, tools, and techniques to design, deploy, and simulate processes to enable a rapid process change in the

2000s	Process-focused IT. Technology support for process improvement.
1980s to 1990s	Business process reengineering (manual).
1960s to 1980s	Automation of parts of business processes. IT as enablers.
1900 to 1960s	Processes embedded in work practices. No link to IT.

IT's scope in business process

Figure 4.1 IT support for business processes–evolution.

organization, aligned to meeting organizational objectives. There is no standard definition yet for BPM that is commonly agreed upon. In this book, however, let us stick to the definition given above.

Figure 4.1 shows the evolution of IT from the perspective of business processes and their improvements. BPM has been around for at least a 100 years. From the early twentieth century, people have been looking at ways to improve their organization's business processes. Some of the methods used were based on mechanization (of certain shop floor work), quality control practices, optimizing specific business functions (department), and *business process reengineering* (BPR). And, these have been applied too with varying results. BPR was more drastic in terms of the changes to the processes since its concept meant discarding the current process totally and thinking afresh to create a new process from scratch. The new process was expected to be free of all the limitations imposed by existing practices, people, and systems. But this turned out to be too expensive for the enterprises and the results were not too successful. An important reason was that the IT systems at that time were not flexible enough to support the massive changes that it brought in.

However, in the last 10 years, especially with the technology changes, BPM has meant a radically different approach to business process change and improvement and this has been looking promising. In the 2000s, BPM has been recommending a strong system-assisted approach to do continuous process improvement in an iterative fashion. Simply put, this means

- Accepting that business processes keep changing.
- Making business processes flexible for change.
- Allowing change and managing the change of business processes with the help of systems.
- Viewing business processes holistically from end-to-end.
- Working with business processes as units of work rather than business functions.
- Going through the full life cycle of the business process and management covering all stages.

- Measuring process performance and optimizing processes in iterations. In each iteration, the process shows improvement. Measure performance, redesign, and deploy—do this continuously. There is no end to this because processes keep changing.
- Considering relation of processes to other processes, levels of processes, and connection to value-chains at the highest levels for process management.
- Business processes drive IT systems.

BPM focuses on the continuous improvement of the business process and not just a one-time big improvement. BPM has two broad aspects: one is the management part and the other is the technology part. Both are important and complementary to each other and together they make BPM complete.

BPM takes an enterprise-wide view of business processes. It looks beyond the individual functions or department units in the enterprise to address enterprise processes holistically to improve process' effectiveness and efficiency. Its view is that what is important to the process is the overall optimization of the output of the overall process and not the individual function's optimization. Optimizing functions within departments of an enterprise need not result in improvement of the process as a whole. In some cases, optimizing a function could drag the performance of the overall process since the subsequent functions (by other departments) in the process may be unable to handle the extra load and the work can get unnecessarily queued up. BPM believes that taking a process scope view for optimization is very important and discourages function-based thinking and divisions from that.

Its approach with a business process is to start with modeling AS-IS process, then analyze it, optimize the process—design the TO-BE process, model the TO-BE process, simulate the TO-BE process, optimize the TO-BE process at design-time, deploy the TO-BE process in production (implement), execute the TO-BE process, monitor the TO-BE process for performance, and analyze it for improvement. The AS-IS process model is the faithful capture of how the business process functions right now in the enterprise and its usefulness is directly related to how accurately it reflects the current process. The entire process life cycle mentioned above is continuous and done iteratively over a number of iterations. The change for a business process can be triggered by many reasons including improving performance of existing business processes, changes in business/market conditions, and launch of new services or products. BPM gives importance to the use of technology (IT systems) in doing all the process management aspects given above, including process execution. It also expects IT systems to help in process automation where more and more activities are performed automatically by processes using systems.

The management side of BPM includes business process architecture, process improvement, process redesign, process optimization, process ownership, process simulation, process monitoring/performance measurement, process analysis, lean, quality methods such as six-sigma, process governance mechanisms, and linkage of process performance metrics to enterprise strategy.

The technology side of BPM is the BPM system (BPMS)—it is the technology part of BPM. BPMS is an architecture concept that takes a process-centric view of applications to provide flexibility and business alignment to applications. It supports the full life cycle management of business processes by providing technology capabilities to manage processes as basic and central entities. It assists the process owner,* process analyst, end-users, and other roles with each stage in the process life cycle. For example, a BPMS would allow the process owner or equivalent roles to monitor executing processes in real time and take management decisions on processes. BPMS would enable process analysts to do simulation of To-Be processes to help optimization of the processes. Evolution-wise, BPMS is a convergence of workflow, EAI, process modeling, and business rules. Due to some legacy-related reasons, the words "workflow" and "BPM," especially in the system context, are used interchangeably by many. However, throughout the book, we shall just stick to the term BPM to avoid any potential confusion. Another term that is commonly used in this context is *BPM suite*—it is used to refer to a suite (combination) of tools, products, and components in the context of BPM such as process modeling, user interface handling, software requirements handling, rules management, workflow management or engines, EAI; underlying platforms such as integrated development environments (e.g., Eclipse™), .Net, Java; and technologies such as XML. BPM suites typically are generic in nature, they do not address specific domains, verticals, or provide canned frameworks for specific processes.

Process improvement can be approached in different ways. However, doing it using BPMS would be the most effective way. BPMS is only a decade old as a concept. Until this arrived, there was no system (including a run time) that was directly supporting BPM and dedicated solely to BPM—this was a cause for the business process–IT system gap and system rigidity. A BPMS assists human roles through the entire life cycle of the business process. It gives the business community and the IT architects a capability to work exclusively with the business process as an entity, thereby helping to make process improvement and management more effective than ever before. For an IT architect, using a BPMS makes it easier to realize system capabilities related to the process layer and the process model, in the IT system. Without a BPMS, all this would have to be implemented in the application by the IT team themselves and it might not finally be as comprehensive, exhaustive, and effective as in a BPMS. And, without a BPMS, it also would mean more time and effort (avoidable) spent on realizing these capabilities instead of better spending

* A "process owner" is a new business role. It is a role that is typically found in enterprises that are organized around processes (more process-oriented) as opposed to the traditional function-oriented organization style. A process owner has the full ownership and overall responsibility of a business process through its entire life cycle.

the same on the core focus of the IT system—which is the design of the specific business process and the design (and implementation) of its individual activities.

4.3 PCA and BPM

Process-centric architecture's roots are partially in BPM too. BPM gives the big picture for PCA.

This influence comes from the technology side of BPM. PCA is a technical perspective of the IT systems, strongly focused on their software architecture, in the overall context of BPM. Though it has roots in process thinking and the BPM movement, PCA is a purely architectural perspective of the enterprise IT systems. It is not the same as BPM though it is under the BPM umbrella due to the importance PCA gives to the business process.

PCA looks at how best to architect IT systems bringing the business process into the center of the IT system's architecture. This architecture ensures that the IT system and the business are fully aligned to each other and it makes the IT system flexible to changes in business process.

PCA's focus is business process as the key architectural component and the driver of the IT system and other components (business). It is not explicitly concerned with process optimization or process improvement or process redesign or process simulation, or process business performance. Its goal is to ensure that the IT system fully reflects, realizes,* and supports the business process faithfully and to allow quick and easy changes to the business process by business. The IT system would be only as good as the business process modeled. This means, if the business process is a process designed after analysis and optimization, the business process would have a better chance of performing well and the IT system would also be good to reflect that improvement. If the business process modeled is basically not an efficient one, the IT system based on PCA would also not be efficient.

BPM, on the other hand, focuses on continuous management of business processes and has a strong objective of improving the business processes. Performance of business processes is of concern to BPM. By itself, PCA does not necessarily improve business processes nor is its objective to improve business processes. If a bad process is modeled, the IT system will still be faithful to that model in PCA. But the business effect of the system would reflect only the quality of the process model that is subpar since the process is subpar.† If a flawed AS-IS process is modeled, no positive difference can be expected to be found in the process performance from the IT system. If a good process is modeled, in PCA, the IT system will stay faithful to it as usual. However, now the business effects of the IT system would be good because of the quality of the process.

---

* Here, we take it to mean that "it implements concretely."

† The "garbage in garbage out" phrase perfectly applies here.

Thus, one would ideally be required to apply BPM to improve processes. Following the principles and practices of BPM makes the business process that the PCA-based IT system needs to support a more effective one, which in turn makes the IT system provide good business performance. Good business process work should ideally precede applying PCA for the IT system's architecture. That is, it is strongly recommended that PCA be used in conjunction with BPM to gain maximum benefits from the PCA architectural style.

A very good (and recommended) way to realize an IT system architected along PCA is to use BPMS, especially its process modeling and execution part. However, BPMS is not a must for realizing PCA-based IT system. Capabilities of a BPMS naturally fit into the core elements of the PCA.

4.4 Business Process Life Cycle

A business process goes through a set of stages in its life cycle. In BPM, that life cycle consists of

- Process design
- Process modeling
- Process simulation
- Process design-time optimization
- Process deployment
- Process execution
- Process monitoring
- Process analysis
- Process optimization

4.4.1 Process Design

The stage is the beginning stage for a process. Typically, there is an existing process, and after analyzing it, the process analyst designs the new process (or changed process in other words). The analyst considers bringing in improvement into the process model, based on the analyst's analysis. Dependencies between activities and extent of human and system participation are considered.

4.4.2 Process Modeling

In this stage, the process analyst models the designed process as an explicit process model. This is typically done as a graphical model using a standard business process modeling notation such as business process modeling notation (BPMN™). This is really the expression of the design model in a concrete form. The analyst also performs some changes to optimize the process model, based on design-time heuristics such as parallelization of activity executions wherever possible, reducing bottlenecks.

4.4.3 Process Simulation

In this stage, the process analyst attempts to do some analysis on the process model that would help the analyst to introduce design-time optimizations into the process model to the extent possible. The process model is simulated in a design-time environment where the analyst plays out "what-if" scenarios on the model. Data from past process executions (process history data) is also made use of for simulation data. The performance of the process model, in various scenarios, is studied and analyzed. The cost of this stage is nothing since there is no impact on production; this is a design-time stage. Simulation of the process is very helpful in studying the process behavior at an earlier stage itself without waiting for the process to be live in production. The latter is more expensive. The observations and the understanding of behavior from process simulation act as inputs for the process analyst/process designer* to improve the process model.

4.4.4 Process Design-Time Optimization

In this stage, the process is redesigned for possible optimization decided based on the analysis during simulation of the process. The process model is modified by the analyst for optimization. Some examples could be changing the branching conditions to more realistic values to reduce bottlenecks, removing unnecessary sequencing, etc.

Whether it is a totally new process or a refinement over the old one, the TO-BE process is expected to get optimized (or improvised) to the extent possible at the design stage itself. Optimizing it at process design stage is a more cost-effective way. This is the preferred option than waiting for the process to be implemented and deployed in production to analyze it, which is naturally more expensive.

4.4.5 Process Deployment

In this stage, the process model is deployed onto the run-time (production), typically a BPMS engine to enable it for execution. If this process already exists in production, the new process model replaces it during deployment.

* A "process designer" is a business role that is concerned with the design of a business process by taking into consideration its business objectives and automation possibilities.

4.4.6 Process Execution

This stage is about the BPMS automatically executing the process model based on triggers to initiate process execution. The process runs in production, performing the activities in it one after the other based on the order specified in the process model involving human and system participants.

4.4.7 Process Monitoring

When the process is executing in production, in this stage, the process executions are monitored by the process manager and/or analyst. The process performance is measured using a useful set of metrics such as average turnaround time for a process, number of processes completed in a unit of time, processes queued with users, and activity completion times.

The process administrator* also gets involved in this stage to take administrative actions on the processes, if required, such as restarting failed process executions.

4.4.8 Process Analysis

The process analyst analyzes the process metrics, the process model from production in this stage. Performance-improvement opportunities are identified and decided by the analyst.

4.4.9 Process Optimization

Here, the process analyst optimizes the process model based on the analysis done. Process redesign is done and changed in the process model. For example, the process logic is changed to reorder some activities, or change business rules, or drop activities.

4.5 Six Sigma

Six sigma comes from the quality control world. It is a management practice (and a methodology) that focuses on business process performance in terms of its product or service quality. It measures performance based on the *defects* found per collection of products. It was first implemented by Motorola. It is essentially a quality management methodology.

---

* This is also a business role that is relevant in a process-aligned organization. A process administrator is concerned with administrating the business processes in operation at run-time. This role monitors what is going on and takes actions such as forcefully terminating a process, initiating specific process executions whenever required, deploying process definitions, mass perform (or global) actions on processes including reassigning activities to a specific user, and scheduling specific processes for execution.

The term *defect* is used in a broader sense in six sigma; it is used to refer to defects in manufactured products, problems faced by the customer accepting a service from the business, a delay in receiving solution from the business, service levels below customer's expectations, or just about anything that makes a customer unhappy with the business of the enterprise.

Six sigma is popularly applied in manufacturing, though it has, in recent decades, been seen to be applicable to various types of business processes in enterprises. It relies on data that is measured and verifiable by concrete means. It minimizes assumptions in process metrics or data. Relentless measurement of performance metrics and the pursuit of measurable improvement in metric is a characteristic of this methodology. Six sigma uses statistical methods heavily to analyze the metrics and defects data.

A key term used is *six sigma quality* that refers to a level of quality an enterprise process has achieved with respect to its efficiency. If a business process produces only less than 3.4 defects per a million units of products produced or services provided to its customers, then it is of six sigma quality. The efforts of six sigma projects in an enterprise that has undertaken this methodology would be to improve their business process's performance so that they reach this (or better) level of quality.

The method consists of various steps that are performed by quality professionals and business managers. The steps include definition of business goals, measurement of quality data, and analysis of the data for potential improvement by identifying causes for performance issues; designing the changed process and implementing it in production, controlling the process in production to catch and act on deviations. BPM exercises in enterprises also involve six sigma methodologies for more successful BPM implementations.

4.6 Lean

There is a school of thought that focuses on reducing waste. It recommends doing more with less. Lean is one process management practice that advocates this. It comes from the manufacturing industry of Japan, where companies such as Toyota adopted lean production systems and practices to improve quality.

As per lean practice, a common-sense-driven approach is to be used whereby waste is identified and eliminated in the process. Any activity done in the process that is not adding value to the customer is considered a waste as per lean and is to be eliminated. It is in a sense reducing the flab from the process.

Some implementations of lean make the process flow smooth by following a constant rate in production of items in the end-to-end process. They also manufacture products to order rather than piling up supply. This inventory is just-in-time (JIT). Nothing much is stocked for a future demand. Many implementations cut wastage in the processes.

As per lean, there could be many types of wastages in processes. Some of them are waiting at activities (considered as a waste because it only reduces the efficiency and reduces value to the customer), overproduction of goods (since it leads to increased inventory and thereby loss of value), and producing an item that is not as per the customer's needs. The practice analyses processes to get rid of these wastages and fill the process with only value-adding activities. Lean has a very strong influence in reducing costs in processes.

Though it is applied more in production oriented processes or manufacturing scenarios, it has been extended to other processes also including service processes such as a BPO process. Lean demands a lot from the employees who are involved in the process. They need to understand the concepts behind lean very well for the process to really derive benefits from lean. Get it right first time is also a waste reduction method as done in lean. Process analysts and process managers involved in applying BPM to their processes can leverage the best of lean while redesigning processes.

4.7 Process Redesign

It is also known as business process reengineering (BPR). It refers to the analysis and redesign of existing business processes in the enterprise to achieve significant improvements in the business process's performance. Performance is measured and compared in terms of standard business metrics for the organization. For example, for a computer manufacturer, the measures could be the number of computers sold per quarter, the average profit per computer, and so on. The redesign effort's objective is to gain remarkable improvements in these measures by changing the process.

BPR is not essentially about incremental improvements in processes, it seeks to drastically improve the process performance by radically redesigning it. Looking at business processes from a "from the scratch" perspective and then designing the processes, without any thinking limitations induced by system constraints or other constraints, without any bias to improve the performance is the philosophy behind BPR. For organizations, it means starting from a clean slate kind of approach. This new design is then implemented in a way that helps the enterprise manage the transition to the new process smoothly. Implementation plays a big role in the success of any BPR exercise. If the implementation is done properly, using proper methods, BPR can result in significant gains for the enterprise. However, in the 1990s a number of its applications have been unsuccessful due to improper implementations. Some of them have failed due to incorrect association of BPR with downsizing.

BPR was a strong movement in the 1990s. In the last 10 years, BPM has come to be considered as succeeding BPR, with BPM bringing in technology support business process change to achieve process performance improvement.

4.8 Process Automation

BPM supports automation of processes to the extent possible. This means that the old paper-based processes can be transformed to automated digital processes where computer-based forms are used and work flows automatically from one participant to another without any paper flowing between them. The idea is not to simply automate the paper trail since that would mean importing all the inefficiencies of the existing process as is too, but only gaining with respect to avoidance of paper movement. Automation can do more here depending on how the process analyst redesigns the business process. The concept is to redesign the process for more effectiveness (optimization) and then automate execution of the process and its steps for efficiency.

Processes describe, in an easily understandable way, the work done in enterprises. Typically, some of that work, which are activities in other words is performed by humans and the others are automated by systems. Also, it would be infeasible to think of automating some human tasks. BPM and any process automation done within its context would be more effective if (and when) it considers both the activities that are/can be automated and the ones that are performed by employees. Instead of looking at automation as a separate objective and proceeding with achieving that, it would be more effective from the enterprise's point of view to enable automation within the BPM umbrella, including work/practices related to business processes, such as BPR, Six sigma, redesigning, Lean, and design-time optimization.

Let us take as an example, a credit card application form filled up by a customer. The form is scanned and captured by the system first in the process. Then the system extracts data from the form and allows the processing clerk to see all the details in electronic forms in system screens. In the subsequent steps, the system could do many automatic works such as validating certain details such as credit history, sending automatic notification mails to the customer as confirmations, and notifying participants. All these automations can be done to handle multiple credit card applications or other service applications at the same time.

4.9 BPMS Products

Let us take a quick look at what some of the available BPMS suites in the market are—the BPMS products. A BPMS supports BPM in all its activities covering design-time as well as run-time (execution). Some examples, in no particular order, are IBM WebSphere business process suite (WebSphere®, FileNet, Ilog®, MQ), Intalio™, Oracle (with Fusion®, Collaxa®, BEA Weblogic®, and Aqualogic®, combined), Pegasystems®, Metastorm®, Microsoft (BizTalk), K2®, SAP Netweaver® (XI/PI), Savvion™, Lombardi®, Sterling Commerce™, and TIBCO-staffware®.

In the context of BPM, process automation refers to automating processes with the use of BPMSs. Process analyst, process owners, business managers, and process administrators all use the BPMS to leverage its capability to do process management. Most of the BPMSs support process management functions to a great extent, providing capabilities such as process simulation, process monitoring, and performance measurement based on predefined metrics, and support process analysis based on various methods including statistical methods. They maintain process history data and provide querying capabilities for reporting and analysis. Querying refers to retrieving specific information about processes from history data as well as current data. People look at the use of BPMS in two perspectives:

The first one is to help analysts and managers to gain better understanding of business processes and that understanding helps them in process analysis to potentially improve the process. Here, the focus is not on whether the process is simple or complex, but the value that they can bring from the process to the enterprise. In this view, the BPMS is thus seen as a software tool that is used to comprehend the process well.

The other is to use BPMS for automating processes. It is not necessarily about eliminating human activities or replacing them with automated ones. The BPMS can assist the users in performing their respective activities. It is also about BPMSs executing the processes involving all participants. In this view, all the processes are expected to be executable by the BPMS.

4.10 BPM Landscape

BPM work in an enterprise happens in various contexts. These contexts are shown in Figure 4.2. Each one typically takes the form of a project. One set of BPM projects are strategic in nature. This work identifies and studies the business strategy of the enterprise. This could be driven by contexts such as mergers and acquisitions, and partnerships with other enterprises. What are the core business processes of the enterprise, what are its support processes? These are questions addressed in such projects.

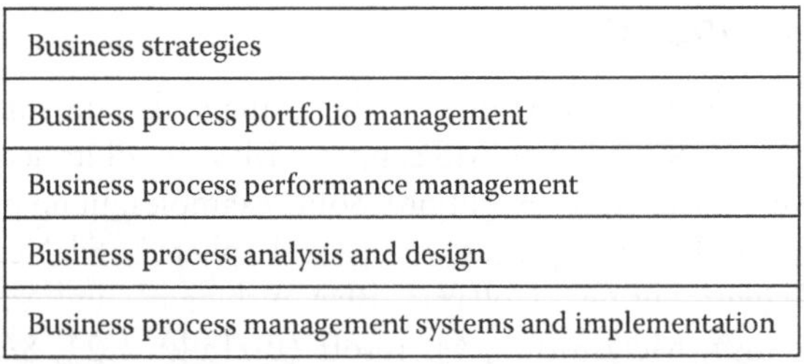

Business strategies
Business process portfolio management
Business process performance management
Business process analysis and design
Business process management systems and implementation

Figure 4.2 BPM work—the context.

Portfolio management for business processes is another set of projects. Here the objective is to identify and catalog all the business processes in the enterprise and take decisions on how they are to be managed. Typical concerns in this work are as follows: what processes can be outsourced, which ones should be insourced, which ones need changes/which ones do not, and which processes can be automated by systems.

Process analysis and design is another context for BPM projects. Business processes, especially the operational ones, are analyzed and redesigned for betterment. This is the core part of process engineering. Processes are looked at hierarchically with value chains (highest level processes) at the top, including supply chains, and then they are broken down into processes at lower levels.

The next context for BPM work is business performance management. For business processes, key performance indicators (KPI) and metrics are defined that reflect their efficiency and effectiveness and help in process improvement efforts. This set of projects also includes the change management effort when business processes are changed for optimization and other reasons.

Implementing a business process using BPMS is another category of BPM projects. These projects involve automation of business processes with the use of BPMS, addressing the life cycle stages process design and execution. BPMS is used to design, deploy, execute, and manage the processes.

4.11 Exercise Questions

1. Do you think systems are a must for business process improvement? Think of a few scenarios from your context where you think process management is better done without involving IT systems.
2. Are there things in BPM that sound too ambitious to you?
3. Have you adopted any specific quality control practice in processes that you are familiar with? How do those fit in a BPM exercise?

Chapter 5

Components of PCA

5.1 Objectives

- To understand the components of PCA in detail
- To understand the concept of business process model and modeling in detail
- To appreciate the need for high-level business and extended technical level business process modeling
- To differentiate between an abstract and a concrete business process model
- To learn the principles related to process modeling
- To learn the techniques related to process modeling
- To understand the relevance of process architecture
- To understand the concept of services
- To learn the principles behind making process definitions executable

5.2 The Business Process Model

The *process model* is the core element of this architectural style. It is the abstraction of the process logic for the system. As we discussed earlier, the IT system that is being architected supports a specific business process of the enterprise. The process model is a representation of what happens in that business process. In this representation, the business process is explicitly defined. It defines (or holds) the system's business objective and purpose.

The process definition describes (encapsulates as a component) the process logic such as control flow, data dependencies, and rules involved in the achievement of the business objective that the specific process is set out for. In this architectural style, the process model is given a well-defined role and place in the architecture of the system. Its role is the primary role in the architecture. This component has design-time (static) as well as run-time presence. It dictates the execution of the business logic and the execution flow in the system.

The definition of the process is in a formal process definition language. This is important to enable the model to become a run-time component in the system and for it to get itself executed. The rigor of formalism makes sure that there are well-defined ways of reducing the model to other forms. It is the process model that determines how the IT system would achieve its business objective.

The process model's objective is to direct the execution order and execution of business logic elements of the IT system so that the business process is performed. The flow of control it brings into effect across the business logic elements is as per the process logic given in the process definition.

Specifically it has the following responsibilities:

- Carry out the intended flow of the business process.
- Coordinate the execution of and follow the order of the execution of various related business functions as required by the business, including branching of the flow based on rules and performance of steps in parallel.
- Maintain the state of the whole business process including its context.
- Handle error situations in the business process.
- Trigger the execution of steps in the process that in turn perform specific business functions.
- Receive messages from processes external to this process and trigger the execution of specific business functions (i.e., steps) corresponding to that. If required, provide response message to the sender process.
- Connect and integrate human roles into relevant points in the flow so that they can perform their respective business function in the context of the overall process.

It abstracts out the process logic for the other components of the IT system so that they focus only on their specific business functions. This allows any changes to the process to be contained within this component itself without impacting other components. It also hides the implementation of the process logic from other elements.

5.2.1 Structure

It is composed of a set of activities, paths involving activities, branches, splits and parallel paths, joins, business rules influencing the branch selections, and process parameters.

Each activity is associated with a specific business function and is considered atomic, whereby the business function is a logically complete operation that typically changes the state of the business entity. An activity does not necessarily need to change the state of an entity or do some update operation. An activity can also perform a non-update (does not affect state of any entity) function such as just an information retrieval function or perform some rule check—check credit history, get item availability etc. are all examples of such activities. The business function is the action performed in the activity.

I. For a user activity, typically the activity itself is composed of one or more tasks that are performed in a sequence to realize the business function for the activity. Each of the tasks is performed by the same user to whom the activity is assigned to. The user activity has specified in it the role of the user or a work allocation specification that would let the activity be assigned to a user at run-time.

II. System activities can be categorized into two types based on the nature of their execution by the system:

    A. The first one is "send" type activities where the process executes the activity by invoking the service associated with the activity (activity-service). The service provider for this service is one of the business logic elements in the architecture. And, the service performs the action expected of this activity. This business logic element may be external or internal to the enterprise and is physically separate from the process.

    B. The other is "receive" type activities, where the process receives invocation for the activity from outside of the process and the process performs the action expected of the activity instead of any service provider (i.e., service) performing it. The invoker (caller) of the activity would typically be another process and only upon this invocation the activity is carried out.

        1. A receive type activity can further be synchronous or asynchronous. It is *synchronous* when the process (from outside) invoking this activity waits for the execution of activity to get completed and the activity to respond back to it with output data. It is *asynchronous* when there is no data expected to be sent back to the invoker and the invoker does not wait for the activity execution to complete.

Process *parameters* make up the context of the process. They are the business data that are relevant to the process and that it deals with. They are also called *process properties*. Their values keep getting updated while the process execution progresses. The state of an active process is primarily defined by the values of process parameters at that point of time.

A *branch* causes the flow in a process path to branch into one or more of the multiple paths ahead of it. In a *conditional branch*, the branching done is based on the branching *condition* specified in the branch. Here, the condition is a business-friendly relational expression* format or an arithmetic expression format or a general expression

* Expressions involving relational operators such as >, <, >=, <=, and, or, true, and false. Relational expressions always result in a true or false value.

format that evaluates some value.* These expressions would make use of the process parameters and their values at run-time. During process execution, based on the evaluated value, the matching path from the set of paths going out from the branch is selected and executed.

The conditional expressions are business rules that influence the flow of the process. These are rules whose scope is at process level. They influence the selection of paths at a branch.

Forks and *joins* enable parallel execution within the process. Forks split a single path into multiple paths that are executed simultaneously by the process. Joins merge the parallel flows at a subsequent point in the process from where the single path execution is further enabled. Joins also merge paths from branches.

To perform the process logic, the process model maintains a list of activities to be performed, their order, and the individual parameters they respectively require. As and when it runs the activities, and also during the course of their execution, it updates their state and the process execution state. It tracks the process parameters for updates from activity executions by synchronizing their updates with the activity executions.

It allows the process layer element in the architecture to carry out process functions such as starting, resuming, and terminating processes by letting the latter interact with it.

5.2.2 Relationships

The process model has interactions with the following elements of the architecture.

5.2.2.1 Business Logic Elements

During process execution, the process model interacts with the respective business logic elements associated with the respective activities for executing the activities. For a system activity, execution of the business logic element performs the business function of the activity automatically, since it is the business logic element that implements the activity. The process model becomes a director and the business logic components become subservient to it. For a user activity, the process model assigns the activity to be performed by a role or a specific user so that the activity can be carried out by the user with the user performing the business function with the help of GUI screens.

5.2.2.2 The Process Layer

The process model is housed in the process layer and the latter interacts with it for the process execution and operations on the executing processes. This interaction

* They need to evaluate into some value at run-time during the process execution. For example, "part amount * number of parts" can be an expression specified for branch.

is enabled through interfaces provided by the process model to the process layer. These interfaces allow the process layer to

- Trigger starting of the execution of a process
- Trigger resumption of a process that has been hibernated
- Handover to the process waiting for a message the message intended for it coming from external sources such as other processes
- Indicate to the active process that the user activity that it is currently waiting for has been completed by the user and provide the parameters supplied by the user activity to the process

The process model also interacts with the process layer to assign user activities to specific users or roles during process execution. It invokes the interfaces provided by the process layer for this purpose. Process model uses the process layer services to invoke the business logic elements corresponding to system activities in the process.

5.2.3 Properties of Processes

Let us look at the key properties, characteristics, constraints, and principles of processes in this architectural style:

1. Processes are executable—Process models have the power of getting executed in a computing environment or platform. The process definition is thus virtually a computer-executable code. They are not just paper models.
2. Formal language must be used for definition—Defined formally, process definitions provide unambiguous understanding and are interoperable with other processes. Reduction of the definition to other forms suitable for computer execution is also helped by formal language use.
3. Processes communicate (or interact) with other processes—A process can be dynamically related to another process. At run-time, the former process communicates with the latter process and this relationship manifests only at the run-time. In other words, they are not bound to each other statically (i.e., during process modeling). Processes can also be composed of other processes at least for managing process-model complexity and improving its maintainability. The inner-level process is called a *subprocess* and the outer-level composed process is called the *parent-process*. This composition can be recursive with the subprocess itself being composed of further processes.
4. Processes are *mobile—Mobility* refers to the ability of processes to communicate with other processes by sending and receiving data to/from them as if those processes were internally part of the process' own environment or of the process itself. It also refers to the nature of the execution whereby at run-time, a single process can execute across multiple machines or environments seamlessly:

  a. Different occurrences of executions of a single process can happen in a different computing environment, that is, each time a new execution of the same process model happens, that process execution can happen in a machine different from the one where it happened for the previous execution.
  b. The *communication channels* used for inter-process communications are themselves treated as data (being moved around within one program) that is just communicated (moved or transferred) between the processes and thus are not bound tight.
  c. Unique identifiers are used for processes that are in execution for making the processes mobile and these process identifiers are dynamically passed around to other processes during run-time. Process identifier is a reference to the entire executing process.
5. Execution of a process is triggered on occurrence of events such as
  a. Request from a user to start
  b. Auto-start based on a schedule set previously
  c. Another process initiating the execution of this one
  d. Arrival of a message from an external source (say an application received by the system from a customer)
6. The process identifier uniquely identifies an execution occurrence of a process.
7. Data flow—Any data flow involved between business logic components in a process model must not be captured separately outside of the process model in any form. The process logic formally includes this flow as well.
8. Business rules applicable to decision points should be part of the process model itself—Rules affecting the flow in the process should be explicitly defined in the process model itself at the respective conditional branches and not anywhere else.
9. Business logic components must not directly interact with each other—They should only interact with the process. Inter-business logic communication should happen only through the process as directed by the process. A business logic element would not know the next business logic element that is to be executed. This is known only to the process model (and driven by the process model alone); the business logic element just returns control back to the process.
10. Processes are loosely coupled with the activity service components of the architecture—At the implementation level, the components implementing the activity services are not bound to the process model. There is no hard coding of the concrete business logic elements in the process. In other words, the business logic elements in the system can be dynamically changed without any change to the process. At the design level, the activities themselves can be rearranged within or dropped from the process.

11. Processes can work across enterprises and departments—Processes can involve multiple departments within an enterprise or multiple enterprises in their scope.
12. Processes have state—State of a process at a point of time includes the context of the process and its execution status at that point of time. Context is the set of business parameters defined for the process and their values at that time. Each process instance is unique and has its own context and state that needs to be maintained throughout. The state of each process instance is required to be stored in the storage medium at logical points during the process execution flow. Some categorize processes mainly from a technical (system) perspective based on the state-related system behavior into the following processes:
    - Stateful processes
      These are business processes that persist their state in a secondary storage medium while they are in execution. This way, stateful business processes preserve their state during their execution by committing the process state at each activity in the process—each activity becomes a different transaction as far as the system is concerned.
    - Stateless processes
      These business processes do not persist their state in any secondary storage during their execution. All the activities in the process are treated as part of one single transaction as far as the system is concerned and they are committed together or rolled-back together. If any activity fails while the process is in execution, the effects of the entire process instance is rolled-back. On the other hand, if the process successfully completes execution through all the activities in the sequence, the effects of the process instance is committed.
13. The process context must not become a dump of all business data—Among the business data applicable to the business functions of the IT system, only those that are key and relevant for the process at the process level should be in the context. All other business data are best confined to the respective business logic elements.
14. Each activity is atomic—Simple activities are atomic. When executed from the process, they either complete total execution successfully or fail fully, rolling back to the state they were in before their execution. Complex activities (activities that contain other activities under them that are to be performed) are not assumed to be atomic. They are expected to take care through their compensation logic and fault handling, faults occurring in them. If any complex activity fails and the state of the complex activity needs to be rolled back to its previous state, the compensation logic should ideally take care of what is to be done.
15. Processes can be hibernated and revived—When they are not active, processes can be hibernated.* By persisting, the state of a process in a medium

* It is also called passivation.

enables resuming the process execution later from the point where it was paused/stopped/hibernated. When the process resumes execution, the state at the time of hibernation is maintained.

16. Processes can have distinct duration characteristics—each business process has a typical duration for its execution. Some of them are short-running processes (also called short-lived processes). They typically run only for a few seconds, or at the maximum, a few minutes—the entire process' execution gets completed within this very short duration. On the other hand, some processes are long-running processes (also called long-lived processes). They have activities that take a longer duration to complete execution, in the order of minutes, hours, or even days. These processes typically involve user activities, receive activities, or parallel flows. Long-running processes are always stateful processes.

5.2.4 Levels of Models

There are two levels of the process model. Both are very relevant and required for the process model to be complete.

5.2.4.1 High-Level Business Process Model

This is a graphical model where the activities of the processes are shown with their ordering. This model is at a higher level of business abstraction and focuses on key business aspects. It captures the control flow and business details of the activities to be performed in the process. It need not have all the details sufficient to let the process be executable in a computing platform. At the minimum, it would have the outline of the process that includes

- The ordered set of activities with the flow details such as sequences, parallel paths, and branches
- Higher level details of the activities such as name, whether the activity is system or manual, the broad set of input business data (input parameters) it needs, the broad set of output business data (output parameters) it provides, and a small description of the business function of the activity, which typically exists as an annotation or property of the activity
- A user role or work allocation specification for user activities that would at process execution cause the process to assign the user activity to a particular user or a set of users for performing the action
- A set of business entities (process parameters) at the process level
- A rough sketch of compensation flow that gives which activities have to be performed and in what order to compensate for the effects of the process execution upon the occurrence of an error
- Business rules for conditional branches in the flow

5.2.4.2 Executable Process Model

The *executable process* is the detailed level version of the high-level process model. It is also called detailed business process model and when this term is used it refers to the graphical version of the process definition. This model has the rigor and required details to make the process model complete-for-execution by a computing platform. The language in which it is modeled would provide clear execution semantics for it. In addition to what the higher-level process model has, details would be available in the executable process model that would enable it to be executed and managed by the run-time platform.

The high-level process model can be seen as an abstract model and the executable process model as a concrete model. This is because the concerns related to the execution of the process in computing systems are not addressed in the high-level model; these aspects are specified in the executable process model. The semantics required for execution need to be accurate and cannot have any ambiguity so that the model can be faithfully reduced to computer instructions.

5.2.4.2.1 Block Structure

A programming language for computers is called a *block-structured* language if it provides constructs for enclosing code segments within well-defined blocks so that the computer program written using it is structured as a set of blocks of code. Most of today's programming languages are block structured. It is a specialization of structured programming. Some examples are the use of "parenthesis" in C language and Java, "begin…end" in PASCAL, and so on. There can be more than one construct in the language for defining blocks. Blocks can also be nested one completely within another, and to multiple levels deep within the program. Also, there can be multiple sections within a block with the use of one construct for each section. One example is "if-then…else if…" in Java. Here, within the single block, each keyword identifies a section and has a code within it.

A program in a block-structured language is easier for computers to understand and operate. The block structure is more intuitive for a computer to execute as it is well structured with no logic flow ambiguities.

5.2.4.2.2 Structural Aspects of Process Model

Executing the process model in a computer is easier if the process model is defined in block-structured fashion. A block-structured process representation would be similar in form to a computer program (in high-level programming language). Unambiguous semantics provided by this structure helps the platform to easily transform (translate) the model into system code for execution. Therefore, a block-structured process model is the most preferred executable process model for business process.

The block-structured process model has the following structural characteristics:

1. The process would be a set of blocks. Each block is a segment of the process where there are one or more fully defined activities.
2. Blocks can be nested one within another to any level.
3. The process must be well-formed. This means that
   a. Every split in the process must be completed by an equivalent join. This would ensure that when a path splits into multiple paths, all of them would merge back into the original path at a subsequent point.
   b. Every conditional branching must be completed by a join down the line where the branches merge, to enable definition of the common path to be followed after the unique path of each branch. This merge point also marks the end point of the entire block for conditional branch.
   c. The process must have a clear start step and all the end steps properly specified.
4. Any block in the program must be closed before its enclosing block is closed. A block cannot span across multiple blocks. A block must either be at the top level of the process or fully enclosed within another block. Blocks cannot cross other block boundaries, that is, a block cannot begin in the middle of one block and end in the middle of another block.
5. All parallel paths must merge at a subsequent point and continue as a single main path.
6. There cannot be any path in the process that is left dangling. No loose ends in the paths. If a path does not join with the parent path, then it must compulsorily have a "process end" step at its end.
7. No infinite loops in the process. The high-level process model must have only acyclic graphs. This would mean that in the graph, the activities cannot get into a loop.
8. Any decision making done in the process must be explicitly represented as a conditional branch or a construct that represents finite repetitive execution of activities.

5.2.4.2.3 Key Aspects of the Executable Process Model

Apart from the block-structure aspects, the executable process model would have the following taken care of in it:

- Completion of the abstract process definition (also, refinement of the partial process model). Addition of missing activities.
- Process parameters and types.
- Complete set of input and output parameters for each activity with their types.
- Technical attributes.
- Service interface for each activity.

- Bindings for activity services.
- Mapping GUI screen details.
- Ensuring atomicity of activities.
- Subprocess creation and mappings, synchronous subprocess invocations versus asynchronous subprocess invocation decisions.
- Completion of the opaque constructs.
- Process deployment details.
- Correlation details for each receive activity including manual activities.
- Process triggering (process execution start) details.
- Compensation flows for undoing effects of execution for failures.
- Fault handling (error handling) flows.
- Scope or context defined for a set of activities (as complex activity). A transaction scope defined for it that applies to all the activities in this complex activity specifying the transaction protocol, the transaction context, and the transaction manager details to be used by them.
- Unique name for the process definition (called process type) and key business entity (such as order id) that would act as a unique business identifier for reference to the run-time occurrence of the process from outside. This enables mobility of process definitions and process instances.
- Mappings between activity and process parameters.
- Rule invocation details for rule activities such as rule identifier.

5.2.4.2.4 Run-Time Manifestation of Process

When a process execution is triggered at run-time, it is considered as an occurrence of the process execution. This is called the *process instance*. Process instance exists as a separate entity with respect to the process model element (process definition). Thus, there can be multiple process instances corresponding to a single process definition. Each process instance is assigned a unique *process id* that uniquely identifies the process instance from other instances. The process parameters are in the form of business data variables of the process that have been defined of a data type. They are actually variables in the executable process model, and as the process execution keeps moving forward, their values undergo change depending on the process logic.

5.2.4.2.5 System Activities

In the executable model, the activity needs to have more details specified in it. Since each send type activity is performed by a service that is outside of the process model, the service interface for the service would have to exist as a part of the activity. The activity output parameters, which are the parameters that would be sent to the service as input message, the activity input parameters, which are the parameters that would be received from the service as output message from the service, need to match with the input and output message in the service interface. The service interface would also have the bindings for the service, for use by the process model in invocation of the service, such as the communication protocols, logical business port for the communication, and in some cases the concrete service port address. The concrete bindings are best known and bound as soon as the control reaches the activity but just before the service invocation, for better mobility.

For receive type activities, it would have the input parameters and output parameters that it would expect to receive from and send to the invoker (which is outside this process), respectively. The receive type activity is thus a service offered to processes (or systems) outside this process that they invoke based on their process logic. The service interface for this service would have been made available to the invoker. The output message described in that service interface would be the input parameters for the activity, and the input message described in that interface would be the output parameters from the activity.

In the case of synchronous receive activities, upon invocation, the activity could be expected to perform some action before the control returns to the invoker. This action is available in the receive activity as a set of system activities that are ordered. In response to the invocation, the process performs these activities in the order and it returns output to the invoker only after that. The invoker would have been waiting to receive this control back till this time.

An important concept in the context of receive activities is *correlation*. It refers to the idea of using a key business data to determine the right process instance from among all live process instances, so that the incoming invocation message can be handed over to the right receive activity. This key business data should uniquely identify a process instance. For example, let us take "cancel order" receive activity in the case of an order process. Let us say we have three instances of it running with the process property "order number" value as 22, 33, and 44, respectively, for each of them. When the customer's process (or system) invokes this activity to cancel the order number 33, the customer invokes the cancel order service provided by the process model. This invocation needs to be rightly mapped to the process instance corresponding to the order number 33 and not to the other instances (22 and 44). The business data order number that would be one of the input parameters for the activity is used for this correlation. This input parameter is identified as the correlation parameter for this activity.

5.2.4.2.6 User Activities

Each user activity would have in it a logical mapping to the GUI screen of the corresponding GUI application for the function to be performed by the user in the activity. The output and input parameters from and to the activity, respectively, would be the input and output parameters for the GUI application, respectively. In this sense, the input parameters for the screen are the parameters used by the GUI application to display business parameters to the user. Similarly, the output parameters from the GUI application are (or based on) the parameters that the user inputs in the screen. Activity is still a service performed by a human role though; therefore, the service interface for the service is also part of the activity. It would have the bindings for the service, for use by the process model run-time, such as the communication protocols, logical business port for the communication. Here too, the concrete bindings to a GUI application's uniform resource identifier (URI) are best known and bound as soon as the process flow reaches the activity, for better mobility.

5.2.4.2.7 Subprocesses

A process model may have subprocesses in its composition, which means that the execution model would have the necessary details to be able to invoke the subprocess and also ensure that the main process' (parent process) context is shared with the subprocess. There would be an activity (*subprocess activity*) in the parent process to invoke the subprocess. Subprocess activity would contain the output and input parameters to be provided to and received back from the subprocess. These would in turn be the input and output parameters, respectively, in the subprocess' process model (and as input and output messages, respectively, in its service interface) and like in send type activities, the service interface for the subprocess is included in the subprocess activity of the main process. The subprocess activity should also have the detail to identify if the subprocess is to be invoked synchronously (where the subprocess activity in the main process would wait till the subprocess' execution is over) or asynchronously (where the subprocess activity just launches the execution of the subprocess as a separate execution and does not wait for the subprocess' execution to get over). In the case of asynchronous subprocesses, there is no output parameter from the subprocess to be received by the subprocess activity in the main process.

5.2.4.2.8 Rules

Rule activities are activities that invoke business rules that are separately kept in the business rules layer. An example of a business rule is "is claim eligible," in an insurance claim process. This business rule is a complex rule that is defined and kept in the business rules layer for execution. Such a rule would have lots of checks to be done, insurance policy clauses to be matched, company claim precedents to be referred to, and based on all this the rule has to arrive at a decision whether this claim qualifies for further processing.

Rule activity would have the output parameters and input parameters to be sent to and received from the rule mapped to the input and output parameters, respectively, of the rule. Bindings provide the activity with details of the rule invocation such as the location and the protocol. For better mobility, concrete bindings are ideally done dynamically as soon as the control reaches the activity.

5.3 Process Layer

Process layer is another key element of this architectural style. This is the architectural layer where the process model is put and kept. It contains the process model and the process instances of the process model. Process layer is the abstraction of the process execution and process management infrastructure for the system. It is the manager for the process model and it is the execution environment for the process model where the process is executed.

5.3.1 Responsibilities

Process layer's high-level responsibility is to manage the life cycle of process instances in the system. As part of this, it performs various functions related to processes.

Specifically, it has the following responsibilities:

1. Trigger the execution of a process by creating and launching the process instance. Do this upon the occurrence of process instantiation triggers, that is, events requiring process instances to be created or conditions that cause new process instances to be launched.
2. Allow the process instance to execute by providing an execution environment for the process instance, within which the process instance can execute its own process logic.
3. Be on the watch for the occurrence of process instantiation triggers, such as
   a. Receipt of message from a source external to the system to start a process. For example, an application for loan received from a customer.
   b. Arrival of request from another process outside the system to start the execution of a process of this system.
   c. Invocation of a subprocess by its parent process in the system.
   d. A user requesting the start of a process, say a leave request.
   e. A time event such as a schedule set previously for starting a process execution. This is considered an auto-start trigger. For example, run the audit-reporting process at the end of every month.
4. Persist the state of each process instance in a persistent medium (storage such as database) at regular logical intervals in the process execution such as at the start of the process, before the execution of activities, and after the execution of activities. As part of this, the process parameters (variables) and their values are captured—this is the process context. Activity states are also captured along with the data items such as timestamps (begin timestamp, end timestamp) that are relevant for process history. The process state information is used by the process layer to faithfully recover/restore and revive a process instance from an exception, or revive a passivated process instance upon the arrival of the message it was waiting

for, and so on, so that the process execution can continue from a logically correct (valid) state.

5. *Hibernate* a process instance when it is in a "waiting" state (it is not doing anything) by persisting the entire process state in a persistent medium and then removing the process instance from run-time. In a waiting state, the process instance would not be doing anything other than waiting for a message to come from outside the process. This happens when the process instance's execution is at a receive activity or a user activity.
6. *Revive* a hibernated process instance, upon the receipt of the intended message it was waiting for and *resume* the execution of the process instance from that point in the flow where it was hibernated.
7. Forcefully *terminate* a process instance if a request is received for premature termination of the process instance.
8. Once a message is received (invocation into a receive process activity), correlate the message to the right process instance. That is, identify which process instance the message is intended for:
    a. Then, hand over the message to this correlated process instance.
    b. If the invocation received is synchronous, once the message is supplied to the correlated process instance, wait for the corresponding receive type activity in the process instance to complete its execution and return the output parameters to it. And, return the output parameters to the invoker.
9. Receive notification from a user that the user has completed performing the user activity. Correlate it to the right process instance and pass on the input message received in the notification to the process instance so that the message reaches the waiting user activity.
10. Provide services through interfaces to the process model to invoke the services corresponding to the system activities (send type).
11. Provide services to the process instance so that a user activity in the process instance is assigned to the specific user or role that has been identified by the work allocation logic of the user activity.
12. Provide process instance/activity instance life cycle-related functions as services to other systems. Some such services are
    a. Trigger new process instance.
    b. Lock a user activity to a user (in the case of user activities that are assigned only to a role) when a user picks up the activity for performing action.
    c. For a user to wait for the next activity that is assigned to the user in the process, after completing the user's current activity in the process. This is relevant in processes that are of the case-handling pattern, where all the activities are assigned to the same user.
    d. For the GUI application to pull its input parameters from the user activity in the process instance, when the user is ready to perform that user activity.
    e. Reassign an already assigned user activity to another user.
    f. Notify that the user activity has been completed.

13. Provide process administration functions on process models and instances as services to other systems. These are services such as
    a. *Deploy* process models so that they are ready to be executed. The process layer translates the process model into executable code.
    b. *Un-deploy* process models so that they cannot be executed in the future. The process layer totally removes the process model from the run-time repository.
    c. List of deployed processes.
    d. Full detail of the process model in its entirety.
    e. Forcefully terminate a process instance.
    f. Resume or restart a system activity that has failed in a process instance. Resume a failed process instance from the point of failure.
14. Provide services for querying such as get the list of user activities assigned to a specific user (or for a role) waiting for action, get process instances currently alive* (meaning instances that have not completed their full execution yet), and get process instances that have failed with some error.

5.3.2 Interrelationships

The process layer being the process execution environment, it interacts with almost all the components of the architecture and vice versa. It is related to the other components of the system in the ways mentioned below.

5.3.2.1 Process Model

The process layer has a "contains" relationship with the process model since the process model is housed in the process layer. Process layer instantiates the process model for execution and initiates the process instance's execution. The entire life cycle of the process instance is controlled and managed by the process layer. The process layer interacts with the executing processes to perform operations such as process hibernation, process resumption, and process and termination (forced). It interacts with the process waiting to receive an external message in the case of a system activity or a user notification message in the case of an active user activity. In this interaction, the process layer hands over the message received to the process through the interface provided.

The process layer provides services to the process model for different functions. One is for assigning user activities to a user or role. After deciding which user or

* Throughout this book, the term "alive" or "active" processes is used to mean the process instances that are currently in execution status. Apart from the process instances that are currently physically running in memory, this also includes the process instances that are currently hibernated, and the ones that are currently down (failed) with error. This does not include the processes that have completed their full execution (from start to end) and those that have been forcefully terminated.

role the user activity needs to be allocated to, the process model interacts with the process layer to actually make that assignment. Another function the process layer provides is invoking business logic elements for system activity services (send type). When the process is at a send type system activity, the process model interacts with the process layer to perform the invocation of the activity's service. The process layer knows how to invoke the business logic element that implements the service, taking care of the communication protocols, service look-ups, transport mechanisms, and data transformations involved in that.

Yet another interaction is when the process model executes the subprocess activity. The process requests the process layer to trigger the instantiation and the execution of the subprocess. Based on whether the subprocess is to be invoked synchronously or asynchronously, the process model waits till the subprocess execution is complete or not, respectively.

5.3.2.2 Business Logic Elements

The process layer interacts with the business logic elements for the system as part of it carrying out the invocation of the activity services on behalf of the process instance. This applies only to the send type activities. It invokes the API exposed by the business logic element passing the output parameters from the activities in the form expected by this API. If it is a synchronous invocation, it waits for the business logic element to complete the operation and return back with the input parameters for the activity.

5.3.2.3 UI Application Layer

Interaction with this layer is applicable (or important? or relevant?) for the user activities in the process. The UI* application that supports the user activity interfaces with the process layer to notify the process layer of the completion of the user's action in the user activity so that this information can be passed on to the process instance.

The UI application for the users also interacts with the process layer to get the work items (list of user activities across process instances) assigned for a particular user or the work items that are marked for a specific role. This list is displayed to the user by the application, so that the user can pick up work items to perform and complete the required action on it. For those work items that the user picks up that were originally not assigned to any specific user, the UI application again interfaces with the process layer to get that user activity locked to this user so that there is no conflict with other users. As part of this, the UI application also fetches the output parameters from the user activity of the process instance by interacting with the process layer.

Interaction the other way round is possible too with certain types of user participation models. Some such models are as follows: The process layer interacts with

* They are mostly graphical interfaces (GUI) today.

the UI application to push the user activity to the user as soon as in the process instance, the user activity is ready for execution and assigned to the user.

5.3.2.4 External Process Systems or Other Processes

These include

- Systems external to the process
- Other processes running external to this process environment
- Other processes running in the same environment as this process, but are not in a main process–subprocess relationship with this process

They interact with the process layer to trigger new process instances, or send message (invoke) to a receive type system activity in an active process instance. These interactions are enabled through the interfaces provided by the process layer to the external systems and processes. An example is, in an order process, after the order has processed the preliminary processing steps and before it proceeds with the final processing, the customer's system (external) might need to send an order confirmation to the process instance to the receive activity "receive order confirmation."

5.3.3 Structure

Figure 5.1 shows the composition of the process layer.

It is composed of

- Process execution layer—concerned with the core execution of the process instances after instantiating them.
- Adapter layer (collaboration layer)—takes care of entire invocation mechanisms and technology aspects such as communication protocols, in the interaction of process layer with the business logic components. Also takes care of the same aspects in the invocations received into the process instances from systems or processes outside.
- Process persistence component—concerned with persisting the state of active process instances in a nonvolatile medium.
- Process repository—this stores the process model and the process run-time data such as full history for each process instance for active as well as completed process instances.
- Correlation component—takes care of correlating an incoming message (invocation) to the matching process instance and activity.
- API layer (interface layer)—concerned with exposing interfaces to components outside the process layer for the various functionalities the process layer offers.

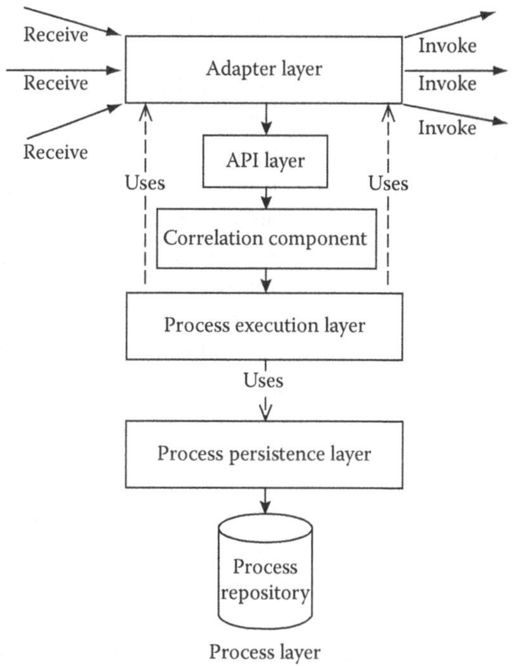

Figure 5.1 Components of process layer.

5.4 Business Logic Elements

Business logic elements (BLE) are concerned purely with their specific business functionality and the business logic for that functionality. They are not supposed to be looking into process logic, data flow, controller functions, or presentation aspects. In the architecture, BLEs support the system activities that are invoked in the process execution. They implement the services corresponding to the activities. Their business logic or how they support the business functionality is purely internal to themselves and not visible to the process. For example, in a purchase order process, the system activity "check inventory" is supported by the service "check inventory" provided by the "inventory services" BLE.

Though a single BLE could provide one or more services, each activity-service is supported by only one BLE and not by a mix of two or more of them. Internally, each BLE is in turn composed of business subcomponents that together implement the functionality expected to be delivered by the BLE. BLEs could be internal to the organization or external. For example, in the purchase order process, the system activity of "validate credit card" is provided by a BLE that is with a third party, the credit card merchant (say Mastercard). Thus, this BLE is from an external organization as far as the process is concerned.

During the run-time, the control comes to the BLE from the executing process instance when the flow reaches the activity with which the service provided by this BLE is associated. As part of this invocation, the BLE would then take in the input parameters supplied by the activity in the process and perform its business logic. After the completion of the business functionality, it returns the control to the process along with it supplying the output parameters from the operation. In the case of the "validate credit card" example, the service would be given the credit card number, card expiry date, and the customer name as its input parameters. The service implementing component would then check the details in the credit card system and validate the credit card limits along with the card's authenticity. Once this validation is complete, it returns its output parameter "Card Validated OK" with true value or false value depending on whether the card is valid or not, to the process with the control.

5.4.1 Principles

BLEs are an abstraction at the business logic level. At this level of abstraction, they are loosely coupled to the activities in the process. The coupling is established dynamically at the time of the execution of the activity and only for the duration of that activity in that process instance.

The service interface for the activity-service should match with what is provided by the BLE. The service interface would be the basis for the coupling between the activity in the process and the BLEs. There can possibly be more than one BLE that implements the service. The choice of the specific BLE is best made dynamically for each process instance and for each occurrence of the activity. The implementation of the service in the BLE and the subcomponents are dependent or based on a specific technology.

The control flow is always top-down from the process to the BLE. There is never a direct relationship between one BLE with another.

The context for the operation of the BLE is provided by the process instance. Each invocation to the service is stateless and it does not assume any specific state or context. The context provided by the process instance is what it uses to operate within and this is lost by the BLE once the control is given back to the process instance after the operation. For example, in the credit card validation service provider BLE, the context includes the credit card number, customer name, and expiry date. The entire validation function is performed fully within this context. However, the BLE is free to use its own data repository for carrying out its operation. That data is purely internal to the BLE and not directly connected with anything that the process is impacted with. For example, it could internally have and use a repository of data (relevant business entities), such as credit card numbers, bank details, transaction data, credit history, and overdue amount.

The granularity of the service would need to be at the level of the activity in the process that is an atomic logically complete business function. *Right-granularity* is the adjective here. This means the granularity of activity-services needs to be sufficiently higher. "Credit amount to the account," "check inventory," "deduct from inventory," or "create account" are some examples here, whereas "update customer record in database," "store line item in database," and "get product name" are bad examples. The bad examples are at lower levels of granularity than is appropriate for the activity.

A BLE offering services at the right-granularity to the activity can be composed of lower-levels of granularity internally in its implementation. This is purely the internal service composition where a right-granular service for a process activity is composed from lower-granular services. And, each of the lower-level services are expected not to be atomic individually. Together they complete the atomic business operation. For example, if the activity-service is "create account," it could be composed of low granular components such as "check completeness of data," "record customer record in database," "update account master record," and "update international banking master." They together achieve the customer account creation as one atomic operation. Also, each of them could in turn be composed of still lower granular services such as *data services*, for example, that just fetch a specific record from a specific database table.

5.5 User Interface Application Layer

User interface (UI) applications are for enabling users to perform the user activities in the process instance. If the user activity involves more than one task, the user activity is logically associated with a *taskflow*. A taskflow is an ordered set of tasks to be performed by this user to complete the action for this activity. The action associated with the user activity is a specific business function, such as "verify application form details" or "enter order details" for example. However, each task in the taskflow would contribute toward that action. The action is completed when all the tasks (as per the order) are performed by the user. As an example, "enter order details," might involve the user entering the purchase order details in three screens. The first screen might be for the task of inputting the customer details, the second one for product details being ordered, and the third one for the delivery details.

Each task is associated with a screen which in turn has a set of business data fields displayed to the user or inputted by the user in the screen. The user moves from one task to the other in the order of the taskflow, completing each task at the same time by doing the actions on the respective screen for each task displayed to the user. The process execution flow has to reach the activity in the process instance for the user to be able to perform the activity. Also, the process flow waits at that point until the user completes the user's action.

The UI application totally concerns itself with the presentation aspects, support for the taskflow, the business logic applicable to the tasks, business data that is relevant only to the specific business functionality that the user needs to perform, and persistence of business data inputted. This separation of the manual activity aspects from other components makes the UI logic/support transparent to the process. The UI application can receive the parameters from the process instance for display in

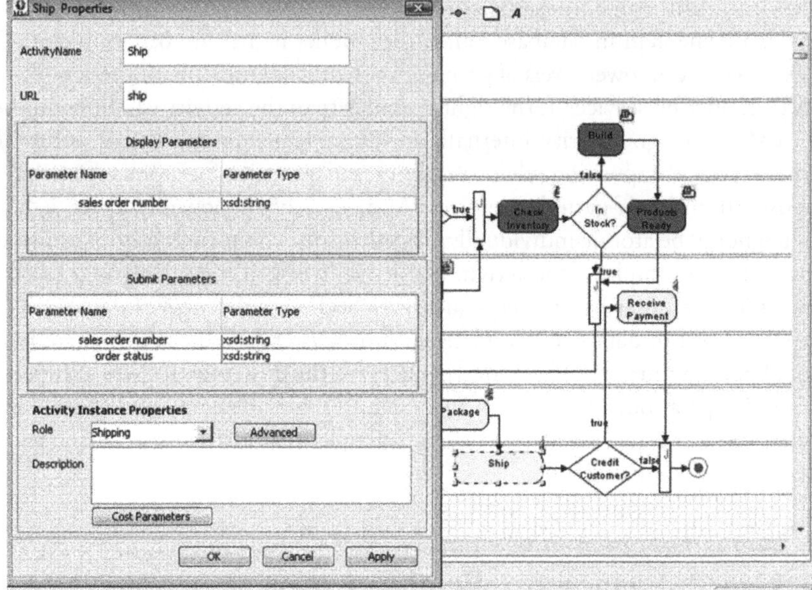

Figure 5.2 A sample user activity.

the screens. This is really the context data that the process supplies and what the user activity is to be performed within. After the user completes all the tasks and thereby completes the action, the parameters that have been input by the user that are directly relevant for the process are passed to the process instance. Taskflow is internal to the supporting UI application and the process is not concerned about it; it is transparent to the process.

An example user activity specification in the process model for an order process is shown in Figure 5.2. In this example, the shipping department ships the package to the customer's delivery address.

5.6 Exercise Questions

1. Why is a pure high-level business process model not sufficient for making it a system executable one?
2. Model an end-to-end business process that you are familiar with in your enterprise at an abstract level using any means you are comfortable with. Study the process in some detail.
   a. Are there decision points in it? Identify those.
   b. How many branches are there in the process? Are the branches converging (joining) at some point in the flow?

   c. Do the branches from decision points merge at some point?
   d. Does the process have multiple end-points?
3. Think of what aspects you would need to specify to make this process enabled for system execution. In other words, identify those details that you think would be required if this process definition had to run in a process execution platform.

Chapter 6

Process Execution

6.1 Objectives

- To learn the principles of process deployment and execution
- To understand the dynamics of processes at run-time
- To understand inter-process communication aspects
- To understand how human participation is enabled in processes
- To be aware of the intricacies in enabling systems participants
- To learn the more detailed concepts of workflows, application integration, and rules

6.2 Deployment

To make the process ready for execution, it needs to be put in the run-time process layer. This procedure is called *deployment*. The entire process model, the service interfaces for activities, bindings/binding policies for activity-services, the subprocess process models, the new executable business logic elements, and the new UI application components are part of the set of elements that is deployed. Existing BLEs and the BLEs that are new but that belong to another organization are excluded from this deployment. The latter ones would have to be deployed and made ready by the other organization if its services are to be invocable by this process.

The process model, the service interfaces, and the binding details are deployed in the process layer. The UI application (with taskflow and screens) is ideally deployed in the run-time UI layer. The business logic elements are typically deployed in the run-tier business logic tier.* The look up details for the business logic elements are

* The concrete realizations of this is given in Chapter 11.

kept in the business logic tier. The process model is persisted in a persistent medium by the process layer. The process layer would fetch the model for execution from the persistent storage.

Deployment ensures that all the references between the process model, the services (including user activities), and to the process model itself (receive activities) are in a resolvable state for execution. This means that the references to the services to be invoked by the process or the receive activities that would get invoked from outside are either available at the deployment time or would become available during the course of the process execution but before the activity becomes active.

Deployment takes care of the static-time validations of the process models and attachments. Validations include potential violations of the executable nature of the processes, dependencies check, and completeness for flow and execution. The dependencies between the various components of the system, such as the process, services, UI layer, and supporting BLEs, are taken care of. During deployment, all the bindings related to these dependencies are preferred to be addressed as "logical" and not concrete. Concrete bindings are postponed (late) to a later stage at run-time for each component individually.

The deployment concept is based on the concept of separation of concerns, where each component of the IT system is housed in separate tiers where they are managed through their run-time life cycles. The is similar to the concept of deploying business components of an application in a JEE application server as Enterprise Java Beans (EJB).

The process model is translated into computer executable code with the deployment. The computer executable code is what is executed by the process layer when process instances need to be launched. Each subprocess is also translated into respective executable code.

Deployment is also a step that addresses the quality of system concerns of the reliability (scalability) and efficiency (performance) of the processes by considering the computing platform aspects such as the number, inter-connections, and sharing and implementing of those decisions accordingly. For example, during deployment, the processes might be so deployed that the process instances are run in a cluster of process layers running in multiple computing machines. The load in this case would be shared between these multiple process layers.

6.3 Execution

If we look at the control flow in the IT system during run-time, the entire execution flow is top-down, where the executing process is at the top and the activities are down in the level. And the process drives the execution of the activities.

Process execution involves the participation of both the system participants and the human participants in the process. The term "system participants" refers to the systems that perform the system activities and "user participants" refers to the users that perform the user activities of the process. The system participants take part in the process automatically by the invocation of the executing process. Execution is automatic in this case and no waiting is involved, unless the activity is a receive activity. Whereas, the human participants participate on their own based on their time availability and priority. The process instance waits for the user to participate and complete the activity before it proceeds with the next activity in the order.

6.3.1 System Participation

We can let systems participate in processes in essentially four different patterns of interaction based on who does the invocation and whether the invocation is synchronous or not. They are *solicit–response, notification, request–response*, and *one-way*.

6.3.1.1 Solicit–Response

Upon the process execution flow reaching this system activity, the process instance takes up the role of invoker and invokes the service* attached to this activity. The process instance invokes the service with output parameters from the activity going to the service as input parameters as per the service interface the service has provided. Here the process instance endpoint of the interaction solicits a response from the service by sending an input to the service. The service performs its expected business function and returns with a response to the process, which is waiting for the call to return. The response received is the set of input parameters for the activity, as per the service interface. The activity parameter ordering in this pattern is always output parameters followed by input parameters. Figure 6.1 demonstrates this.

An example is a "make payment using credit card" activity in an order handling process. The process instance while processing the order reaches this activity where the customer payment needs to be accepted and invokes the service with the output parameters credit card number, payment amount, customer name, card expiry date, and customer authentication code. The service debits the amount from the

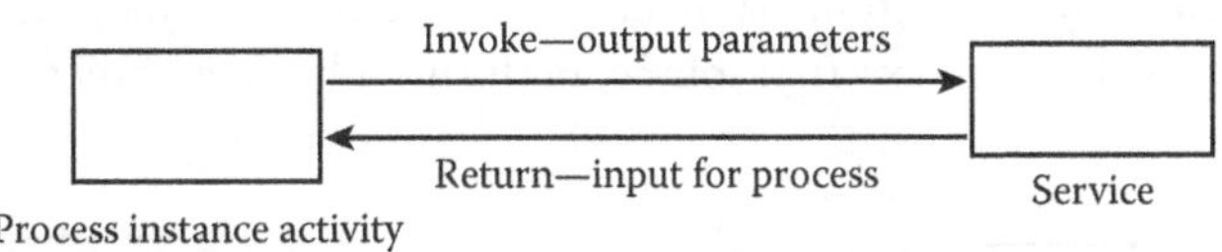

Figure 6.1 Solicit–response pattern.

* In this book at most places the terms service and operation are not explicitly differentiated. However, in some places in the book, where such distinction is important for the concept at the place, the differentiation for these terms has been provided.

credit card account balance and then returns to the activity with a transaction ID and a success indicator code.

This pattern requires that the process instance and the service be synchronized during the execution of the service. That means, at this activity, the process instance needs to wait for the control to come back to it from the service before the process instance can move ahead. Thus, it is a synchronous invocation.

6.3.1.2 Notification

This is similar to the solicit–response patterns in that the process instance is still the invoker. However, the interaction ends as soon as the process sends the activity's output parameters to the service endpoint. The activity has only output parameters and no input parameters. The process instance just notifies the service and does not wait for any response. In fact, no response is expected from the service as per this interaction model. The process instance immediately proceeds with the execution of the process to the next activity in the order as soon as it sends the message to the service. Figure 6.2 demonstrates this.

The service on its part executes its function asynchronously to the process instance. Upon receiving the input message, the service proceeds independently of the process instance. Thus, this pattern is called asynchronous invocation.

An example for this is an "alert inventory replenishment" activity in the purchase order handling process. After the handling of its specific order, in the case of inventory going below a reasonable threshold, the process instance simply sends a message to the alert service of the inventory system with the "current inventory value" output parameter of the activity and moves on. After receiving the notification, the alert service proceeds independently to handle inventory replenishment.

6.3.1.3 Request–Response

The invoker is an external system or another process here. The activity in this process is the receiver of the invocation. Here, the order of the activity parameters is input followed by the output parameters. The activity in the process instance receives a request from an external source, performs a business function, and then

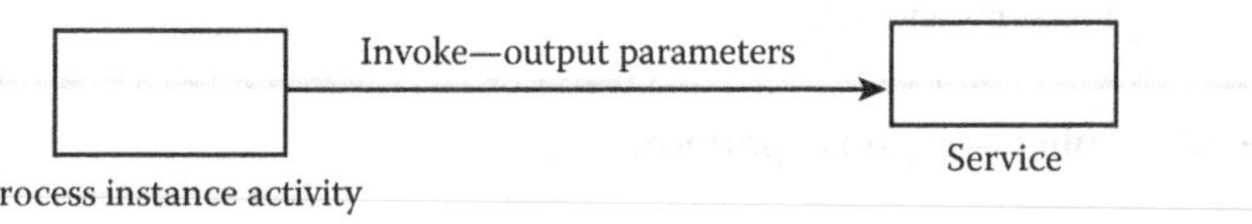

Figure 6.2 Notification pattern.

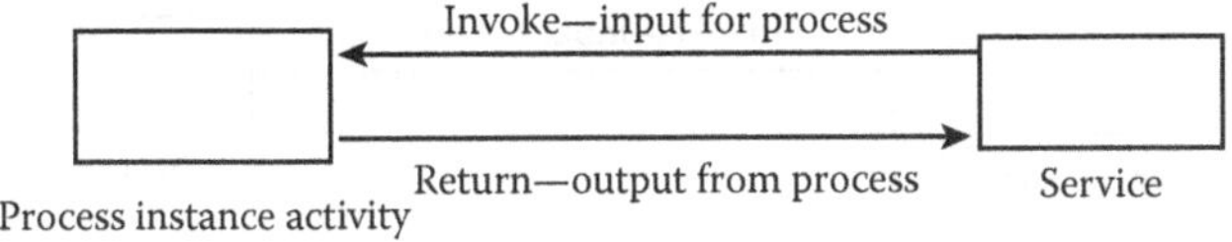

Figure 6.3 Request–response pattern.

returns a response to the external source. That is, the activity first receives the input parameters and then after performing its operation, sends the response back as output parameters from it to the invoker. The external source keeps waiting for the response to come from the activity before moving on with the rest of its execution. Figure 6.3 demonstrates this.

As an example of this, let us consider the process of a computer parts supplier that interacts with an inter-enterprise process of a computer manufacturer that procures various parts from external suppliers. The supplier's process, would get triggered when the computer manufacturer's process makes an invocation to the supplier's service to request a quote for the parts. The supplier process sends a quote back (with a quotation number) to the manufacturer's process and then waits at the "receive order request" activity (which is a receive activity) for the order to be received from the manufacturer. The manufacturer process then places the order with the supplier by invoking this service "receive order request" exposed by the supplier process. This invocation is done by supplying the same quotation number as one of the invocation parameters, so that correlation to the supplier process instance is enabled. The "receive order request" activity creates an order in the supplier system and returns the order id as confirmation to the manufacturer process. Thus, the "receive order request" activity here is an example of the request–response pattern. The invoker in this case is the manufacturer's process.

6.3.1.4 One-Way

One-way is similar to the request–response pattern in that the invoker is an external source and the invocation comes into the activity. The difference is that there is no output to be sent back to the invoker. The parameters for the activity are input only and no output is expected to be sent from it.

Thus, it can be called the *asynchronous receive* model. An example for this pattern is a "receive alert for inventory replenishment" activity in an inventory management process. The external source simply sends the message to this process instance with the "current inventory value" as an input parameter to the activity and the external source moves on. After receiving the notification, the receive alert activity lets the inventory replenishment process instance proceed with the subsequent activities to handle inventory replenishment. Figure 6.4 demonstrates this.

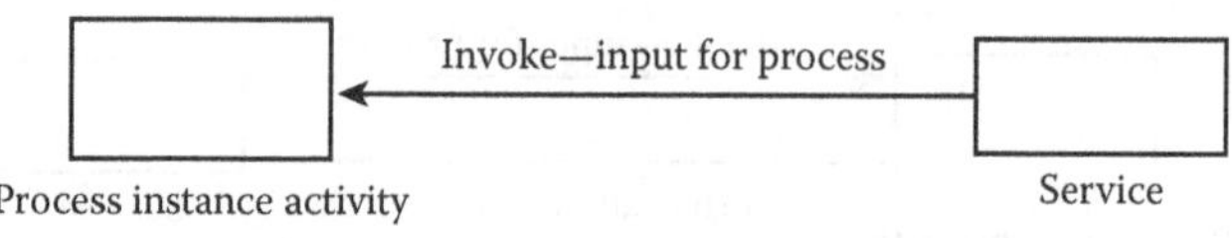

Figure 6.4 One-way pattern.

6.3.2 Critical Aspects at Run-Time

The execution of processes brings with it the run-time aspects that need to be handled. Some of the important aspects of those are *errors*, *transactions*, *compensation*, *monitoring*, and *correlation*.

6.3.2.1 Errors

A process model's execution is considered to be *normal execution* flow when the process instance executes fine from the start step of the process to its end step passing through one of the many possible logical paths in the process. And that is what we have assumed so far in the discussion about the processes. However, a process often faces situations that are exceptions to the normal during the execution of the process instance. These could be business error conditions, an unexpected situation for the IT system, a scenario undefined for the system, or an abnormal condition. Such situation occurrences are called errors. The cause for an error could be system related or business related and the error disrupts the normal flow of the steps in the process.

Some examples of errors are as follows:

- In a purchase order process, a product is found to be out of stock.
- While ordering a book in a book order process, the book is found to be out of print.
- While submitting a claims request in an insurance claims process, the claim submission is found to be invalid since the claim form used was wrong.
- A service corresponding to a system activity is found to be not available at the time when the process instance attempts the invocation.
- In a banking process, while withdrawing money, there is an error because of an insufficient balance in the account.
- In a loan request process for an existing customer, the customer number provided does not exist.

The process ideally needs to handle errors and take actions to cope with the situation so that the process can reach a logically meaningful state or fail (or exit) gracefully. This means, the process needs to detect the error situation, figure out what action to take to deal with this occurrence, and perform the required action to recover.

An error could occur at any level in the process; it could be within an activity, in the process flow, within a subprocess, or in a conditional branch. Some examples of errors in the process flow are as follows:

- Invalid data received by the process instance for a receive activity
- Unable to carry out invocation of a service for a send activity because sufficient concrete invocation details are not available or wrong invocation details are given
- Infinite loops in the process at run-time
- An unexpected value (or invalid value) in a process parameter that causes a condition branch to fail

The process is expected to handle the errors when they occur and if it does not handle them, the process execution will fail crashing the IT system. Generally, process crashes are not acceptable. Even if there is a failure, they are expected to fail gracefully.

6.3.2.1.1 System Handling the Errors

To handle errors, the process model would have error handler flows* in it that specify the ordered set of activities to be performed to handle each specific error. This prevents the process from failing and the IT system from crashing. The principle here is that the error handler portion in the process handles error cases that are recoverable. That is, those situations where the process can take a relevant action to undo the effects of the unsuccessful step of the process where the error has occurred. Some actions as part of the error handling could be business actions such as sending a message to the external system indicating an inability to successfully complete the business objective. In the case of unrecoverable cases, at a minimum, the process fails gracefully. That is, its execution ends with nothing left hanging. Post the error-handling action, once the error causing condition has been addressed, say stock for the product has been replenished, we could restart the process to continue execution from the step where it encountered the error.

The errors discussed above are typically errors that are generated from within the activities (services) and the process. Some of these could be system errors encountered by the activity but are further transformed into business errors and then raised to the process. Such errors are expected to be handled by the process. However, there could be errors that are generated from outside this IT system in the system environment that indicate serious problems and abnormal conditions impacting this IT system and others. Ideally, the process is expected not to attempt handling these types of errors. Some examples here are, the computing environment is in serious problem state or the system environment crashes. In such cases, typically the process (or the process layer) itself has no way of catching the error happening since the environment that contains it would have crashed and died.

* Also called exception flows or fault handling flows.

In the case of such errors, the overall system administrator would need to look into the computing platform level issues to resolve them. Once those are resolved, and after addressing any business inconsistencies, the processes could be restarted to resume from a logical point,* which in most cases is the point of failure itself.

For example, let us say a travel booking process fails due to a system environment crash in the middle of the system activity "get quote from different airlines." The system administrators, after they fix the system issues and bring the system up, need to restart the travel booking process instance from this activity "get quote from different airlines." This is because till the previous activity to this one in the process flow, the process has completed execution and the logical point for restart is from the beginning of the "get quote from different airlines" activity.

6.3.2.1.2 Manual Handling

So far we have discussed error situations where the error-handling is done by the system. In some cases, the process would require manual intervention. That means a business user handles the error and the carrying-out of the rest of the business process logic. Here, outside of this process (in this IT system), the user corrects the condition causing the error, say the business data, and bypassing the process instance, the user takes over the process and manually performs the process steps to fulfill the objective of the business process and completes it. For example, in the case of bulk mutual funds transactions processing, let us assume that one of the process instances failed with an error because of an invalid detail (say amount and account number) in the process data. This is considered as a business exception and is expected to be handled by a business user. The user would take over the execution of the process, verify the details from the relevant sources including systems and the customer, get the correct data, and carry out the entire transaction processing manually. This would ensure that the mutual funds transaction is completed for the customer.

6.3.2.2 Transactions

Transaction handling is a run-time aspect in an IT system that is process-centric. Here, the term transaction† is used in its classical meaning as used in the software application context, which is it is a single unit of business work. The transaction is handled at the activity level. In the context of activities, transaction handling ensures that the effects of the execution of an activity is seen by others only after the execution of the activity is completed and at no point are any partial results seen by other activities, process instances, or systems. If there is any failure in the activity, the transaction is rolled back causing all the changes made by the activity to be

* In some cases, this logical point could be a step before the point of failure or after it.

† With ACID properties being exhibited.

discarded. The objective of transaction handling in a process is to make sure that the process instance does not end up in an inconsistent state in case of any failure.

6.3.2.2.1 Simple Activity

Each simple activity is generally considered to have atomic property. It is because the activities in a process are at a high-level of granularity that it is just right for a logical business function that can be carried out on its own and still bring about a well-defined business state. This atomicity means that when the activity is executed, the business function associated with it is either executed in its entirety or not executed at all. If this function's execution is successful, the activity (transaction) is committed. If the function's execution is not successful, the activity (transaction) is rolled back. For the process instance, it would be as if this activity has not been executed at all, thus in the restart the activity can be executed again. In the case of a simple receive activity, the arrival of a message, the process instance performing the activity, and the sending of the response message are all tied into one atomic operation. That is, the input message is considered to have been received successfully only if the activity is successfully completed.

It is possible to have a simple activity that is nonatomic. In this case, its transaction will get executed in a transaction context of another activity. Typically in such cases, a set of consecutive simple activities are marked nonatomic and grouped to be under one transaction context. This makes all of them execute their respective transactions in the same transaction context and they are committed together or rolled back together, depending on the success of all the activities or the failure of even one activity in this group. In case of a failure, a restart of the process would resume the execution from the first activity in this group all over again.

6.3.2.2.2 Complex Activity

Complex activities* are not expected to be atomic. Each activity "A" that is inside the complex activity is in turn considered atomic if A is a simple activity. During the execution of the complex activity, if there is a failure somewhere in the middle of the set of activities, then all the activities (transactions) executed up to the failure point would have been committed by the time this failing activity started execution; thus, only the failing activity transaction would be rolled-back. When the process is restarted after failure, by default, the execution resumes from the activity that failed inside the complex activity. If the restart (business need) requires the complex activity to be executed fresh from its beginning, then at the time of failure, the complex activity would need to have a flow logic in it to handle the failure and reverse the business effects of the execution of all the activities in the complex

* A complex activity can even be a block in the process model that contains a set of activities within the block. In such a case, it is mainly used as a structuring element.

activity prior to the failed one. This is so that during the restart after failure, the complex activity can begin as if it is has not been executed.

On the other hand, if the complex activity has atomic property, then all the activities under this activity would be executed in the same transaction context and as one transaction. That is, they are all committed together on the success or failure of any one activity. Thus, the commit and roll back is synchronized across all these activities inside the complex activity. In this case, the restart of the process after failure would make the execution resume from the complex activity and it would be a fresh execution of the complex activity from its beginning.

6.3.2.2.3 Subprocess Activity

A subprocess activity in the process instance is not normally considered to be atomic. This activity invokes a subprocess. If the subprocess fails in the middle after executing some activities within it, these executed activities would have been committed as and when the activity was completed, with them being individually atomic. A restart of the process, by default, would cause the execution to resume from the failed activity in the subprocess. If the business requirement of the IT system requires that the subprocess be able to be restarted from its beginning, then the subprocess is expected to handle the failure and reverse the business effects of its execution to bring it back to the initial state prior to the beginning of the start of the subprocess execution, so that the subprocess activity can invoke this subprocess again.

If the subprocess activity is marked atomic, it commits all the activities inside the subprocess together or rolls them back together, similar to the way an atomic complex activity does, based on the success of all or a failure of one, respectively.

6.3.2.2.4 Choice

Thus having the transaction attribute specified in the process model at various steps in the process is a good choice to handle transactions effectively. The details would include items such as the transaction context, transaction span, transaction protocols, and the transaction managers. The transaction details for each activity would determine how its transaction would be handled in the success or failure of the step itself or of other activities before the step. A sound principle with respect to transactions is that atomic transactions should be applied only for short running processes and activities. Short running processes are expected to complete execution in a very short time and thus are atomic, and such processes do not include the activities such as user activities or receive activities that involve waiting. For long running processes, meaning those processes that have activities that are expected to take a longer duration to complete execution (e.g., minutes, hours, or days), transactions should not be atomic for those activities. It would result in unacceptable delays due to the time spent waiting for locked resources by activities executing in parallel and would prevent an executing activity from completing before others have completed, even though this activity's business operation may have been over.

6.3.2.3 Compensation

While transactions address the completion of a unit of work within a process, compensation addresses the completion of a process in the case of errors or exceptional conditions occurring while the process instance is in execution. Let us call them compensation triggers. Here, the exceptional conditions are situations such as a cancel request arriving for the process and the process is unable to meet the physical constraints, say the time-limit. Compensation undoes the effects of the process execution that has happened until that point. If an error or such an event has happened in an executing process and that condition prevents the process from completing its normal execution, then compensation gets activated to compensate for the business effects that the process has brought about and abort the process after that. Execution of the compensation logic for a failed process cancels out the entire process so that for the system or user that initiated the process, it is as good as the process instance having not been executed at all. That would allow the initiator of the process to initiate a new process instance for the same request. As an example, if an order process fails after payment but before shipping the product due to some problem, the compensation for the process would send a refund to the customer of the amount that was paid when initiating this order process instance.

As part of backing out the process, the compensation work takes care of reversing the activities (undo their business impact) that have already been executed and releasing all the resources the process instance is holding. This will enable other processes to use those resources for their work. Since atomic activities, existing in the flow until the point of execution where the compensation trigger arrived in the process instance, would have been committed, and a roll-back in the transaction sense of the word is not possible, the compensation needs to reverse its respective work by compensating for what has already happened by invoking or performing reversal business operations. The reversal business operations reverse the effect of the execution of those already completed activities.

Compensation logic for a process is explicitly specified as a set of activities to be performed (along with the flow) in the process model. The conditions in the process instance under which this flow would get triggered are also specified in the process model. The compensation flow gets triggered only when any of those conditions occur during the process instance execution. Some of these conditions could be error conditions and in such a case the trigger for the compensation flow is specified in the fault handler for the error. A subprocess encountering an error condition preventing it from completing can use compensation to undo itself and bring itself back to its initial state so that it can be invoked again by having the compensation flow triggered from within the fault handler for that error in the subprocess' process model.

6.3.2.4 Correlation

At any point in time, the process layer in the system would be running a number of process instances. If there are receive type activities in the process, external systems or processes could be sending messages into the system to invoke these receive activities. These invokers might invoke the same activity in multiple process instances with which they interact. However, for each request, such invokers cannot be expected to be aware of any specific technical attributes (including the process instance ID) of the process instance that they need to interact with so that they can include those attributes in their message (request) to address the specific process instance uniquely. If they were to do that, then the incoming message would become very specifically bound to that system where the process instance is running, which would no longer be a generic service (that can be invoked by any invoking system and one that can be implemented and provided by other service providers too), curtailing the freedom of the invokers to easily (and dynamically) shift to other service providers providing the same service. If it were a generic service, the invoker would not have needed to change the message type for the invocation message for each service provider.

We desire loose coupling between the invoking system/process and this process instance containing the receive activity. Given all this, a very good option is to use the business parameter(s) of the process for the process instance identification purposes. Such a set of business parameters need to be able to uniquely identify a process instance from among the many process instances that are active at any point in time. This is regardless of where the process instance is currently executing or where the invoker is located. One key principle is that this set of business parameters is key business data for the process (such as order number, request number, application number, and customer account number), and this set is a small set. A single parameter used for correlation is preferred; anything above three is large and best avoided.

Correlation is the method of figuring out the right process instance that the incoming message is really addressed to, from the business information provided in the message. To do correlation, the process layer looks at the values of those business parameters in the incoming message that have been identified as correlation parameters in the process model. If these values match those of a process instance, the message is correlated to that process instance by the process layer. The message is then handed over to that process instance for the receive activity to receive it.

As an example, let us take an order process that has a receive type activity for confirmation of the order—a confirmation message is expected from the customer that indicates the order is confirmed. The order process can proceed to completion once the customer sends this message. Since there could be multiple order process instances active in the system, the incoming message has a parameter named order number with the value of the order that is being confirmed, say 22. This is the correlation parameter defined in the process model as this uniquely identifies a process instance. Since each instance of a order process would mean a new order and consequently a new order number, the order number would uniquely identify an order process instance. The other parameters in the incoming message such as "confirmed by" and "confirmation date" are not correlation parameters, they are input to the activity.

Systems and processes communicating with a process instance need correlation to be able to address the specific process instance with which they are interacting. In addition to the receive activities, correlation applies in the same way to user activities when the UI application sends a notification to the process instance indicating completion of the user activity by the user.

Correlation done this way means any invoker would simply continue to send only business data in the message and not any technical attribute for identification of the process instance. This allows it to dynamically go with other service providers and for this IT system to maintain a generic service interface that other service invokers can also use. It also improves the mobility of the process since only the business reference is used to refer to the process by the interacting processes. This reference remains constant independent of where these processes and the interacting processes are located for execution at that moment, which is an aspect that keeps changing during the process executions.

6.3.3 Human Participation

User activities involve a human performing the activity. The process instance would have to wait at the user activity until the user completes performing it. This wait is similar to the wait in a receive activity and the status of the process instance would be "waiting." Let us take the example of the purchase order process. The activity "approve order" is a user activity. When the execution reaches this activity, it is given to the manager to perform. Until the manager completes the action, the process instance would be in a waiting state.

A user activity may involve a set of tasks in the form of a taskflow where one task corresponds to one screen in the UI application. Such a user activity is completed only when the user goes through the entire taskflow (one or more screens). For example, the customer account creation activity in an account process may involve a set of screens for capturing the customer information, account information, confirmations, etc. In some cases, each task might be one page of a multipage input. An example is a new member registration activity in a library. There may be multiple pages that need to be filled with user input data one after the other. Each such page is a task in the taskflow for the activity. The activity gets completed only when the user reaches the last page (last task) and indicates submission of work on that page. There are three aspects in human participation: allocation, execution, and notification.

6.3.3.1 Allocation

Allocation refers to the identification of a user to do a user activity that is ready to be performed and assigning that user activity to that user so that the user can perform it. Once it is assigned, the activity becomes a work item for that user. The work allocation specification for the activity in the process model specifies how (and to whom) the allocation must be done by the process layer. Broadly, there are two types: static allocation and dynamic allocation.

In *static allocation*, the activity is allocated to a role specified statically. During the execution time, any user that performs that role picks it up as a work item and acts on it. For example, in the case of an order process, the activity "pack and ship items" may be allocated to the role "packing group." Anyone who is part of the packing group role performs it. This allocation is called role-based allocation.

In *dynamic allocation*, the user to whom the activity is to be allocated is decided at run-time when the process execution reaches the activity. An example is the "approve order" activity in the order process. It could be so specified that the activity must be assigned to the person (user) that has been specified in the approver input field in the previous activity "review order" by the user of the "review order" activity.

There are some common patterns that we come across in allocation:

- Deferred allocation—a user ID value is obtained from the process parameter.
- Separation of duties—the current activity should not be done by the person who has done a previous activity in the same process instance. This typically is used in review activities where the reviewer needs to be different from the user who input the loan application.
- Case handling—the same person handling all activities in the process. Allocations are implied or specified at the process level here. For example, a customer service request in a bank or a call center process.
- Organizational allocation—this is relationship based; for example, approval of the order has to be done by the manager of the person who performed the order submission activity.
- Shortest queue—the ability to allocate a work item to the resource that has the least number of work items allocated to it. This is relevant in business process outsourcing scenarios.
- Capability-based allocation—the work is assigned based on skills either to a person or a group. For example, in a financial data analysis process, the context for a case to be analyzed is so complex that the person who has the maximum experience is required to perform it.
- Round-robin allocation—work is allocated to each person in a group on a cyclic basis.
- Retain familiar—assign the activity to the person who performed a specific previous activity. For example, the person who performed the activity invoice generation is the one that should perform the activity receive payment activity.

It is possible to specify soft goals for allocation by using soft constraints. Soft constraints allow more flexibility in work allocation. If there is a hard constraint, such as "credit approval," it must be performed by the role "manager." We could add an additional soft constraint saying "prefer a manager located in the same region as the customer." This soft constraint is only a goal that the process layer tries to meet while doing the allocation; if it is possible, it is done. If no such manager is available, then this soft constraint is not applied and the activity goes to the role manager and any manger may be able to pick it up.

6.3.3.2 Execution

This is about how a user to whom the work (the activity) has been assigned performs the actual work. There are two models of relevance here: the push and the pull.

6.3.3.2.1 Push Model

In this model, as soon as the process layer completes the work allocation for the activity, it pushes the work item directly to the user. The business parameters required as input (display) for the work item are also pushed along with the work item. Here it is assumed that the user's location (address) is known to the process layer through some means. This push is to an agent on the user's computing device. The agent is typically a fat client here. The device at the user's end could be a handheld device such as a cell phone. This agent brings the user interface to the user for the activity and the user performs action on the screens provided to complete the activity. This model does not work well for user activities that need users to input a lot of information.

6.3.3.2.2 Pull Model

In this model, the process layer completes the work allocation for the activity and expects the user to pull the activity (work item) from the process layer when the user is ready for performing the activity. The user does it through a UI application that lists the work items that the user is assigned or the ones, the user can pick up for performing. Once the user selects the item to work on, he or she pulls the input parameters (to be used for display) for the UI task from the process instance and works on the tasks of the activity one by one.

6.3.3.3 Notification

Notification is about signaling the completion of activity by the user's UI application to the process layer through a message, once the user actually performs the user activity and logically completes it. The notification message should contain the output parameters (user inputted key parameters) from the user to the process. All along, the process instance in the engine would have been in a waiting state until the user activity is completed by the user. Whether it is the pull or the push model, for the entire duration of the user's execution of the activity, the interaction of the user is with the UI application and this is separate from the process layer. And, it is an off-line execution as far as the process layer is concerned because it is not the one performing the action. Upon receiving the notification, the engine correlates this message (the correlation is based on a key business parameter(s) in the process) to the right process instance. The engine then resumes the process execution from the next activity in the sequence.

In a way, a user activity's execution can be considered as a combination of an asynchronous invocation (notification pattern) to the user followed by an asynchronous receive (one-way pattern) from the user.

6.3.4 Life-Cycle Stages

A process instance goes through a set of stages in its life cycle. Figure 6.5 shows the life-cycle stages of a process instance. The instance is created when triggers for process execution occur. During the creation, the instance is created by the process layer from the process model and then it initializes the process parameters in the instance. After that, the process layer launches the execution of the process instance separately from other process instances in the environment.

The next stage is the executing stage. In this stage, the process instance executes its activities one-by-one in the sequence given. The parallel paths are executed in parallel. System activities are performed automatically and transactions are committed along the way as specified. As far as the normal flow is concerned, execution

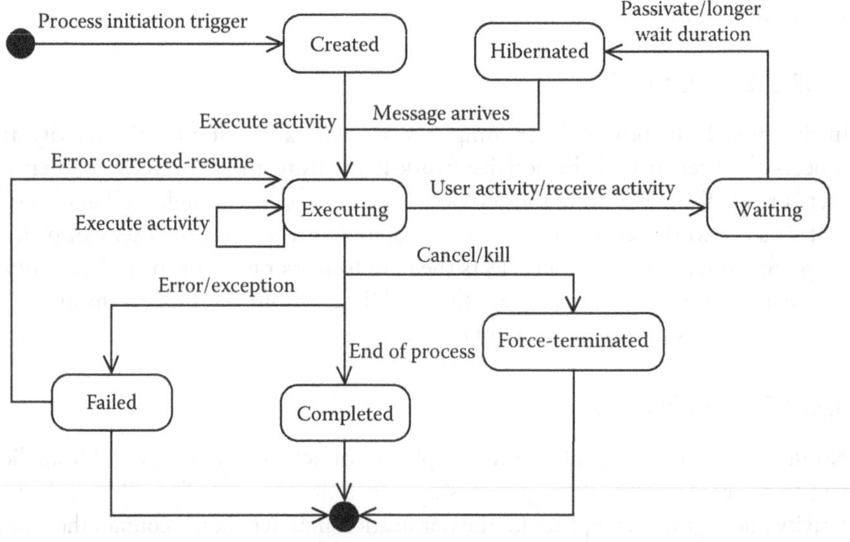

Figure 6.5 Life-cycle stages of a process instance.

proceeds until a user activity or a receive type activity is encountered. Once the user activity or the receive activity is reached, the process instance enters into another stage. It enters the "waiting" stage, where all it does is wait for the input message to come from a user or an external system or process. This might take a longer time (minutes, hours, or even days).

At this stage, the process instance can be hibernated by the process layer. In hibernation, its entire state as of that point in time is persisted in a persistent medium. The process instance would have a logically consistent state. The state information also includes the full process context as of that point in time and the process instance is removed from run-time.

The next stage is when the message for the waiting activity in the process instance arrives in the process layer—the passivated process instance is revived and made active in run-time. The process layer re-creates the process instance and revives it to the same state that it was before it was hibernated. The process layer indicates to the process instance to resume execution and hand over the incoming message to the process instance. The process execution resumes, proceeds with the current activity that received the message, and after completing it, the process instance moves on executing subsequent activities.

The next stage in normal execution is the process instance reaching the last step of the process during execution. At this point, the process reaches the end of the process and the process instance successfully terminates its execution. This is the last stage called "completed."

If there are errors or exceptional conditions happening while the process instance is executing, the process takes alternate flows (such as compensation flows, error handling for recovery). Depending on these situations, the process state can be "Failed with error," "Forcefully terminated," or "Canceled." If a process instance is in error and the error handler logic has recovered it to a consistent state, then the process could be restarted to resume from the point of failure. The process layer does the restart of the process.

6.4 Addressing Integration

In an IT system that is process-centric in its architecture, multiple applications can come together to participate and perform in the process. The BLEs of the IT system, which are the components that are invoked by the process instance, could be one of the following at the time of architecting the IT system:

- New business components to implement the activity services
- Existing applications in the enterprise that provide activity services
- Existing applications in the enterprise that are service-enabled for the process
- Existing systems outside this enterprise that provide activity services
- New systems developed and owned by other enterprises that would provide the services for activities

Thus, each BLE could be a separate application. The already existing applications among the above list could be as follows:

- Custom developed applications in the enterprise; they are also referred to as in-house applications
- Legacy applications in the enterprise (example Mainframe applications, Client–server applications on ORACLE-PowerBuilder, etc.)
- Application packages such as ERP packages; some examples are SAP, ORACLE apps, CRM packages, SIEBEL®, and PeopleSoft; packaged-applications is another term for these applications
- Content Management Systems (CMS)

Getting the multiple applications (regardless of their underlying technology environments) to work together is called Enterprise Application Integration (EAI). The focus of EAI is on the flows where predominantly applications (systems in other words) are involved in interactions and there is no or minimal human intervention; systems send messages to each other and complete business function. For example, a mutual funds transaction process that happens totally without any human intervention whose instances are typically executed in batch with other mutual funds transaction process instances. The process-centric architecture (PCA) integrates all of them (the systems) holistically in a process-driven way where the process instance interacts with each of them through their links to activities, with the context of the process. The objective of the integration is to let the applications participate in the process by playing their individual roles providing the service required by the activities—this leads to the achievement of the business objective of the process.

Let us consider the example of an sales order process, where the order is placed by the customer and the process gets completed when the payment is received. As one of the initial activities of the process, if the customer is a new customer ("check new customer" activity), the customer is created in the CRM application ("create customer account" activity) and a customer ID is generated for the customer. These two activities are performed by the CRM application when the process instance invokes it. Then, in the "check inventory" activity, the inventory is checked for the availability of the products ordered by the customer. This activity is performed by the SAP application. If the inventory is short of the products, the next activity "replenish inventory" is invoked by the process instance, which is supported (performed) by the SAP application that triggers the manufacturing application to manufacture the inventory threshold quantity of products. When the process reaches the "make payment" activity, after taking in the customer's validated credit card information, the activity processes the payment in the account receivables application. This activity is performed by the account receivables application, which is a custom-developed in-house application in the enterprise. Then finally, the last activity in the process "schedule delivery of products to customer," is executed, which is performed by another application, the SAP package itself (fulfillment application). In all of these cases, the respective service for each activity is provided by a packaged-application. The activities were executed with the process instance invoking the corresponding service provided by the packaged-application.

In this way of integration, that is process-driven integration, these applications are all part of the IT system that is as a whole process centric, but they play individual roles in the process as individual applications providing specific business services.

The applications become active only when they are invoked by the process instance for performing a specific activity. They need to maintain all the business data associated with the specific action they are performing and only that business data—this data is hidden from the process and other applications. For example, the inventory management packaged application would only maintain inventory data and will not maintain other data such as customer information and payable information for money owed to suppliers or partners. Such data are respectively maintained only by the CRM application and the Financials (accounts payable) applications, respectively. It does away with data redundancy. This model of integration also does away with the need for a central data source that all the applications in the enterprise feed their respective data to and the need for any synchronization of redundant data between various disparate applications in the enterprise. The context for execution is provided by the process instance to the application that the application uses to understand the state of the business entities and perform the application's specific job, which is implementing the service for the activity. As each application maintains and owns respective business data, there is no room available for data inconsistencies, since other applications would not be handling such data. The required business data for each service is provided from the process context by the process instance to the service-implementing application through the input invocation message that the application receives from the process during execution. For example, the accounts receivable application that performs the payment activity receives the customer account ID and name from the process instance to carry out the payment.

The applications are connected and disconnected from the process instances dynamically. Once the execution of the service is complete, that application is disconnected from the process instance. The process model also statically is open to change. The activities in the process, to which the applications are attached, can also be dropped from or rearranged in the process to alter the process logic. But, this does not cause any change in those applications. They get attached or reattached without being aware. During the activity service invocations in process execution, the process layer handles all communication mechanisms–related responsibilities by decoupling the activity-service and the implementation of the service by the application, be it packaged, in-house, or third-party and irrespective of the technologies (heterogeneous) involved.

6.5 Workflow

Workflows in the traditional sense involved flows of work or a business entity (such as a loan application, a customer complaint for the customer services department of a company, a case that is handed in a BPO organization, etc.) from one person to another where each person acts on the business entity (work item). The work item's status changes while it moves through the flow and eventually the item gets completed when it reaches the last step in the flow. Hand-offs from one user to another user, of the work item, is a key characteristic of workflows.

In PCA, the workflows are treated as processes where each user is a participant who participates and performs action on the respective user activity using a UI application. The process instance executes, moving control (the work item in other words) from one user activity to the other. The process instance does the hand-off of the work item from user to user until the end of the process. The key attributes of the entity, such as application number, case number, complaint number, and complaint date, are included as process parameters. The full details of the entity (or the entity itself), such as the application form and complaint form, are stored and maintained in the UI application itself and not the process layer. Typically, a reference to the business entity, say the document ID of the document (application form) stored in a document management system, is provided to the process instance and is available as a process parameter serving as the key or reference to the entity itself. This key is passed around in the process instance from one activity to the other.

In a workflow scenario, the PCA-based IT system would have the following:

- The process model reflecting the flow of work
- A user activity representing each step in the workflow
- At run-time, a person (user) assigned to perform each user activity, in which the person plays a specific role that is relevant for the activity and the work item
- A UI application corresponding to each user activity that the user uses to perform the activity
- Multiple user activities can be supported by one UI application; thus, the IT system would have one or more UI application
- The UI application would have a component to show to the user, a list of work items from across process instances assigned to the user

The UI application can be a new UI application developed for this IT system or it can be an existing UI application in the enterprise. It could also be a mobile UI application in case the push model of user activities is followed. The bindings for the user activities with the UI application(s) can be done late at run-time in a dynamic way. This decouples the user activity from the technology and implementation details of the UI application. Technically, the UI application could be a JSP/servlet application based on Java, a .Net application or a Java mobile application, a mainframe application with a character user interface screen (CICS based for example), or a PowerBuilder client application, and so on.

To understand the dynamics of workflow, let us the take the example of a customer complaint process. The process is triggered when a complaint is received from the customer by phone, e-mail, or other communication methods. The first step in the process is the user activity that captures the details of the complaint and the generation of a complaint number. Now it becomes a work item. This user activity is performed by a customer service representative (CSR). The e-mail or the written complaint if provided by a customer, is scanned and stored in a document management system (DMS), and a unique reference number is provided by the DMS. This upload to the DMS can be done by the same user as part of the first activity using the UI application in which the UI application invokes the DMS interface. Or preferably, storing in the DMS can be the next system activity, where the DMS interface is invoked and the document is stored.

The next activity is one in which the complaint is looked into by support personnel who get this work item after it was assigned to him or her by the process layer or by the specification of the CSR. The UI application shows the complaint details to this user, who studies the details and takes further action. Either this user resolves the reported problem or reassigns the work item to another person for deeper investigation. The next activity could be one where a technical engineer gets the work item. This user updates the UI application with the investigation results and changes the status to "resolved pending review" if the problem gets resolved. The next activity would be the review activity, now the process instance moves the work item from the engineer to the manager, who is the reviewer. The manager uses the UI application, checks the details of the complaint and the actions that have happened on the work item so far, and updates the work item status as "resolved" if it is OK and the process ends successfully. If the review is not OK, then the manager updates the status of the complaint to "needs reinvestigation" and assigns it to a technical expert to look into the problem. The process instance now assigns the work item to the technical expert by assigning the next user activity "expert investigation" to the user who performs this activity. The expert uses a UI application and provides investigation notes and updates the status to "resolved" after resolving the work item. In this example, the UI application used by all the users in the process is the same since all of them work with the same details.

All along the process instance, the status of the work item (i.e., complaint here) keeps changing from "registered" at the beginning, to "assigned," to "in progress," to "escalated," to "awaiting spare parts from supplier," to "waiting for confirmation from customer," and finally "resolved." All the details of the complaint are stored and maintained by the UI application in a database attached to it. These details include: the complaint number, the nature of the complaint, the product or service that is the subject of the complaint, the customer name, the customer account number, the customer's contact details, the address for any visit, a detailed description of the problem, the date when the problem occurred, whether under warranty, the warranty period, whether under a maintenance contract, the maintenance contract number, and the validity period. The process would have only the key data, such as the complaint number, under warranty or not flag, under contract or not flag, customer account number, and date of complaint as process parameters.

6.6 Business Rules

Some applications abstract out the business rule part of the program logic and put it in a separate component called rules layer. The rules layer houses the business rule and manages its entire life cycle. This design allows the rules to be modified separately from the application core components without directly impacting the application code. At the appropriate point, the code in the application invokes the business rule in the rule layer and the rule layer executes the rule and returns the results of the rule execution to the application in the invocation itself.

In PCA, the business rule is expressed in a business-friendly way and the process model brings the business rule execution into the process context so that the rule, when it gets executed, always has the context provided by the process. In PCA, the rule abstraction is taken another level higher. The process level that is the highest abstraction incorporates those business rules or parts of business rules that directly affect the process flow, as conditional branches. An example is shown in Figure 6.6. In this example, the condition checks if the customer is a new customer or not in the order process. Depending on the value of this expression, the flow branches into the appropriate path.

The other business rules or parts are expressed in a business-friendly way and are kept in the business rules layer for full management and they become rule activities in the process.

At the rule activity in a process, the process instance invokes the rule residing in the rules layer. A rule activity is associated with a specific business rule and it can get results from the execution of the rule. The rule is invoked only by the process instance and not by any other component. Business rules leverage all the services provided by the rules layer, such as rule translation into executable code, run-time rule instances, and isolation from other executing rule instances. For the invocation at the rules activity, the process instance communicates with the rules layer providing it with the details of the rule to be executed including rule name (rule definition identifier) and the input parameters for the rule, which are those process parameters in the process context that are relevant for the business rule. Once the business rules invocation is over, the process instance disconnects from the rule layer and proceeds to execute the next activity in the sequence. Thus, the process integrates business rules into the flow in an effective way.

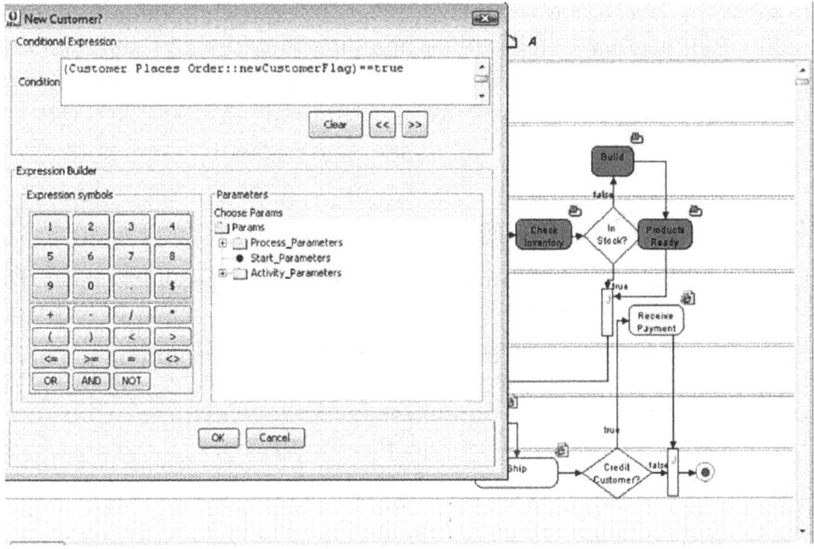

Figure 6.6 A conditional branch.

6.7 Flows Handled in a Process

We saw a different nature of flows that can happen in processes including workflows, application integration, and rules; some of them involving human participants and some of them involving only system participants. PCA can handle the processes various interaction possibilities between the participants and holistically.

These are as follows:

- P2P—person to person—Here the interactions are between humans and systems and are almost not involved or involved very minimally. The process contains user activities and the control flow is between them, involving multiple users. The flow progresses from one person to the other in the context of the process.
- A2A—application to application—Here the interactions are between systems. Multiple applications interact with each other but in the context of the business process and under the orchestration of the process. System receive from and give control back to the process in the control flow of the process. Unlike in human participants, no waiting is involved in the process since the systems invoked return control immediately back to the process.
- P2A—person to application—Here the interactions involve humans and systems in any combination. The process, while executing, integrates each user and system into the process flow. At any point in time in the process instance, the control could be with a system or a user depending on the activity being performed in the process at that time. Flow orchestration is totally managed by the process model and the systems receive and release control.

Thus, we see the integration achieved by a PCA-based system is holistic and comprehensive incorporating system participants, human participants, and rules rather than addressing them in parts. The participants take part in the process instance only when their contribution is required as determined by the process.

6.8 Exercise Questions

1. In your organization, identify processes that span across applications. How do they interact with each other today? How do they know of each other? Identify the dependencies they have with each other.
2. How do we ensure that our process does not have to change, if we move from one third party service provider to another for a service?
3. Think of some work allocation rules that you have seen in your organization for processes that involve human participation. Which are the most complex ones? Do you think there is some allocation in this list that a human would address more effectively than a process-centric system? And, why is it so?

Chapter 7

Benefits of Process-Centric Architecture

7.1 Objectives

- To understand why an enterprise should go with process-centric architecture (PCA)
- To understand the benefits from the business perspective
- To understand the IT benefits

7.2 Business Benefits

There are significant benefits to the business from the PCA style of IT systems. These provide compelling answers as to why PCA is a style worth applying to IT systems in an enterprise. The key benefits are discussed in Sections 7.2.1 through 7.2.6.

7.2.1 Business–IT Alignment

Through the focus on and the centrality of the business process in the architecture, business and IT systems align better in this architecture. The gap between the business process/business specifications/requirements and the IT system is directly confronted by this architecture and the architecture with its approach leaves minimum scope for the gap to even exist in the first place—by avoiding the translation (that has been largely manual), by the IT analyst/programmers, of business process specifications captured by IT analysts to the system code.

It is the business process that drives the system architecture, design, and execution of the whole IT system. Business processes can be rapidly changed to meet the change in business requirements involving zero or minimal changes to the application(s) code. Typical changes that are necessitated in the IT system due to changes in the business, such as changes to the process logic including changes in process flow, flow of control, adding or removing steps in the flow, or changes in business rules, can be done in the process layer itself without involving changes to the code in the application. The application code would only need to be changed if there is a change needed in the specific business functionality (this is the application logic). The model-driven approach advocated by PCA, right from the concept stage of the system, through the architecture stage and coding stage all the way to the deployment stage provides better linkage between the business and business artifacts with the IT system and artifacts in the IT system development.

The IT system code in this architectural style no longer has the potential to evolve independently of the business process nor does the business process evolve separately from the system. The process is actively pinned to the IT system programs through the business process model.

7.2.2 Better Control for Business

As should be the case, business gets more control over the business processes in a PCA-based IT system. It enables them to quickly make changes to the process when needed without necessarily involving IT changes all the time. In traditional architectures, it often necessitates the involvement of an IT person and the IT person making changes in the application code. This is made possible by making the process visible to the business, allowing them to monitor the processes (executions) at run-time, measure their metrics, and take action in real-time.

7.2.3 Reuse

The concept of services is strongly used with PCA. This promotes reuse of business components in the architecture across processes. The processes themselves are reusable entities. PCA, therefore, leverages all the reuse benefits brought by services such as the reuse, interoperability, and utilization of existing system assets.

Whether processes or activities in processes are reused outside the enterprise or even within the enterprise, the processes are not directly exposed—the processes themselves or activities (if activities are being reused) are exposed as business services through only the defined service interface. The service implementations for the business services are not exposed to the external or internal processes/systems using them. This is important from an intellectual property (IP) perspective for the organization. As explained in Chapter 5, processes are defined as abstract and concrete (executable) processes. Concrete process definitions are associated as the IP of the company and they are not exposed to other systems. An abstract definition of the process is what is exposed and provided to the other enterprises and external systems (and internal systems too) that are going to use the process. Abstract processes by definition mask all IP and details of the process.

7.2.4 Central Store of Processes

When IT systems are architected based on PCA, the business process definitions (process logic) are moved out of the applications scope and kept in the process layer. This process layer would hold all the business processes of the enterprise making this a centralized repository of business processes for the enterprise. From this, the processes are used uniformly across the enterprise.

7.2.5 Process Management

PCA enables better management of business processes by allowing the managers to take an overall process view that clearly conveys to them how well a process is doing. PCA plays an important contributing role to the business process management (BPM) exercises in the enterprise. PCA helps automate and optimize the end-to-end processes such as "order to cash."

7.2.6 Mergers and Acquisitions

A typical enterprise can go through efforts related to mergers and acquisitions (M&A) where multiple enterprises join to become one. It could lead to big changes in the business processes of the enterprise including the integration of processes and systems across merging enterprises. IT systems based on PCA enable such integrations to be smooth. Such IT systems can be quickly changed to integrate with other systems based on process-driven integration.

In M&A, the business processes of the entities concerned in the operations need to integrate. The combined business entity decides what the business processes would look like for the resulting new organization (new entity). It is strongly recommended to use BPM in this exercise—the objective of the exercise is business process consolidation and business process integration—for the best value. PCA is to be used in conjunction with BPM in the architecture exercise for the IT systems concerned with the business processes of the new entity. This typically involves the following:

1. Identify, list, and analyze the existing business processes of each entity.
2. Decide on the new business processes that will apply for and run in the new entity.

3. Design the new business processes for the new entity with the activity details (business operations).
4. Identify the existing application portfolios of both the entities.
5. For the new business processes designed, architect the IT systems required to support them.
6. While doing the architecture
   a. Analyze the existing applications for suitability in the supporting steps of the new process.
   b. Do application rationalization to take care of application overlaps and getting rid of duplicate and redundant applications.
   c. In the exercise done in step (b), some applications from both the entities may get eliminated. The result of the rationalization is the set of applications from both the entities that have been found to be useful in the new context of the merged entity.
   d. Map the applications and the steps of the business processes for supporting the process.
   e. Even when there are no duplicates, some applications may get eliminated (sunsetted) if they are not found suitable and appropriate for the new context.
   f. Identify the gaps in business processes, where the process steps do not have existing applications supporting them.
   g. Design the business logic components for the steps that have been identified in step (d) above. These will need to be designed and implemented anew.
7. Implement the IT systems and the related business processes in a phased manner ensuring a proper transition.
8. During the transition period, the new IT system that has been architected in the above mentioned steps based on PCA (for the new enterprise), as well as the old IT system (that has been marked to be eliminated) may coexist and support respective business processes (new and old, respectively). The old systems and consequently the associated business processes may get transitioned out gradually.
9. For the transition period, based on PCA, the new business processes can be incrementally changed and implemented as an IT system. The new process and the IT system thus architected progressively reaches the final new process model instead of one big jump from the existing business process to the expected final state business process.

PCA makes this whole exercise easier than other approaches by providing a clear process-based integration approach rather than the conventional hard integration approaches. The process-based approach is more flexible and more manageable thereby helping the M&A complexities and the consequent transition.

7.3 Benefits to IT Systems

Just as PCA benefits business, PCA also provides great benefits to IT personnel and to the implemented systems themselves. It makes the IT systems flexible, agile, interoperable, scalable, and maintainable. The benefits are explained below.

7.3.1 Flexibility

In this architecture, the process logic is clearly separated from the business logic so that as far as the components of the systems go, there is good separation of concerns with respect to these. This makes the system more flexible. The process components, the rules components, the business components, the user interaction components, and the applications involved can be modified independently of the other components. Each of these components are loosely-coupled to the others.

Also, contributing to this improved flexibility of the system is the fact that the business process is made explicit and it is described in a formal specification.

7.3.2 Agility

PCA leads to agile IT systems—systems that can respond faster to the changes necessitated in the business processes by the business environment, strategy, or market conditions. The system adapts faster to the changes because a change to the business process specification directly results in a change in the system's behavior.

7.3.3 Interoperability

The architecture does not make any assumptions on the technical nature of the applications that become part of the process in the PCA-based IT system. The principle that it follows in the interactions of the process with the applications is that the interactions are service-based. That is, the process would execute in the IT system by invoking the services provided by the applications for specific steps in the process. This enables interoperability in a great way since the applications that are integrated into the process flow can be of any technological environment and heterogeneous. They can be external to the enterprise or belong within the enterprise.

For the integration of the applications, PCA offers a more effective process-driven way of integration. This concept naturally helps overcome interoperability problems with applications running on disparate technologies.

PCA encourages the collaboration between different applications by making them work under the common context of the business process. The IT system becomes more of an open system in this architecture because of the stress on clear interface specifications by each application component for the service provided to the process.

7.3.4 Scalability of the IT System Is Improved

The IT system becomes more scalable. The additional tiering in the architecture that brings better separation of concerns enables this. New layers such as the process layer and the business rules layer allow the process components and the rule components of the system to be physically separated from the other components (such as business components, presentation components, user interaction components, and data components) and thus allow them to be scaled independently of other components or applications.

7.3.5 Maintainability

In PCA, the business process underlying the system is made explicit and is formally specified. The concerns of process logic are clearly separated out from the business logic of the application components. This makes the IT system more easily maintainable. Changes to the process logic can be quickly done to the process model and confined to the process model only. Changes to any business functionality can be done confining it to only the application component that handles that functionality without impacting any other component including the process model.

The clear separation that PCA brings can also be helpful to move certain user-interface (UI)-based functionalities from a legacy application to a more user-friendly UI application. An example would be a mainframe-based UI application that may not be very user-friendly. It can be part of the process flow initially. Then at a later point in time, the architecture would allow its replacement with one based on more UI-friendly technology. All this is done without changing anything else in other components of the architecture.

7.4 Scalability of the PCA Style and Approach

PCA, being rooted in business process focus, is inherently scalable for addressing the business processes of businesses of different sizes—be it a small-scale business, a medium-sized business, or a large business enterprise. This architecture is not constrained by the size of the organization or the complexity of the processes in a large organization because the process layer is going to hold the process flow instead of the hard-coded flow ingrained in the applications supporting the business process in the conventional architecture. With respect to scalability for the run-time system, process layer components and the business logic components being separate concerns are physically independent of each other and they can scale up or scale out separately as per the load.

For example, in the case of a full end-to-end process, such as order-to-cash in a large transportation services company, the process layer would include the end-to-end process model housed in it having the steps corresponding to various activities such as sales, order placement, invoicing, payment, order fulfillment, and accounting entry. This process is typically decomposed as a set of subprocesses for each distinct part of the process such as order creation, order fulfillment, and financial processing. Each such subprocess is itself a process and may have another level of decomposition, which is further composed as a subprocess. For example, the finance process in the end-to-end process may be decomposed into activities related to payment processing, making general ledger (G/L) entries, invoice account payable to receivable matching/netting, providing receipts to the customers, etc. In the PCA for this IT system, the end-to-end process exists in the run-time and so do the process instances corresponding to each of the subprocesses that it is composed of down to the lowest level subprocess—all of these process instances are executed seamlessly and in the right sequence inside the process layer.

In the previous example, the entire process would interact with business logic components supporting the various activities that are part of sales operations, order creation, order processing, finance operations, and so on. These business logic components may be supported by existing applications or new applications depending on how well they provide the respective services to the process. The architecture inherently enables the components to be scalable in such a large end-to-end process in such a big enterprise. To handle a larger number of orders received by the company, the process layer could be scaled up/out so that more process instances are executed and load managed. Components that are supporting business functionalities, such as payment processing, can also be separately scaled up if there are more loads related to payments or finance work. The seamless integration of all the applications involved in this end-to-end process is enabled by PCA, and this ensures the scalability of the approach itself whether the process is a small one in a small enterprise or is a complex large process in a large enterprise. The PCA approach supports them equally well.

There are essentially two types of processes in an enterprise: operational processes and management processes. Though PCA supports both of them, operational processes are the best candidates for PCA as of now, because of their direct involvement in the core operations of the business and they involve more repetitive, well-defined activities that can be more amenable to be supported by systems. Management processes involve a good amount of knowledge-intensive work and activities that are more ambiguous, less structured, and abstract when compared with other processes. Also included in this broad category are processes such as product development, research and development related work, and other strategic processes—these are knowledge-intensive processes. PCA may fit IT systems supporting such processes to some extent. For example, reporting processes or monitoring processes for managers could be architected as IT systems based on PCA. Computer systems have also been evolving to handle work that is more abstract and knowledge-driven. As they become more and more capable, PCA would scale to support knowledge-intensive processes (management processes) too.

7.5 Complexity versus Manageability

While following the PCA style to architect an IT system, the unrelenting focus is on the business process at hand. It can be an intra-department business process, say a loan disbursement process that focuses on the activities to be done as part of a service provided by a specific department—a relatively less complex process. Or, the process can be an organization-wide end-to-end process say the order-to-cash process that covers the entire scope of the enterprise. Such an enterprise-wide process could appear complex to deal with especially since it would mean modeling most of the activities of the value chain in the enterprise and involving multiple applications or systems in the architecture—the entire process design and modeling itself could be felt to be a daunting task.

This complexity can be well handled in the PCA approach while at the same time keeping the architecture manageable. PCA provides the best manageability and ability to address process-design complexity when it is applied in conjunction with the BPM program in the enterprise. Organization-wide BPM implementations facilitate a structured approach to process improvement, process-design, and process management. BPM greatly helps address complexities with respect to process design and the architecture work for PCA. BPM implementations typically happen over a period of time in the organization to address the complexity of moving the organization from a function-based to a process-aligned one.

When applying PCA to architect systems in the enterprise, especially the large- and medium-sized businesses, it is more pragmatic to avoid going for a big-bang approach—that is attempting to apply PCA for all the systems in the enterprise overhauling the existing architecture. It would be more manageable to apply it first to smaller-scope processes, say new IT systems, that need to be built for a new process that is within a small department of the enterprise or to re-architect an existing system supporting an intra-department process. An example here would be a new mutual fund plan that could result in a new fund process. It is best to do one pilot with a relatively smaller process and then use this learning experience to architect more and more processes in an incremental way thereby gradually covering the entire enterprise and end-to-end processes. Thus, it is suggested to start from one IT system, apply PCA for its architecture, and then move to another IT system (one process at a time in the initial projects) instead of attempting a big-bang. That way it would be manageable.

Complexity associated with business process design is best managed by applying PCA together with BPM. If BPM is not already in place in the enterprise, it would be worthwhile to move the enterprise processes toward BPM for better long-term value. This is true especially for medium-to-large businesses.

Another method of dealing with complexity and making the whole architecture and implementation work for the IT system is *process modularization*. Processes are modularized into smaller processes or subprocesses. Since PCA supports process composition and process hierarchy, complexity can be directly addressed with the concept of abstraction. Even within the process layer that is an abstraction above the business logic and user interface logic, more levels of abstractions are possible at varying levels of granularity—the lowest level process will have relatively the highest level of details. An end-to-end process that spans across the functions (and departments) of the enterprise is broken down into subprocesses of lower-scope and specific business objectives at each level. Each lower level is incrementally more in detail and less in scope than the higher levels. What becomes more important here in managing this process design complexity is the granularity of activities in the process. Even at the lowest level of process abstraction, the granularity of each activity in the process is ideally kept at the right level so as to keep the process manageable and maintainable. The level of detail at this level of granularity for the activity needs to be just right and it needs to avoid too many details—this level of granularity for the activities in the process is called business service granularity. At this level, the activity performs a logically complete business function that is recognizable from the perspective of a business user or a business manager. Some examples of activities (business services) at the right granularity are: adding a new customer, updating an existing customer's details, approving a loan request, withdrawing money from an account, depositing money to an account, redeeming a specified number of units from a mutual fund held by the customer, and placing an order. Chapter 9, SOA for services, discusses the right granularity for the process activities in more detail. These levels of process abstraction in the process help us handle their complexity better, making them not difficult to manage and maintain.

Most enterprises would have some already existing means of managing their business processes with an objective to improve them and the business processes would have been getting managed based on those ways. And, process management has been complex for most of the enterprises. Now with PCA, business managers and IT personnel get more power and effectiveness in managing those very same business processes and effect appropriate IT changes so that IT systems are better aligned to business. As far as manageability and complexity are concerned, the only thing that PCA (and BPM) introduces is a bit more formalism, a more effective method for the business to impact IT behavior with the very similar kind of process design and modeling the business is already used to. Thus, PCA will be only as complex as, if not less than, the existing process design and modeling approaches.

7.6 Raised Level of Abstraction for the IT System

Historically, programming and design for software-intensive systems have been going higher and higher in abstraction. This movement in abstraction has been in the direction toward the human (or the business user of the system or stakeholders of the system) and away from the machine. With each higher abstraction, systems are becoming increasingly closer to the human than they were before—with respect to the ability they provide to the human to build them, work with them, understand them, change them, or fix problems in them.

Let us look at the programming-related abstractions. The first-generation systems were programmed in machine languages—they were the closest to the machine but the farthest from humans. Then assembly languages took the programming abstraction a bit higher with the introduction of mnemonics replacing machine instruction code—which made it a bit easier for programmers to program (or change) the system, relative to the previous abstraction. After that came the third-generation languages (3GLs) that took abstraction to the next higher level with a jump with the name high-level programming languages—programming was taken to a level of ease where more people could write programs and build systems with a syntax that was distinctly different from machines and more friendly to humans. However, the people doing this were expected to be technically oriented or programmers and it was clearly not for the business-oriented people. With the advent of fourth-generation languages (4GLs), the level of abstraction went up still higher where the programs, to a great extent, were expected to be written by business folks themselves. Structured query language (SQL) is a good example of this. 4GLs provided the ability for people to store, retrieve, and update information from databases in an easier way using a language they are more comfortable with than high-level programming languages.

But, 4GLs are considered to be a failure by some because business folks still did not find 4GLs that easy to use or very friendly to program. This is mainly because it still involved programming business logic, which is beyond just data access, into the systems. This still required the use of 3GLs. And, more importantly the abstraction was an abstraction only at the programming level and not at the system architecture level.

Given this history, it is reasonable to be concerned about whether PCA, by moving the abstraction of the system to the business process level, would still be effective as far as the friendliness to and use by business folks goes. The abstraction PCA introduces is unlikely to be a failure given the following:

- It is an architectural abstraction. It has raised the architecture abstraction from the current business-logic or component level to the business process level that is closer to the way business folks see the systems.
- It allows the business folks to directly drive the architecture by specifying, all on their own, the business process (this avoids all lost-in-translation gaps from business requirements to the system design/implementation) that would become the center of the architecture of the system and that would drive the behavior of the system. The previous level of abstraction allowed them to only specify business requirements that merely became (and remained) passive documents later as far as the system's architecture was concerned.
- It allows businesses to change the behavior of the system by changing its architecture through the business process model. They can directly change

the business process of the system. PCA takes the abstraction closer to the WYSIWYG (what-you-see-is-what-you-get) philosophy, where the business process that the business folks design and specify is the business process that the system actually runs and is based on.

- PCA does not expect the business folks to learn any new programming paradigm or any new programming oriented method. For architecting the system, it lets them directly use the terms and notations that they normally use in their day-to-day parlance and also lets them see the system in the same way. They can now relate well to the architecture of the system and the concepts in it. All this means businesses also do the architecture work for the system; that makes it very different from and more powerful than the earlier abstractions.

7.7 Exercise Questions

1. What process would you to pick in your organization to demonstrate the benefits of PCA?
2. Pick up a business process that you are familiar with and visualize the benefits that would come if that is architected on PCA. Do those benefits justify the decision to architect it this way?

II

ARCHITECTING IT SYSTEMS, THE PROCESS-CENTRIC STYLE (DESIGNING PCA)

Chapter 8

The Approach

8.1 Objectives

- To understand how the architecture of an IT system looks in the process-centric style
- To appreciate the different components and their roles in the architecture
- To be introduced to the architectural design behind process-centric architecture (PCA)

8.2 A Typical Manifestation of Process-Centric Architecture

8.2.1 The Architecture

Let us take a look at an architecture that embodies the PCA style. This example involves order processing.

Figure 8.1 shows the process model of an order process. The static and dynamic views of the architecture are shown in Figures 8.2 and 8.3.

In this manifestation, we have the following components. The process engine of a business process management system (BPMS), the process model inside the process engine, the application components that support the business, the application server (JEE), the web server, the web application, an application package, the process repository, and the business rules engine. This is one possible manifestation of the architecture for the business process.

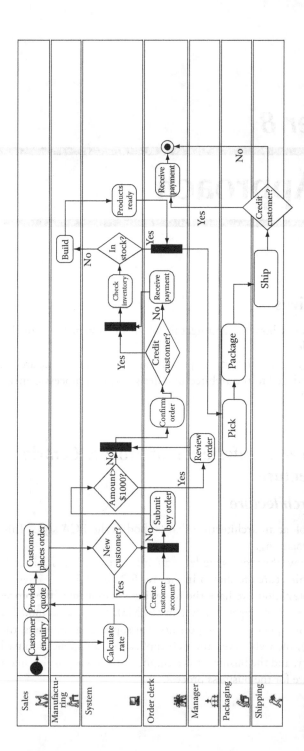

Figure 8.1 A manifestation of PCA—the business process model.

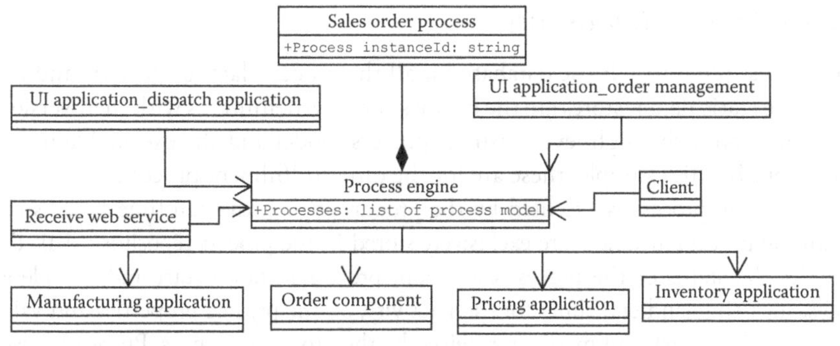

Figure 8.2 A manifestation of PCA—static view.

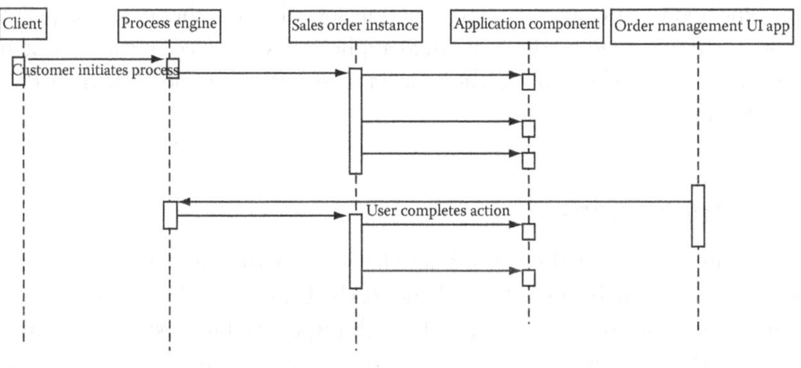

Figure 8.3 A manifestation of PCA—dynamic view.

8.2.1.1 Process Engine

The process server (also called process engine) is the embodiment of the process layer in the architecture. It is provided by a BPMS here. Its role is to implement all the services and functionalities of the process layer including creating process instances, initiating their execution, and managing their life cycle. It houses the process model and provides the environment for the process model to execute.

The process server is at the center of this architecture and it holds the IT system's core component, the business process, for example, the handle order process. Run-time manifestations of the process are also created by the process server. It is a layer separate from the application server.

It implements the entire infrastructure required for process deployments and executions. It takes care of the needs of the executing process instances including receiving messages and invocations to the business components seamlessly across technologies and communication protocols.

8.2.1.2 Process Repository

The process repository is the database for all the process data, both static and run-time. The static data it stores are the business process definitions with their versions. It includes both the high-level business process model and the executable process definition. In this example, these are for the order fulfillment process.

When the process is executed by the process engine, the run-time process data for all the process instances are exclusively stored in the process repository. This data includes the status of the process execution, process instance start and completion times, start time and end times for each activity, all the process properties and values (process parameters), and messages received by the process instances. Process hibernation and process resumption are carried out using the data from the process repository.

The process engine owns the process repository and is the one that updates it as the process instances move along with their executions. The process repository is not expected to store any business function specific data, that data is expected to be stored and managed by the individual applications involved in the IT system. It stores only process-related data. The process repository is provided by the BPMS in this architecture.

8.2.1.3 Applications

Applications implement the various activity-services that are part of the business process. They are the business logic elements (BLEs) for the IT system. Each application supports one or more services through respective business components that implement the services. They include in-house applications, application packages (commercial off-the-shelf [COTS] packages), legacy applications, and third-party service providers. For example, the inventory application, pricing application, order management application, and CRM package.

Each application implements the services that are in the business scope of its specific area, say inventory. And it maintains and manages all the business data related to that area in the application database. The application database stores the application data and is used by all the applications. This database is separate from the process repository. The application database is owned by the applications and access to it is only through the applications. Only the applications or business reporting applications directly access this data.

The business components in some of those applications are Enterprise Java Beans (EJB) components; for example, inventory application services, order management application services, and pricing services. Each of the services is implemented by an EJB component (high-granular) that in turn uses other EJB components that are low-granular business components right down to the level of business entities, such as the EJB component for order entity (in the database).

Some of the business components that implement services could be web service implementations (not shown here in this example) that use SOAP over HTTP.

Another application that is part of this IT system is the customer relationship management (CRM) application package. That application implements the customer information and management related activity-services for the process in this IT system; for example, the prepare shipment for deliver activity. A legacy application could also be part of the process by implementing an activity-service in the process.

All these service implementing application components are invoked by the process instance executing in the process engine at the right points in the process.

8.2.1.4 Application Server

The applications with the EJB components are kept in a JEE application server in this manifestation. The application components are managed by the application server. The service implementing the EJB components of the inventory application, pricing application, and order management application are the ones hosted by the application server. It concerns itself totally with supporting the life cycle of these business components and providing them with a system infrastructure for carrying out their business logic. Some of the infrastructure services offered are transaction management, database access, application level security, redundancy, performance related support, etc.

It enables access to the application database for the individual applications through a separate data abstraction layer within it. The process engine interacts with the application server to execute the EJB components that implement the activity-service in the process during the process execution.

8.2.1.5 Adapter Layer

The adapter layer is a part of the process server. It is concerned with handling all communication-related aspects of the interaction of process instances with the business logic components. This includes communication protocols, transport/network protocols, technologies, data transformations, character encodings (EBCDIC, ASCII), and so on that are involved in the invocation of the activity-services and the invocations received into the system. It enables the process server to invoke the services corresponding to the system activities. This adapter layer would be capable of interfacing with a wide variety of systems spanning across disparate technologies.

The adapter layer takes care of the invocation of different types of services including web services (standard), EJB components, legacy application, packaged applications (such as SAP, ERP, CRM), etc. by taking care of the necessary interoperability requirements. In this example, the business components of order management, pricing, and inventory applications are EJB components in the application server. It would perform the necessary EJB look ups and the invocation on the remote interface. In the case of the package application, it would connect to the service exposed by the package or the wrapper created to expose the package services, then performs necessary data transformations from the format that the process instance uses to the format that the package requires, then invokes the service, and after that it performs reverse transformation of the data received from the package to one that the process uses. It does a similar thing with legacy, for example mainframe, applications. Also, it would use the gateways provided by a mainframe to access the mainframe applications.

The adapter layer would most effortlessly invoke services that are based on standards-based protocols such as web services based on SOAP over HTTP and in XML, as they are inherently non-technology specific. Such services are naturally preferred for the services and their invocation. The adapter layer can be an Enterprise Service Bus (ESB) that is either part of the BPMS or a separate entity such as Mule.

8.2.1.6 Business Rules Engine

The business rules engine houses the explicitly defined business rules that govern the business functionality of individual activities (e.g., claims approval rules). By invoking the rules engine, the process server gets the rules executed by the rules engine. For example, the "calculate rate" activity shown in Figure 8.1 can be realized as a business rule and be deployed in the rules engine. All the rules that are applicable in calculating the effective price of the items in the customer's order is defined in this business rule. During the process execution, this rule is then invoked from the process when the process reaches the "calculate rate" activity step.

The process server uses its adapter layer to handle the technical concerns of the rules invocation such as data transformations. A rules engine allows the business rule to be defined in a business-friendly format using business terms and to be deployed in it with a unique rule identifier. The rule identifier is used by the process to invoke the rule during execution. The input arguments it requires and the output arguments that it returns are specified in the rule. The process engine interacts with the rules engine. For example, the "calculate rate" activity shown in Figure 8.1 can be realized as a business rule and be deployed in the rules engine. All the rules that are applicable in calculating the effective price of the items in the customer's order is defined in this business rule. During the process execution, this rule is then invoked from the process when the process reaches the "calculate rate" activity step.

8.2.1.7 Web Server

The web server realizes the user interface (UI) application layer of the architecture. It uses the HTTP protocol and serves HTML pages. The web UI applications for the manual activities in the process are housed on this server. The users perform all the manual activities (such as reviewing orders, delivering to customers) using the web-based user interfaces providing the web UI applications. The UI application runs in the web server and shows HTML pages on the user's workstation.

The user participation portal is the web-based UI application that the BPMS provides, which also runs on the web server to enable the user to see the activities that he or she needs to take part in at any point in time. The user may have to take part in more than one order fulfillment process instance or more than one type of process itself (say a loan process too). All this is shown in the user portal for the user's convenience. The actual functionality corresponding to the user activity is handled by the user interacting with the web UI application itself (e.g., order management application as shown).

The process monitoring portal is a component that is provided by the BPMS. It allows process managers and business managers to monitor the details of the executing processes and take any action required on them including forceful termination of a process instance if there is a problem. It can show data from the process repository including the process history for executed processes.

8.2.2 Legacy Components

These are applications that have already existed in the enterprise for a long time but serve useful business functions. They are typically developed in-house. These applications have complex business logic coded in them (implicit) and are difficult to rewrite or replace. It often makes more sense to reuse them as they have been serving the business functions well rather than replacing or rewriting them. Documentation would be absent or minimally available. Logic is implicit in the code; it requires code to be read to understand the business logic. All these are their key characteristics.

Some system activities in the process could be performed by the legacy application. They are service-enabled so that their business functionalities could be invoked by the process. Invocations are handled by the adapter layer of the process server.

One example of a legacy component is a mainframe application. The application would typically be a CICS/COBOL application or a COBOL based application. The business logic of the CICS application is separated from the presentation (CICS maps) of it and is made as invocable separately outside of the CICS screen environment as a screen-less CICS transaction. Using the CICS gateway provided by the mainframe is one of the ways to achieve this invocation from the adapter layer by invoking it as an external business interface. Another way is to expose the CICS application's business functionality as a service using the SOAP gateway provided by the CICS server on the mainframe (SOAP engine running on mainframe). Here, the services are invocable by the adapter layer using SOAP over HTTP.

A plain COBOL application in the mainframe can be invoked by exposing it as a service on the mainframe using the SOAP engine on the mainframe. It would be an external business interface to the COBOL application's business logic for the benefit of outside systems.

Whether the mainframe application is an online CICS or a batch COBOL application, the application can be modularized to separate the business logic into a COBOL subroutine. The COBOL subroutine can be invoked from the existing CICS application as well as the batch application (that is the job). This subroutine can be service enabled to be invoked from outside via gateways to CICS, for example. Another option is to use a Java Transaction Adapter (JTA™) to bridge its invocation from an EJB component in the application server to the mainframe COBOL subroutine. In this procedure, the copy books are converted to equivalent JAVA objects and vice versa during the invocation.

8.3 Architectural Design in PCA

8.3.1 When to Apply?

PCA is applicable only to IT systems in the enterprise. An enterprise could be a corporation or a government agency. Whenever flexibility of the business processes and business–IT alignment are overriding concerns for the system, PCA is the right architecture style. Here are some of the right scenarios where PCA can be applied:

- Architecting new systems in the enterprise to support new business process(es). Example, a new service is being launched by the enterprise.
- Architecting new systems in the enterprise to support existing business process(es). Here the entire system is architected and built new. For example, the existing loan application processing system in a bank is being scrapped and it is going to be designed newly from scratch. The architectural approach here would proceed as if a new system has to be designed from scratch—the existing applications concerned with the loan process do not get considered and thereby do not influence the design.
- The current IT system(s) or the set of applications in the enterprise do not link up well to the business processes that they are intended to support. There are business process–IT alignment issues. Therefore, the IT system needs to be re-architected. For example, the auto insurance claim process in an insurance company is supported by an application and is found to be less flexible to adapt to changes in the process. Some of the existing application components might get reused in some form in the new architecture.
- BPM exercise (or BPM project(s)) is going on in the enterprise and business processes are being re-designed or changed as part of that. The IT systems concerned in the enterprise will then need to be architected or re-architected to support the new business processes. The scope of the BPM program can be the process architecture for the entire enterprise. Or, the scope can be a specific business process or a set of processes taken up for improvement. PCA applies directly (of course at the system level) in the context of any BPM effort in the organization—be it process monitoring, process measurement, performance management, or analysis.
- In the application at hand, there is a flow of work involved between human roles or systems, or both. These flows might cover multiple business functions or just one business function.

- Processes within the enterprise need to be integrated. This also involves applications getting integrated.
- Processes need to be automated.
- Processes to be supported are inter-enterprise processes. There are inter-process relationships—processes might interact with each other.

In short, in the context of the enterprise, when we have the need to architect systems where the scope is a business process, PCA can be applied—this means it applies to almost all the systems in an enterprise because they will all be involved in the context of some business process or the other.

8.3.2 How to Apply?

Let us now look at how to apply PCA and design the architecture of the IT system. The approach to target the architecture development is primarily *top-down*. The architecture work starts with the modeling of the business process and then it proceeds down to the design of the components of the architecture. The business process that the system to be created needs to support may be one that already exists in the enterprise or a new one required for it.

For an existing process, the current state needs to be analyzed. Process models or architecture assets for the existing process may not exist or may be little. However, the current state process analysis is often done bottom-up because the process models need to be re-created from the study of the tasks that happen in the context of the process and the functions (workings) of the applications that currently exist. This is the baseline description of the architecture. Working assumptions are made about the top-level architecture for the existing process and it is refined as more ground evidence comes in.

8.3.2.1 Modeling Business Processes—Prerequisites

As far as the business process for the IT system is concerned, it could be a new process if the enterprise is entering a new business by launching a new service or product. In this case, what is described is only the *TO-BE process* model.

In the other case, the business process is typically being modified, reengineered, or tailored for improvement, optimization, and efficiency.

The *AS-IS process* is important in this situation. The process as it is currently performed is modeled first and this is called the AS-IS process. The AS-IS process modeling is a faithful capture of how the business process functions right now and its usefulness is directly related to how accurately it reflects the current process.

The AS-IS process is then used as the basis for understanding the existing business, activities, and work. This leads to an analysis of the AS-IS process for potential improvement and optimization. It is strongly recommended to follow the BPM practices and approach for this optimization. The practices applied include

Six sigma, lean, and business process reengineering. Otherwise, the value from the business process implementation through this architecture would not be significant. The architecture would be only as good as the quality of the business process specified.

The business analyst then creates and models the TO-BE process as an improved process over the one before. Among the things that the analyst considers for process optimization are design heuristics, such as identification and the possible removal of potential bottlenecks based on dependency analysis, improving parallelization of activities in the process, increasing automation, changing the ordering of activities, and relooking at business rules governing the process flow to potentially change them to effect optimal flows. At this point, one additional analysis and optimization method that the analyst can use is simulation. They can do simulations with the process model to study the behavior of the process model in various scenarios and come up with further optimizations on the process.

Whether it is a totally new process or a refinement over the old one, the TO-BE process is expected to have been optimized (or improvised) to the extent possible at the design stage itself. This is the preferred option rather than waiting for the process to be implemented and deployed in production to analyze it, which is more expensive. The process modeling and improvement is primarily done by the process analyst.

8.3.2.2 Top-Down Approach (or Leaned to Top Approach)

The architectural design follows a top-down approach when applying the PCA style. We always start at the top, with the business process to be supported (to-be process). The steps involved in this architecture creation are performed by the process analyst and the system architect(s). The business process focus remains through system implementation, deployment, run-time execution, and monitoring stages. This is irrespective of whether IT systems are already available and running or not.

1. The to-be business process would have been arrived at after analyzing the as-is process for optimization. The to-be process could also be a totally new process.
2. Model the business process graphically with all the paths and decision points.
3. Capture the rule for each decision point as specified by the business.
4. Consider the activities that the process is composed of.
5. For each system activity, associate with it the service that provides the logical business functionality of the activity. The service supports the activity. If the service is not already available in the enterprise, consider consuming it from a third-party service provider or create the service.
6. Describe the service interface in a standard format such as WSDL.
7. For each service, identify the application that provides the service or could be enhanced or created to provide the service.

8. Service enable the application if it does not provide the service in the standard business format; for example, legacy service enablement.
9. Consider reusability characteristics of services and take actions to improve reusability. The context of business process driven SOA or the process driving the services provides opportunities to improve reusability. For example, the business analyst makes the call that the credit card validation step will pass credit card number, customer name, expiry date, CVV number, and billing address of the customer to the credit card validation service and not just credit card number and expiry date. If there is a service already available in the enterprise that takes only these two as inputs, then the business process would lead the analyst to decide that this service is to be extended to take in the additional parameters or that a new service be created to take all the five parameters as inputs.
10. Keep the following things in mind while identifying the services:
    a. Reusability is of prime concern and essence; that would allow more leverage from IT systems.
    b. Be flexible with the service interface (in/out parameters) requirements of the activity especially if a service is already available; otherwise, it becomes just another procedural programming.
    c. Be willing to tailor the interfacing parameters list of the activity if the service is already available and has good potential for fitment here.
    d. Refrain from creating new services on impulse due to the over-focus on the need for perfect process orchestration.
    e. Consider the use of object-oriented programming system (OOPS) polymorphism principles in creating redundant service interfaces supported by single service implementation to encourage the maximum number of activities to reuse the same service, and they need not request for a new service just because the service interface does not match exactly though the service functionality matches fine. Only the parameters listed in the service interfaces would be different.
    f. Merge the concepts of OOPS and procedure-oriented programming.
    g. It would be best to survey a set of business processes in the same domain to identify if there are standardized services (for standardized activities). If standardized services are available, attempt and intend to stick with that standard service definition and tweak the activity parameters to match the same. Refrain from nonstandardizing behavior as much as possible. Do it easily for non-core processes.
11. If feasible, identify and extract common process flows from a set of processes in the enterprise that have some overlapping set of steps or actions and make the common process flow into a new process. This new process can be used as a sub-process by other processes that need its functionality. For example, if the flow for approval is common across processes such as travel, expense settlement, leave, order form processing, and timesheets, then it can be made

into a new process named approval that can then be invoked as a sub-process from these processes mentioned above.

12. While working on one process and identifying services for that process, consider the set of business processes in the enterprise that could be related in some way. Look for overlapping activities. Standardize the service that all of them require to one service where all these activities, after some tweaking in their definition, can use this single service rather than creating a new service for each of them. This step actually suggests a way to identify potential for reuse. Reuse potential identification needs some bit of bottom-up approach, where you look at all the components already built with an objective of reuse across the organization.
13. The danger in not doing this reuse identification is that it can take the enterprise IT back to the problems in the old days, where each department or function created programs and routines they wanted just because the program they wanted did not exactly match the function signature of their program in an existing program in another department.
14. For a new service, design the business logic components (based on the platform of choice) that will together deliver the business function. Implement the service based on the components.
15. Each component needs to be designed to perform the algorithm associated with the business functionality it is supposed to take care of.
16. If complex business rules are involved, implement the component on a business rule engine as a rule.
17. Define the rules in a business-friendly language in a rules engine and host the rules on the rules engine.
18. The rules are made invocable by the rules engine at run-time.
19. Specify the rules invocation identification (rule ID) in the activity of the process for invocation by the process layer or invoke the rule from the service implementation component.
20. If the service is one that is going to be provided by a third party, identify the quality of service requirements (SLA) for the run-time service provider selection.
21. For each user activity, specify the user role that is expected to provide that service by performing the business function of the activity.
22. Specify the work allocation rules for the activity so that at run-time, the activity gets assigned to a specific user.
23. Identify an existing GUI application that provides support for the user function.
    a. The screens of the application correspond to each different task of the activity.
    b. Chain the begin and end application screens to the activity in the process if the application functionality is multipage.

c. Otherwise, chain the application screen page to the activity in the process, if single-page.
d. Modify the application screen logic on the last page to send a notification to the process indicating the completion of the activity.

24. If an existing GUI application is not available or not suited, design a new one.
    a. Design the GUI screens for the activity tasks, one for each task, for example, HTML/JSP pages.
    b. Design the task level flow logic to move from one screen to next.
    c. Implement the task flow as a screen flow specified in the controller part of the GUI application, say Java servlets and a screen flow control framework, such as Struts™.
25. Another aspect is the granularity of the processes or the levels of processes. Processes can have a hierarchical relationship to each other and this means there can be multiple levels of processes. An activity in a process that is at a higher level of granularity may be a lower-level process itself, i.e., it is a subprocess of the former process. This is recursive and can go on and on. At the lowest level of granularity, the activities are all specific logical business functions and not subprocesses. The right number for the levels of processes is something to be decided and determined based on the context of the enterprise. To not make it too complicated (to manage), a hierarchy, four or five levels of granularity, is considered appropriate and effective.

If a top-down approach is not followed, the enterprise IT can end up with thousands of services designed and implemented, but the business processes might need only some hundreds of them. The rest of the services would just be a waste. And, a huge investment would already have been made on them.

There is a downside and this might sound contradictory. To ensure maximum reusability, we need to have business people who know about most (if not all) of the business processes in the enterprise and they would need to scan the entire set of processes in the company to identify which functions are common and so reusable. In a way, this would mean that all these processes are modeled first. Services are mapped to activities next. Looking at it realistically, such people are hard to find in the organization.

One rule of thumb is to go with standards or best practice services wherever possible. That will open up more reuse from not only within the enterprise but also from outside through third-party services or partner services.

A guiding principle is to strike a bit of middle path with strong leaning towards the processes and top-level, eventhough the architectural design always starts from the top. It cannot be totally bottom-up driven nor can it be totally top-down driven since both are extremes. Some flexibility and adaptability is required from both sides whereby the process activities consider the need for reuse as also important and trade some interface customization (but not functionality) for this. SOA, on the other hand, needs to be more oriented to the needs of the process and not remain very strict on perfect reusability up to the point of matching the functionality and the parameters and their data type 100% perfectly. With this flexibility, we can achieve substantial benefit (maybe 80% as a rule of thumb) of business IT alignment and IT flexibility but not a perfect world of 100% business IT alignment where each service is perfectly reused and each activity perfectly fits the service. So, there is a need to be realistic about the alignment aspect. It is caused or it comes from the basic trade-off of customizability versus maintainability and reusability. That cannot simply be wished away. Take the analogy of the reliability and security quality goals for a system that are inversely related to each other and the trade-off is classical. To make it more reliable, we improve the availability by adding redundancy but this inversely affects the security of the system as there are now more points of security vulnerability, and instead of an attack coming from a single point of entry (which is easy to make secure), now it can come from multiple redundancy points.

A mix of standard-mindedness, pragmatism, core versus non-core differentiation, harmonization across geographies, forward thought, long-term oriented thinking, and strong business need focus is preferable during the architecture stage.

Earlier applications were centered on data and information. It was assumed that data and information were central to the application's architecture. Now it is acknowledged that the business process is central to IT systems and their architecture and not data. So, the business process should be given the first importance in architecture. Entities related to data should be considered only later. Process precedes information in the new paradigm.

8.3.3 Levels of Models

While modeling the TO-BE business processes, there are two levels of modeling performed. One is the higher-level business process and the other is the executable process definition.

8.3.3.1 High-Level Business Process Modeling

In the high-level modeling, the process analyst or the process designer defines the business process by graphically modeling the business process as a set of activities chained together in the order that determines the achievement of the business objective of the process. The activity construct is used to model the activities and for each of the activities, a business label or name is specified. Typically, the name of the activity (or the identity of the activity) is a verb such as "purchase spares." It (the verb) indicates the action taken in the activity; it is the intent of the activity. Additionally, a small description of the business function of the activity is also specified as an annotation or as a property of the activity.

Identifying each activity in a TO-BE process is an important step in the modeling. Here, the analyst looks at which business functions achieve logically complete business operations and each of those functions becomes an activity in the process. The decision related to the right granularity of each activity and the breakdown of the activity into tasks (especially the user activities) is taken by the process analyst. Each activity is considered to be atomic. As an example, in a purchase order process, the state of the process is changed to "order verified" on completion of the "verify order" activity. For each activity, the analyst mentions on the activity construct if it is a manual activity or a system activity. For manual activities, the role that is expected to perform the activity is also specified in the activity details.

Parallel flows (or concurrent flows in other words) are identified and modeled by a "fork" construct that splits the main process path into multiple parallel flows. The parallel flows are merged at a subsequent point using the "join" construct. Parallel flows allow activities to be performed in parallel. That is, they can be executed simultaneously.

One key thing that determines the extent of the parallelization of process flows is the potential dependency between the activities. For example, the activity "Review purchase order" depends on the business data output from another activity "Prepare purchase order" and thus they cannot be performed in parallel. The dependency here is a data dependency. Another possible dependency between activities is control dependency where one activity does not depend on any data to be produced by another activity, but is still dependent on the completion of the other for the control flow. For example, the activity "reserve the room" can be completed without requiring any data from the "receive payment from customer" activity. But, the "reserve the room" activity can be performed only after the "receive payment from customer" activity is completed, which is a control dependency.

The analyst models conditional branching constructs to indicate branches in the process flow or in any of the parallel flows. Analysts specify the condition for a branch in a business-friendly relational expression format, an arithmetic expression format, or a general expression format that evaluates to some value and also specify the possible values for the expression and marks them on the branches (paths) going out of the condition. These expressions would make use of the process parameters of the process.

At this point, the analyst and the IT architect together may introduce some programming-driven thinking to chunk and separate process parts to manage the complexity of the overall process. In some cases, the process calls another process. An example is, the sales order process calling a purchase parts process that is under some other department in the organization.

In some cases, the business process may be complex or just too huge to manage in its modeling. Some parts of the process, those that may get repeated or that are logical chunks, are removed from the process and made subprocesses. This is more for structuring the processes for handling complexity and to make it more modular, readable, and maintainable, similar to coding best practices in high-level programming. The subprocess activity in the process represents the invocation of the process associated with the subprocess. The subprocess, of course, needs to be defined as a separate process model that is a self-contained process in itself with its own set of activities. In a graphical process model, the usage of subprocesses leads to the de-cluttering of the process to make it more readable.

The subprocess may itself be nested, whereby it is composed of further levels of subprocesses. Refer to Figure 8.1 for a sample higher-level business process model.

During the high-level business process design, it is important not to be influenced by any implementation considerations or constraints whether those are technology related or not. Rather, the focus of the business process design would best be in describing the process, the parts it is composed of, and the connections (i.e., sequencing) between the parts.

There could be two types of high-level diagrams. One is called process architecture, where the processes in the organization are listed out with their interrelationships and hierarchy. The other is the process model where each process is individually detailed out as an activity chain; some activities may involve interaction with another process.

But the goal of the process model is not primarily the representation of interactions with other processes; it is in the flow of activities. The goal of process architecture is to clearly show a view of the enterprise business processes where we can see how the processes are interrelated. It is an enterprise-wide view and is important for enterprise-wide business process improvements.

The process analyst or process owner specifies the details of how the errors and special conditions (exceptional conditions) in the process are to be handled at a high-level. Flows are modeled for handling these conditions. Compensation flows are modeled at a high-level.

Identify similar business sub-functions, though the processes may be different. For example, be it the loan application process or the purchase order process, the user credentials validation and the creation of fulfillment request are common. The submission of fulfillment request and entitlements check activities are similar in both the processes.

Approving an order fulfillment request or forwarding an order fulfillment request is also similar in the case of other processes, such as the leave application process. The approvers are different, though, in these two processes. For this, the activity can have specified the role (the manager of the employee applying for leave) that performs the approval. In the loans process, the approver role is a guarantor and this is specified in the activity in the process model.

8.3.3.2 Executable Business Process Modeling

A detailed process model is derived from the high-level process model. This model is the executable process model that has the required details (technical too) to make the process model executable by a computer system. To the high-level process model, technical details are specified that would enable the process to be executed and managed by the run-time process execution platform.

Here, the IT architect is primarily involved and each activity is seen as a service being offered by a human or a system. The architect performs the following functions:

1. For each activity, he or she
   a. Completes the input and output parameters with their data types
   b. Specifies the service interface for the activity in a format such as WSDL
   c. Specifies the bindings in the WSDL for the service endpoints (service providers) wherever possible and includes concrete bindings for the services if possible
2. Ensures the process definition is block structured
3. Specifies and completes the input and output parameters for the subprocesses
4. Ensures the correctness of the conditional expressions specified for the branches, iterations
5. For each user activity, provides the mappings to the UI application that includes the starting screen's URL (servlet URL) or a logical name mapped to the starting screen's URL
6. For each user activity, take care that only those parameters that are required by the UI corresponding to the activity are specified as output parameters in the activity. These parameters are the key parameters that the UI would use to pull up data from the UI application's database, for populating its screen display fields. That is, ideally the activity should not supply data for each field in the UI screen—if it did, that would make the process take up a responsibility that is not actually the UI application's and make the process unnecessarily bloated in memory at runtime. The data displayed in the screens by the UI application should be kept and fetched from the UI application's database. For example, in the user activity for approval in a travel booking process, the approval activity would have travel request id, employee id, travel date, and project code as output parameters. The UI application for this activity, would fetch all the travel request data such as travel purpose, travel legs, origin, destination, duration, employee name, and address details from its own application database and display them in the screen fields of the "approval" UI screen.
7. For each user activity, verifies the correlation parameters specified and ensures their uniqueness property for the process; specifies them if not already specified
8. For each receive type activity, identifies the correlation parameters ensuring their uniqueness for the process and specifies them

9. For synchronous receive type activities, specifies the set of activities (actions) that are required to be performed as part of the receipt of the message to this activity
10. Verifies the correctness and the completeness of the error handling flows, compensation flows, and exception handling flows; completes them as required if incomplete
11. For each activity, specifies the transaction attributes including the transaction nature (atomic or not), transaction protocol, the transaction context, and the transaction manager

8.4 Re-Architecting an Existing IT System for PCA

The previous section talked about how to architect a new IT system based on the PCA style, such as, for example, a new loan processing system or a new mutual fund processing system. However, it is common to find IT systems already existing in the enterprise. They would have architectures different from PCA. This would, therefore, involve re-architecting the IT system based on PCA.

8.4.1 A Scenario

For example, the enterprise (a bank) could have an existing banking application that has been taking care of its core banking operations for quite some time, say a decade. This system might have been architected based on a conventional architecture style, such as a client–server, where there is a tight coupling of the elements such as screens and their flow, or between the functionality elements on the server side. Some of the existing problems with the system are as follows:

- Due to the tight coupling between the screens, it becomes very hard to customize it for a change of task flow. Any new presentation layer or new GUI screens for the system cannot be adapted to the system easily. Integration with new screens also becomes hard. The system is not flexible enough and not easily maintainable.
- An employee working on a banking related request would need to move, as part of the request processing flow, from one screen to another manually or in some cases it is taken care of automatically in the form of some hard-coded screen-dependent scripting. Due to this inflexibility of the system, extensibility suffers.
- Depending on the geographical location or the region, the banking operation flows have variations and the screens involved could also be slightly different. The agility of the system becomes an issue. It takes lot of effort to make the system meet the demands to support variant flows and flexible request flows for region-based support.

8.4.2 Approach

It is important to consider what is involved in transitioning that IT system from the old architecture to an architecture that is based on PCA.

8.4.2.1 Justification

In such a context, it is most pertinent to see if the effort (and thus the investment) that needs to go into this migration is justified by the potential benefits that arise from the PCA-based architecture.

In this example scenario of the banking application, there are great benefits to be gained from moving its architecture to PCA. Some of these are as follows:

- Configurability—the workflows related to banking operations become flexible and easily configurable; they can be changed to support different types of banking processes and banking workflows tailored for regions
- Better agility and flexibility
- Better maintainability of the system—the flows are not hard-coded in the screen code any more
- Improved portability—the system would now integrate and adapt easily with other systems in the bank including applications specific to a region; it can easily accept new screens without having to change the code
- Better manageability of the banking processes; this will enable continuous process improvement

8.4.2.2 Re-Architecture

Once this cost–benefit justification is made, then the next step is to do the re-architecture for the system. The existing system's architecture needs to be process-enabled. This involves the following steps:

1. Analyze the existing process flow (AS-IS) with the help of available documentation and with the business manager/end-user support and also by extracting the flows hard-coded in the application that are already existing in the form of screen scripts or program code.
2. Model the AS-IS process flow for the processes currently supported by the system.
3. Identify the existing application parts or components that currently support parts (steps) of the process.
4. Clean up the user interface modules—separate out the presentation logic from the business and process logic.

   a. Make sure each UI element has only the presentation logic specified.
   b. Make sure all the business logic is removed from the UI element and is made into a business element that is invocable by other elements in the application.
   c. Make sure that at no point does the UI element call any business function not directly associated with it. It may call the business function in the business logic module that is directly relevant to the specific business function that the UI element is expected to perform. This includes data access modules—to fetch application specific business data to be shown in the screen and also to update the business data entered by the user—that are connected with the data items being worked with in the screen.
5. Introduce tiered architecture.
   a. Separate business components of the application from any other responsibilities and make them easily invocable business components with appropriate interfaces defined and exposed; make them into separate modules called business function modules.
   b. Separate all data-access and data manipulation program elements out of the existing system and make them a separate data module that is used only for data and database operations and is invoked by business modules.
   c. Introduce the process tier; put the process models in this tier.
6. Convert each business function component in the business function modules into an invocable business service. If necessary, such a service may be formed by grouping together more than one low-granular business function to make it a reusable process-level service. Make sure that the business service is not tied to any other business service in any way; that means, there should be no invocation from this service to any other business service.
7. Map each user activity in the process to the appropriate screen. If there are a set of screens for the activity, map the first screen to the user activity and ensure the last screen for this activity does an invocation to the process layer to indicate that the activity is complete.
8. Map each system activity in the process to the appropriate business service created in the above steps.
9. As far as possible, have the business functions only get invoked from the process in the process layer as business services and not directly from the UI code.

8.5 Addition of an IT Subsystem to an Existing IT System

It is common to find, as part of acquisitions, that an IT subsystem or product may get acquired and then get added to the existing IT system of the acquiring company. Following PCA here means that the architecture of the existing system (let us call it “System A”) in the acquiring company integrates into it the new IT subsystem (let us call it “System B”) coming from outside. This integration is still done in a top-down manner. Let us assume System A is already architected in the lines of PCA—there would be a business process model (say “Process A”) that would have been driving the system. There could be the following scenarios here with respect to System B:

1. There may be steps in Process A that are currently being supported by some existing BLEs, and those steps could be supported by System B if System B has been analyzed and found to be a better option for those steps. The integration now involves one or more of the following:
   a. System B might need to be extended to expose the service interfaces expected by those process steps.
   b. A service-wrapper for System B might need to be implemented to business service-enable it.
   c. No re-architecture for System A is needed.
   d. Leaving open the option of using System B services or the current services for supporting the same steps in the process. This decision could be left to be taken at run-time. Those particular steps in the process could be made dynamically to use at run-time, either the business service exposed by System B or the ones exposed by the existing BLEs. The executing process can decide this based on various factors such as cost, efficiency required, and customer requirements.
   e. Of all the steps in the process that System B can potentially support, a subset of those (partial steps) could be made to be supported by System B if it provides better support of those steps compared with the current System A.
2. System B may be supporting business functionalities that are separate from (or outside of) the current System A. Those functions are extra to the existing process, but nevertheless, it might be beneficial to make use of them. In this case,
   a. The business process of System A can get extended with the addition of extra steps that enhances the business process—resulting in a new extended business process. This could provide a better overall and enhanced experience to the customer and the business.
   b. The process model of System A would need to change a little—new activities related to the functions in System B would get introduced, a potential reordering of existing activities could be done, and new decision points might get introduced in the process model to direct the flow to functions supported by System B.

In all of the above scenarios, System B may not need to undergo a total re-architecture to make its architecture a PCA-based one. It would only need to get enabled to be invocable as business services from the process in System A. All the integration-related changes mentioned above are easily enabled by PCA as it follows business process-driven integration and not hard integration. Here, PCA makes the entire integrated system (System A and B combined) a more flexible system, even for the future changes with respect to the integration of System A and System B.

8.6 Exercise Questions

1. Do you agree that process redesign/optimization is a must before architecting the IT system based on PCA? Why?
2. If you disagree with 1 above, why?
3. What is the role of an IT architect in the architecture creation process here? What are the differences between an architect's conventional role and what is done here?

Chapter 9

SOA for Services

9.1 Objectives

- To understand the concept of services and SOA
- To appreciate the role for SOA in process-centric architecture

9.2 Services

The concept of *services* is an important aspect of the process-centric architecture. A service is a software element that is reusable by other software. Each service has a well-published interface and the service provides a well-defined functionality to the service requesters (clients or service consumers). The service interface is abstracted out and separated from the design and implementation of the functionality of the service. Service implementations of a service are not exposed to the invokers of the service. Service interface is the only public aspect of the service and acts as the binding contract between the service requester and the service provider.

Some examples of services are validate credit card service, get stock quote service, payment gateway service, and funds transfer service. In each of these cases, the service provides a well-defined function to the service-invoking system such as validation of a credit card based on the details provided.

The service interface of a service lists the operations it would perform, the input parameters that it expects to be supplied by the caller, the output parameters that the service would return to the caller after completing the operation, the protocols to be used for communication, etc. The implementations of a service are those systems that provide/support the service and expose the service to the potential invokers. There can be more than one system that exposes the same service to the invokers. However, their implementations of the service on the back end would be different, not just in the business logic or algorithm but also in the technology used for implementation. For example, a credit card validation service could be implemented by one service provider, say a bank 1, by using a JAVA application and by using an algorithm internal to bank 1. Another service provider bank 2 could also implement the same service by using another algorithm and it could realize as a mainframe program(s) in COBOL. This is shielded from the invoker. The invoker would only be relying on the service interface for the invocation.

9.3 Service-Oriented Architecture

SOA is an architectural pattern that promotes the design of software as a set of elements where each software element is a service. The service provider and the service consumer are loosely coupled with each other. This makes them detachable, removable, and replaceable.

SOA-based architecture makes IT systems agile by allowing applications or components to loosely couple to each other through the service interfaces. It allows the concept of composite application, where the application is created quickly by chaining together such services to service a business need. The service invocations are orchestrated at run-time. SOA offers a value proposition of assembling an IT system from a set of available services as opposed to writing much code for the system. Of course, if the services are not preexisting, code needs to be written for implementing the service at the service provider component end.

Such services whether they are new or preexisting become available to the entire enterprise and some of them even to the external world to customers, partners, or suppliers. A service would have service legal agreements (SLAs) that it needs to adhere to while providing the service to the consumer. Examples for such SLAs could be the service should complete the operation in sub-second time, and the service should be available 24 × 5 and 99.9% of the time. Services thus also need to be managed and supported to ensure that they adhere to the committed SLAs. Service management also includes managing the evolution of the service and the implementation, typically including version management, etc., and without impacting the consumers of the service.

SOA is based on certain principles:

- Reusability of services
- Services can be at various levels of granularity
- Services are composable; a service is composable from other services
- Interoperability of services
- Stress on standards
- Service interaction is based on contract

9.4 Bottom-Up Approach

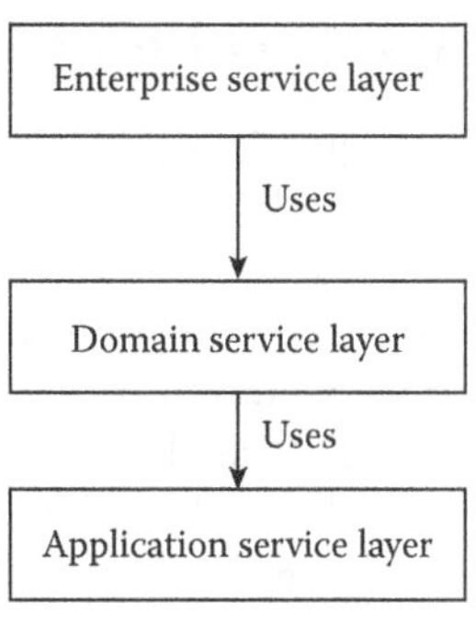

Figure 9.1 Layers in SOA architecture.

SOA follows a bottom-up approach in architecture. The view of the architecture is bottom up. Looking at what the business functions and technical functions are that can be exposed as services for reuse and consumption by all systems commonly is where the focus of the architecture work lies.

Figure 9.1 shows the different layers in the SOA-based architecture. The topmost layer is the enterprise service layer that directly exposes services for use at the enterprise level and intra-department level. The layer lower to it is the domain service layer that consists of services that are applicable within a domain, say sales. The lowest layer is the application service layer that provides services usable within a particular application.

While designing services in SOA, the services are organized (or composed) in a service hierarchy. Each level is a layer, where the services in a layer reuse services from the lower layer. The level of granularity reduces as we go down the layers. At the lowest level are those services that are application-specific services or technical services. These are typically reused within the scope of only a specific application. An example is reusable infrastructure service such as logging service that provides an architectural function. Another example is a data access service that connects to the application's database and gets specific information from the database tables such as a customer details when given a customer ID as input.

At the middle level, the services are composed from the lowest layer. The scope of the services at this level is the domain or a business area (department/function), and they can be called domain services and the layer the domain layer. Within the context of the domain, the services would be reused across the applications. As an example within the finance domain, a general ledger check service can be reused by the accounts receivable application as well as the accounts payable application.

The highest level is the enterprise layer. Services at this level are composed of services from the domain layer. The scope of this layer is enterprise-wide; the service can be reused within the scope of the entire enterprise across domains and applications. Their granularity is the highest and purely at a logical business function level. Hence, their identification and interface contract design would be influenced by procedures spanning departments. An example is the deposit money into bank account service. This can be used by an account opening procedure as well as a purchase procedure. Some of the services can also be wrapper services to service-enable a legacy functionality.

9.5 Need for SOA in PCA

PCA provides a high-level abstraction named the process layer for architecting and building IT systems. When seen from the perspective of business, the level in the system at which the business can more effectively participate in the creation and evolution of the IT system is the process layer. This is because the process layer is at the business' abstraction level itself and its embodiment is business-friendly.

In PCA, the activities in the business process are expected to be componentized, high-granular services (can also be called coarse-grained) that perform a complete business operation that is atomic. They are called activity services in this architecture. The system activities among them are the ones expected to be supported by business components following the SOA pattern.

As an example, let us take the account opening process in a bank. One of the system activities that are part of this process is the "deposit money into account" activity. This activity needs to be performed by a system component and the process needs it in the form of a service provided to the process. Thus, the activity is associated with (or linked to) the service in the process model where the operation of the service is to update the amount in the customer account maintained in the system. This service is expected to perform the complete business function expected of the activity by the process. For example, here the service needs to perform the following logic as part of deposit money service:

1. Perform required validations such as
   a. Account status
   b. Applicability of differential interest rates
2. Make the customer's account reflect the money deposited by updating the data

Since this is business logic, the activity in the process is not concerned with the way the operation is carried out, on the other hand the process expects the service to be concerned with this logic, the exact manner in which it is performed, the lower level components involved, and so on. The process would be the client for these business services and needs them to be exposed to it so that it can consume the services as part of the orchestration of the activities in the business process flow.

Figure 9.2 shows the business process involving activity services, they in turn use the domain services that in turn use the lower-level application-specific services at the resources platform level: DB, legacy app, etc.

SOA plays the service provider role to the core element of this architecture. It is the underlying model enabling the activities in the process. It is direct in the case of system activities. For manual activities, the concept of SOA still applies in the identification/design of manual activities; however, the only difference is that the service is provided by a human playing an appropriate role.

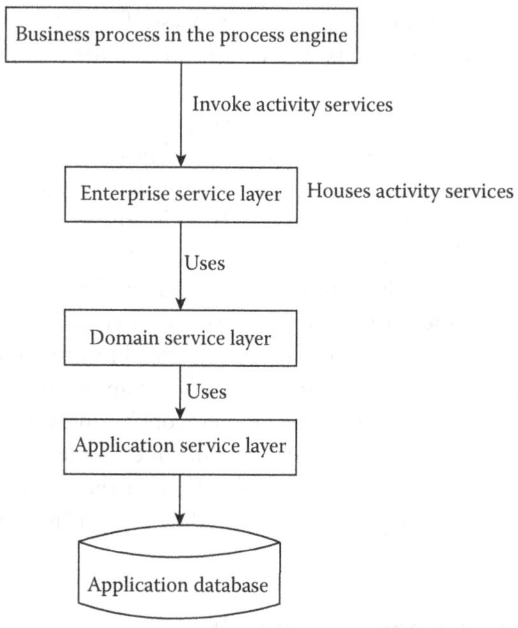

Figure 9.2 Platform view.

Another reason why PCA needs SOA is in the aspect of reuse. Since the activity services are at a high level of granularity, they are reusable at the process level. Across processes, the same activity service can be applicable if the same business function needs to be performed in those processes as well. The deposit money into account service in the above example can be reused in another process, say manage customer account process or funds transfer process. These two processes also involve the money deposit business operation, though their contexts are different from the account opening process. For this, the architecture needs to have the business components supporting the activities to be decoupled from the specific objective of the process or the context of the process and operate as stateless. To truly enable such reusable components, PCA relies on the underpinnings of SOA and the concept of services that SOA advocates. This reusability framework can be provided by SOA to the architecture so that the activity services (or the activities themselves to put directly) in a particular business process can get reused easily in other processes instead of having to implement them as functions that are bound to one process' specific context and business requirements alone.

Another reuse characteristic in PCA it helps to enable is process reuse. SOA lets the process on the whole be viewed as a service that can be used by other processes. This is very important for inter-process interactions and thus for relationship between processes. Through SOA, the process is exposed as a service, where the details of how this process achieves its business objective are not exposed to the invoking process that consumes this reused process. Those details are internal and encapsulated in the reused process; the reused process becomes an activity in the other process.

If the invoking process is at a higher level of process granularity than the reused process, then the reused process is treated as a subprocess leading to process hierarchy. The process exposed as a service can be provided as external service to other processes such as in business to business (B2B) or business to customer (B2C) integration scenarios. In this case, the process as an external service is invoked by the processes of customers, suppliers, or partners to achieve integration.

Loose-coupling of the activities to the process is helped by the SOA approach. PCA takes a process-driven integration approach to addressing integration of applications and it does away with hard-coupling between applications. SOA lets this be realized through the applications exposing their core business functions as services. The order in which they are orchestrated at run-time is determined by the process and this makes the chaining highly flexible. Though the order of invocation can change in the process, the applications involved do not get impacted.

9.6 Complementary Approach to Architectural Design

9.6.1 Context

In PCA, the macro context needed by the business services (activity services) for their execution is provided by the business process at run-time, as specified by the business analysts or managers formally during the design-time. This context presents and dictates the way these services are to be chained together to deliver value. And, the process maintains the state of the interactions with the services involved in it. The true value of a service is realized when a client (it is the process here in PCA) orchestrates its invocation with other services; that is, how the services serve its business need. And, without the context provided by the process, its existence would not have much meaning.

9.6.2 Top-Down

When seen purely from the SOA perspective, services need to be built first. However, when we view at an enterprise-wide scope and attempt to visualize all the services that would be required by applications in the enterprise and then build those services, it turns out to be neither a feasible approach nor a cost-effective effort. There are some reasons for this. Functionality to be supported by a service is best determined by the business based on what the business thinks the business process must be doing. It comes from the business requirements for the IT systems. But, these business requirements keep evolving and consequently the expectations from the functionalities of the system also change. And thus the services identified would be subject to continuous change. It stresses more on commonality among available functions (reuse and leverage what is already available) than on looking at what the business processes need, because ultimately the users of services are business processes.

A more feasible approach instead is

1. Let the business design the business processes according to the business need.
2. Let the business determine the activity services for the process, looking at each activity identified for the process.
3. Identify the reusability potential of the activity services across processes. The business needs to involve here with visualizing the various different process contexts where the same business functionality at the same high granularity is required.
4. Services identified thus are reusable across processes.

This means a top-down approach that PCA uses would provide more value out of SOA. The number of such business services thus identified and to be implemented subsequently would only be small especially when we compare it to what we would have ended up having had we identified the services from bottom-up. It is obviously cost-effective, designing them top down as opposed to creating the full set of services from bottom-up approach and often ending up using only a small number of them in the systems.

The key message is, when embarking on architecting IT systems, sound redesign of the as-is business process should precede the design of business services. This would ensure that the SOA part of the architecture effort does not get wasted in attempting to support flawed as-is processes (or wrong processes).

9.6.3 Design of Services in the Context of PCA

The services need to be designed and implemented based on SOA principles. Each activity service (i.e., a business service) can be composed from low-granular services. What is mapped to the activities in the process as activity services are business services in the services hierarchy. It is best to follow the top-down approach further down too to design the activity service. It can be designed by breaking the coarse-grained activity service down to a set of finer grained business tasks that are again services. Reusability across activity services in the domain would be a major consideration while doing this. The finer-grained domain services can further be designed as a set of still finer granular (low granular) services with reusability within the level in mind. The low-granular services might make use of technology services such as infrastructure services and data access services. In some cases, it would make sense to design some lower-level services in a bottom-up way rather than totally top down. To achieve reuse and time-to-market benefits at minimal cost, horizontal services that can be commonly used enterprise-wide as utilities are better designed bottom-up. Examples of such utility services are currency conversion, zip code lookup/check, address validation, etc. Also, following the bottom-up fashion, some legacy functions are service-enabled through the use of wrappers on them so that their existing functions are reused and exposed as services. Being legacy, the existing application might not offer much flexibility to change; however, its functionality could still be really useful in the context of the business process.

9.6.4 Leverage What Is Available

A principle that would be useful is to leverage existing applications in the enterprise wherever possible, irrespective of whether they are legacy, application packages, or custom built in-house applications—it would bring cost gains. This means, at the lower level of services, include wrapper services that wrap legacy functionalities to service-enable them. Wrappers might also be required to service-enable the packages or in-house applications. The wrapper services can be used by the higher granular services or coarse-grained business services to implement their function.

Maintaining a single point of truth for business information is another important principle. This primarily applies to data-access services. Along with single point of truth, uniform semantics must be used and maintained for all business data (entities). As an example, the customer profile information should ideally be made available through a single data-access service. This service should access it only from one data source, and the customer data that it provides (comes back with) should mean the same customer when viewed throughout the enterprise regardless of which departmental function's context the system is performing in. Simply put, this means that when the accounts receivables application refers to a customer name and address, and the sales system also is referring to the same customer for its operation, they both should be working with the same customer name and address.

9.6.5 Binding

At run-time, the executable process model needs to have concrete bindings* to the activity services, at least at the time of invoking the service as part of the process orchestration. The process model may have abstract bindings for activity services at design-time or even till some point at run-time. Loose coupling is at its best when the concrete binding is as late as possible. At run-time, the process may get the concrete binding for an activity service dynamically from the execution of prior

* Binding means tying the location of a service provider with the consumer of the service. When it is concrete, the binding gives full locational details of the service provider so that the consumer can directly connect with the service.

services in the order as provided by one of those service providers involved. Or, the process takes the help of the process layer to use the details provided in the abstract binding to discover, negotiate, and select the right service provider for an activity service that it is ready to invoke. For this purpose, the process layer could also use an infrastructure such as an enterprise service bus (ESB) for the same if that is available in the architecture. Once this is done, the process activity binds concretely to the selected service provider and invokes the activity service. The binding is released after the invocation or retained, depending on the preference of the process.

9.6.6 *Complementary*

Any software application can be architected and built using SOA; however, the best use-case for SOA is in process-centric architectures. SOA has become an increasingly popular approach to connect the activities in business processes to systems implementing them in the form of services.

Thus, PCA and SOA enable each other and provide the best value realization when combined together and approached holistically. SOA delivers a reusable service foundation that the process component and layer in the architecture should leverage, so that the IT system delivers a more effective business process with business value. Services delivered through SOA must be flexible enough to enable process changes to support business needs. SOA and PCA are complementary in this architecture.

9.7 Exercise Questions

1. Identify the set of services that a process you are familiar with needs.
2. Come up with a hierarchy of services for these services.
3. What are the considerations you made to decide on the reuse of some of those services?
4. What are the key things that made you decide the right level of granularity for each service?
5. Have you used any technology services in the above hierarchy? If yes, why?

Chapter 10

Standards and Technologies

10.1 Objectives

- To be aware of the standards in the area
- To be aware of the technologies involved in the implementation of the architecture
- To get introduced to the various standards and their role in the realization of the architecture

10.2 Standards

A specific way of performing some action or communicating (whether between humans or systems), that has been agreed upon by all,* results in a *standard*. An Internet communication protocol HTTP is one example of a popularly followed standard.

In PCA, standards help in the implementation of the architecture. Following these standards helps make the IT system

- More open
- Interoperable, compatible with other systems
- Handle interoperable processes with more ease
- Executing environment uniform

---

* In practice, it means a majority of people have agreed to it.

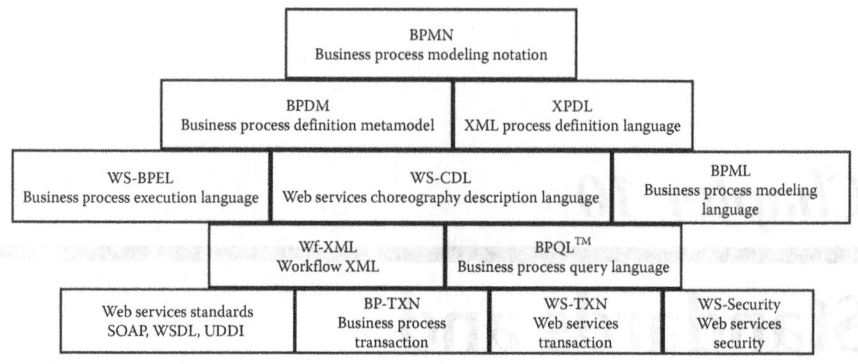

Figure 10.1 Standards stack for BPM.

- Frees the IT system from being locked in to a specific vendor and minimizes the risk of vendor failures
- Enables reuse
- Provides implementation options for the IT system without affecting the architecture

In the context of PCA, there are a host of standards that are applicable and can be used. These are at various levels of the architecture and also pertain to specific aspects of the architecture and the process life cycle. We shall look at some of the more popular ones here. Figure 10.1 shows the stack of standards in the BPM area. Most of these standards are applicable in the context of PCA.

10.3 Process Modeling Standards

There are standards that address the modeling of business processes—specifically they show how each part of the process is to be visually represented and what the semantics of each such representation construct are. These are also called notation standards. While realizing PCA, these standards (one of them) are used to specify the business process. It becomes the manifestation of the process model component of the architecture and will sit in the process layer.

10.3.1 BPMN

Business Process Modeling Notation (BPMN) is a popular standard for modeling business processes graphically. It helps the business processes to be interoperable at the human level where the process can be understood by any person whether business or technical; thus the process definition can be communicated between various people. It provides graphical constructs or notations for specific aspects of the process such as the start of the process, activities, subprocesses, conditional branches, splits, joins, and the end of process that can be used while modeling the process. The BPMN process definition is a graphical process modeling notation where the entire process is modeled as a graph and the result is a formal Business Process Diagram (BPD) that is the representation of the process. BPMN is from the Object Management Group (OMG) and the OMG supports its evolution. A sample BPMN process is given in Figure 10.2.

BPMN provides a set of basic flow elements in the form of *events*, *activities*, and *gateways*. The process model would have the flow elements connected using *connecting objects*. The *artifacts* are used for capturing extra information about the process such as *annotations* (free text notes for information), the business data entities (called *data objects*) involved in the process, and grouping (as *groups*) of a set of flow objects or other elements of the BPD. BPMS provides swim lanes in the diagram for each specific participating role in the process. That is, the users, roles, departments, or systems that perform activities in the process are identified in their respective *swimlanes*. Activities that each user or role is expected to perform are organized into one group and shown in the swim lane corresponding to that role. Directed edges show the order of the activities or the control flow in the process. The process looks like a network of objects (that are activities) and is similar to a flowchart diagram. Activities are rectangular graphic elements (rounded corners). There are separate symbols provided to represent types of activities such as *timer* activities (timed or scheduled activities), a task, or a subprocess. Conditional branches (or decisions) are diamond-shaped elements. These are called gateways. Gateways are used to specify decision points in the flow, forking, and merging. Events are used to represent message arrivals or such events happening in the duration of the process.

BPMN process model can be translated into an executable process definition such as WS-BPEL™ so that the process becomes executable in the system. Mappings are defined between the symbols of BPMN and the constructs of WS-BPEL. BPMN is extensible by modelers to add nonstandard elements for specific needs, say unique requirements of a domain such as finance.

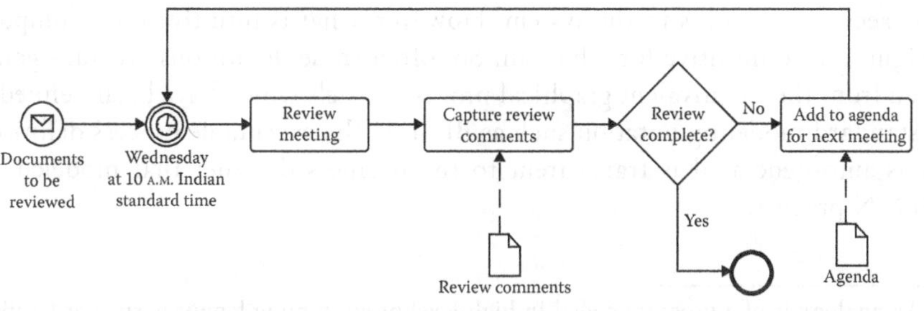

Figure 10.2 Sample BPMN process.

10.3.2 XPDL™

XPDL is another process notation standard. It is expanded as the XML Process Definition Language (XPDL). This is a standard from the Workflow Management Coalition (WfMC) aimed at enabling transferability of process definitions from one system to another. It provides a predefined XML schema using which the business process definition's graphic aspects such as the positions and the semantic aspects such as the control flow and activity execution details, can be captured. This definition can then be exchanged with another system. The XPDL definition is purely XML based, which is yet another standard for interoperability at the data level. Strictly speaking, it is also an execution notation standard.

10.4 Process Execution Standards

There are standards at the level of process execution. They address executable process definitions and impact the process layer of the architecture. Process definitions made in these standard languages are executable in computers. Some also call them integration standards since they integrate the process model to the execution platform. These are languages that can be used to define business processes formally. One of these languages is used to realize the executable process definition, in PCA. The process model defined in the graphical modeling standard such as BPMN is translated into the equivalent executable process definition in the executable process language standard. At runtime, this executable process definition sits in the process layer and manifests as multiple runtime components for process executions after the process layer parses the definition into executable code.

These standard languages have been optimized, right from their design, for the computation in computers and for the interoperability among such systems. Some of them such as BPML™, WS-BPEL are rooted in formal mathematical models for systems such as the pi-calculus. These mathematical underpinnings enable their execution capability in today's computers since they can be reduced to executable chunks in the system. However, what is intuitive for a computer might not be intuitive for a human. So, often these definitions are auto-generated from their equivalent graphical process models which have been defined in a standard modeling notation such as BPMN. The executable process definition thus auto-generated is transparent to the business designer that modeled the BPMN process.*

* An analogy is of a program coded in high-level programming language such as COBOL and the compiler-generated machine code equivalent of that program. What finally runs in the computer is the machine code. What the programmer works with is the COBOL program.

10.4.1 WS-BPEL

Web services Business Process Execution Language (WS-BPEL) is the de facto standard and a popular one for defining executable business process definitions. WS-BPEL is from OASIS.

WS-BPEL is a language based on XML, using which the behavior of a business process can be described based on the interaction of the process with the participants of the process to achieve the business goal of the process. The interactions are described in the form of service interactions, assuming web service interfaces.

10.4.1.1 A Combination of Interoperability Standards

In simpler terms, in WS-BPEL, each activity in the process is described as a service to be invoked from the process (*invoke* action in the WS-BPEL). Thus, the activities are client end points of web services. Any step in the process where there is invocation into the process is a service provided by the process and thus is described as a *receive* activity. Thus, these steps are service end points of web services. Each service, whether it invokes or receives from the process perspective is described using web services description language (WSDL) standard. Associated standard of Universal Description, Discovery, and Integration (UDDI) is used for the discovery of the services (and publishing) and invocation from/into the process. Other standards used in conjunction with WS-BPEL are XML Schema 1.0, XPath 1.0, and XSLT 1.0.

The entire process definition made in WS-BPEL would be an XML document. Expressions related to branch conditions in the process, assignments of values to parameters in the process are all recommended to be made based on XPath. Any transformation to be applied on data as part of assignments is recommended to be done by using XSLT.

10.4.1.2 Structure

WS-BPEL is a block-structured language and thus suits computer execution very well. It includes only executable operations in the business process definition. The graph part of the process model is irrelevant for execution in such a language and thus is not contained in the WS-BPEL definition of the process. It provides an XML schema for the language that includes the elements such as `<sequence>`, `<flow>`, `<receive>`, `<reply>`, `<invoke>`, `<switch>`, `<assign>`, `<faulthandlers>`, and `<partnerlinks>`. The process definition is structured as an XML document composed of sections, one for the variables (process parameters) in the process, one for the process flow definition itself, one for the parties that interact with the process at various activities, and one for the process logic that handles faults happening in the process. A sample WS-BPEL process definition is given in Figure 10.3.

```
<process name="purchaseOrderProcess"
   targetNamespace="http://example.com/ws-bp/purchase"
   xmlns="http://docs.oasis-open.org/wsbpel/2.0/process/executable"
   xmlns:lns="http://manufacturing.org/wsdl/purchase">

   <documentation xml:lang="EN">
      A simple example of a WS-BPEL process for handling a purchase
      order.
   </documentation>

   <partnerLinks>
      <partnerLink name="purchasing"
         partnerLinkType="lns:purchasingLT" myRole="purchaseService" />
      <partnerLink name="invoicing" partnerLinkType="lns:invoicingLT"
         myRole="invoiceRequester" partnerRole="invoiceService" />
      <partnerLink name="shipping" partnerLinkType="lns:shippingLT"
         myRole="shippingRequester" partnerRole="shippingService" />
      <partnerLink name="scheduling"
         partnerLinkType="lns:schedulingLT"
         partnerRole="schedulingService" />
   </partnerLinks>

   <variables>
      <variable name="PO" messageType="lns:POMessage" />
      <variable name="Invoice" messageType="lns:InvMessage" />
      <variable name="shippingRequest"
         messageType="lns:shippingRequestMessage" />
      <variable name="shippingInfo"
         messageType="lns:shippingInfoMessage" />
      <variable name="shippingSchedule"
         messageType="lns:scheduleMessage" />
   </variables>

   <faultHandlers>
      <catch faultName="lns:cannotCompleteOrder"
         faultVariable="POFault"
         faultMessageType="lns:orderFaultType">
         <reply partnerLink="purchasing"
            portType="lns:purchaseOrderPT"
            operation="sendPurchaseOrder" variable="POFault"
            faultName="cannotCompleteOrder" />
      </catch>
   </faultHandlers>

   <sequence>
      <receive partnerLink="purchasing" portType="lns:purchaseOrderPT"
         operation="sendPurchaseOrder" variable="PO"
         createInstance="yes">
         <documentation>Receive Purchase Order</documentation>
      </receive>
```

Figure 10.3 A sample WS-BPEL process definition. (From WS-BPEL documentation. Copyright © OASIS® 1993–2007.)

```
<flow>
   <documentation>
      A parallel flow to handle shipping, invoicing and
      scheduling
   </documentation>
   <links>
      <link name="ship-to-invoice" />
      <link name="ship-to-scheduling" />
   </links>
   <sequence>
      <assign>
         <copy>
            <from>$PO.customerInfo</from>
            <to>$shippingRequest.customerInfo</to>
         </copy>
      </assign>
      <invoke partnerLink="shipping" portType="lns:shippingPT"
         operation="requestShipping"
         inputVariable="shippingRequest"
         outputVariable="shippingInfo">
         <documentation>Decide On Shipper</documentation>
         <sources>
            <source linkName="ship-to-invoice" />
         </sources>
      </invoke>
      <receive partnerLink="shipping"
         portType="lns:shippingCallbackPT"
         operation="sendSchedule" variable="shippingSchedule">
         <documentation>Arrange Logistics</documentation>
         <sources>
            <source linkName="ship-to-scheduling" />
         </sources>
      </receive>
   </sequence>
   <sequence>
      <invoke partnerLink="invoicing"
         portType="lns:computePricePT"
         operation="initiatePriceCalculation"
         inputVariable="PO">
         <documentation>
            Initial Price Calculation
         </documentation>
      </invoke>
      <invoke partnerLink="invoicing"
         portType="lns:computePricePT"
         operation="sendShippingPrice"
         inputVariable="shippingInfo">
         <documentation>
            Complete Price Calculation
         </documentation>
```

Figure 10.3 (continued)

(*continued*)

```
            <targets>
               <target linkName="ship-to-invoice" />
            </targets>
         </invoke>
         <receive partnerLink="invoicing"
            portType="lns:invoiceCallbackPT"
            operation="sendInvoice" variable="Invoice" />
      </sequence>
      <sequence>
         <invoke partnerLink="scheduling"
            portType="lns:schedulingPT"
            operation="requestProductionScheduling"
            inputVariable="PO">
            <documentation>
               Initiate Production Scheduling
            </documentation>
         </invoke>
         <invoke partnerLink="scheduling"
            portType="lns:schedulingPT"
            operation="sendShippingSchedule"
            inputVariable="shippingSchedule">
            <documentation>
               Complete Production Scheduling
            </documentation>
            <targets>
               <target linkName="ship-to-scheduling" />
            </targets>
         </invoke>
      </sequence>
   </flow>
   <reply partnerLink="purchasing" portType="lns:purchaseOrderPT"
      operation="sendPurchaseOrder" variable="Invoice">
      <documentation>Invoice Processing</documentation>
   </reply>
</sequence>

</process>
```

Figure 10.3 (continued)

Each activity in the process becomes an invoke element or a receive element depending on whether it is a send-type activity or receive-type activity, respectively. A <reply> element always is associated with an inbound invocation activity such as a <receive> that happened before it; together a receive–reply combination can signify a receive-type activity in the process that is a complex activity containing the set of activities to be performed before returning to the caller (synchronous). It could also mean a combination (asynchronous) of a one-way receive-type activity and followed by a notification operation that is invoked after performing a set of activities in between the <receive> and the <reply>.

10.4.1.3 Bindings

Each activity is bound to a service using the definition provided in the WSDL document for the service, referencing its `<operation>`, `<porttype>`, `<message>` from the WSDL. These are still abstract bindings providing the definition independence from a specific actual service provider. A sample WSDL is shown in Figure 10.4.

Though the name suggests web services, any implementation of the service is possible for the service. For example, the service could be implemented as a web service involving HTTP/SOAP, or a Java EJB involving the EJB protocol and RMI™, or mail service involving SOAP and SMTP, or a SOAP over Java messaging service (JMS) or a .NET service, and so on. This invocation mechanism detail comes from concrete bindings. Concrete bindings are best avoided at the process definition stage and postponed to runtime. In WS-BPEL, to enable resolution of bindings at runtime, partner links are used to refer to partners of this process, i.e., the service providers that are invoked by the process and the service consumers that invoke the process activities. They have an abstract part and a concrete part. The abstract part of a partner link only refers to the abstract part of the WSDL for the service (message, operation, and porttype). Concrete part of a partner link at runtime refers to a concrete binding to the location (including the message protocol such as SOAP, the transport protocol such as HTTP, and the URL address of the partner (service provider or consumer)) for that particular service. Setting of this concrete part of a partner link is preferably postponed to the runtime (late binding) and made dynamic and handled by the process layer.

10.4.1.4 Extensions

WS-BPEL allows optional extensibility to the language by implementations to take care of specific needs. Manual activities are not explicitly supported in WS-BPEL. Implementations typically support manual activities, with extension; some may add new elements to the WS-BPEL set, others may add new attributes to existing `<invoke>` or `<receive>` elements. These attributes capture the user activity specific details such as location details and work allocation specification.

10.4.2 BPML

Business Process Modeling Language (BPML) is another standard language for executable process definitions. This came from BPMI.org, which is now a part of OMG. This standard does not officially exist anymore since BPMI.org and OMG has endorsed WS-BPEL as the de facto standard. Still, it is worth getting an idea of BPML since it explicitly supports some concepts such as process instances, nested processes, process packages, calling and spawning of subprocesses, transactions and atomic activities, and signals. These concepts are very relevant and useful in the IT system's context.

```
<wsdl:definitions
   targetNamespace="http://manufacturing.org/wsdl/purchase"
   xmlns:sns="http://manufacturing.org/xsd/purchase"
   xmlns:pos="http://manufacturing.org/wsdl/purchase"
   xmlns:wsdl="http://schemas.xmlsoap.org/wsdl/"
   xmlns:plnk="http://docs.oasis-open.org/wsbpel/2.0/plnktype"
   xmlns:xsd="http://www.w3.org/2001/XMLSchema">

   <wsdl:types>
      <xsd:schema>
         <xsd:import namespace="http://manufacturing.org/xsd/purchase"
          schemaLocation="http://manufacturing.org/xsd/purchase.xsd" />
      </xsd:schema>
   </wsdl:types>

   <wsdl:message name="POMessage">
      <wsdl:part name="customerInfo" type="sns:customerInfoType" />
      <wsdl:part name="purchaseOrder" type="sns:purchaseOrderType" />
   </wsdl:message>
   <wsdl:message name="InvMessage">
      <wsdl:part name="IVC" type="sns:InvoiceType" />
   </wsdl:message>
   <wsdl:message name="orderFaultType">
      <wsdl:part name="problemInfo" element="sns:OrderFault " />
   </wsdl:message>
   <wsdl:message name="shippingRequestMessage">
      <wsdl:part name="customerInfo" element="sns:customerInfo" />
   </wsdl:message>
   <wsdl:message name="shippingInfoMessage">
      <wsdl:part name="shippingInfo" element="sns:shippingInfo" />
   </wsdl:message>
   <wsdl:message name="scheduleMessage">
      <wsdl:part name="schedule" element="sns:scheduleInfo" />
   </wsdl:message>

   <!-- portTypes supported by the purchase order process -->
   <wsdl:portType name="purchaseOrderPT">
      <wsdl:operation name="sendPurchaseOrder">
         <wsdl:input message="pos:POMessage" />
         <wsdl:output message="pos:InvMessage" />
         <wsdl:fault name="cannotCompleteOrder"
            message="pos:orderFaultType" />
      </wsdl:operation>
   </wsdl:portType>
   <wsdl:portType name="invoiceCallbackPT">
      <wsdl:operation name="sendInvoice">
         <wsdl:input message="pos:InvMessage" />
      </wsdl:operation>
   </wsdl:portType>
```

Figure 10.4 Sample WSDL. (From WS-BPEL specifications. Copyright © OASIS® 1993–2007.)

```
<wsdl:portType name="shippingCallbackPT">
   <wsdl:operation name="sendSchedule">
      <wsdl:input message="pos:scheduleMessage" />
   </wsdl:operation>
</wsdl:portType>

<!-- portType supported by the invoice services -->
<wsdl:portType name="computePricePT">
   <wsdl:operation name="initiatePriceCalculation">
      <wsdl:input message="pos:POMessage" />
   </wsdl:operation>
   <wsdl:operation name="sendShippingPrice">
      <wsdl:input message="pos:shippingInfoMessage" />
   </wsdl:operation>
</wsdl:portType>

<!-- portType supported by the shipping service -->
<wsdl:portType name="shippingPT">
   <wsdl:operation name="requestShipping">
      <wsdl:input message="pos:shippingRequestMessage" />
      <wsdl:output message="pos:shippingInfoMessage" />
      <wsdl:fault name="cannotCompleteOrder"
         message="pos:orderFaultType" />
   </wsdl:operation>
</wsdl:portType>

<!-- portType supported by the production scheduling process -->
<wsdl:portType name="schedulingPT">
   <wsdl:operation name="requestProductionScheduling">
      <wsdl:input message="pos:POMessage" />
   </wsdl:operation>
   <wsdl:operation name="sendShippingSchedule">
      <wsdl:input message="pos:scheduleMessage" />
   </wsdl:operation>
</wsdl:portType>

<plnk:partnerLinkType name="purchasingLT">
   <plnk:role name="purchaseService"
      portType="pos:purchaseOrderPT" />
</plnk:partnerLinkType>

<plnk:partnerLinkType name="invoicingLT">
   <plnk:role name="invoiceService"
      portType="pos:computePricePT" />
   <plnk:role name="invoiceRequester"
      portType="pos:invoiceCallbackPT" />
</plnk:partnerLinkType>
```

Figure 10.4 (continued)

(continued)

```
    <plnk:partnerLinkType name="shippingLT">
       <plnk:role name="shippingService"
          portType="pos:shippingPT" />
       <plnk:role name="shippingRequester"
          portType="pos:shippingCallbackPT" />
    </plnk:partnerLinkType>

    <plnk:partnerLinkType name="schedulingLT">
       <plnk:role name="schedulingService"
          portType="pos:schedulingPT" />
    </plnk:partnerLinkType>

</wsdl:definitions>
```

Figure 10.4 (continued)

BPML also follows the XML standard and is defined based on an XML-Schema. The process definitions have to be well-formed XML documents based on this schema. BPML also uses associated specification standards such as WSDL and XPath. The entire executable process model is a package comprising of the BPML process definition, and WSDL files corresponding to the activity-services in the process (and to other related processes).

Here too, each activity is an `<activity>` element in the process definition with linkages to a service interface described as a WSDL with the abstract bindings. A process can be nested with other processes (called subprocesses) within it to any number of levels. The subprocess is also defined as a separate BPML process definition and this is invoked by the main process using the "call" activity that synchronously invokes the subprocess at runtime. In the case of call activity, the subprocess executes in the same context as the main process, and thus has access to the properties of the main process. Its execution will be thus dependent on the main process and vice-versa. The subprocess also can be asynchronously invoked (the main process does not wait for the subprocess to complete), using the "spawn" activity of BPML. In the case of spawn, the subprocess is launched for execution separate from the main process and it executes in a totally new context, independent of the main process.

A good feature of BPML is the "signal" concept, which allows a set of activities in the same executing process to synchronize execution of activities in the process within the context (scope) of the activities. This is relevant for those activities that are in parallel paths and have execution dependencies between some of them.

In BPML, each execution occurrence of a process definition at runtime is a process instance. And, the process instance identifier is a parameter that has unique value for each process instance. This is used to uniquely identify a process instance at runtime. BPML advocates persistence of processes where the process state is preserved in a nonvolatile medium for later process instance reconstruction and resumption. Process instance identifier plays a role in identifying the instances in this. It plays an important role in the semantics of some process functions (called instance functions) that can be used in the process definition.

Process definitions are organized in the form of packages similar to the way high-level programming languages allow the programmers to organize the programs to achieve modularization. A package organizes a set of related process definitions. A process is statically identified along with the name of the package it belongs to.

BPML addresses the handling of transactions in activities by allowing transaction scopes (transaction context) to be indicated. It supports the notion of atomicity in activities. A transaction completing across a group of non-activities is also supported; these activities commit together or rollback together. BPML, however, does not mandate that any particular transaction protocol be used in the process. The process layer is left to leverage any existing transaction protocols such as WS-Transaction, X/Open XA, BTP, and OTS.

10.5 Inter-Process Layer Interactions

This is to address the possibility that multiple IT systems could have their respective process layer implementations supporting different executable process definition notations (including competing standards) and that they may want to interact with each other in the course of process executions and especially when the participants in the same enterprise need to take part in processes that together involve multiple process layer implementations. The Wf-XML standard from WfMC addresses this. It is for BPM systems (or workflow systems) interoperability. It defines a set of common interfaces that each BPM system needs to implement for enabling interactions between process engines.

10.6 Business Logic Interaction Standards

There are a number of standards available that can be used in the interaction and implementation of the business logic elements in the process-centric architecture. Web services are a very popular standard for implementing the activity-services. This includes the HTTP, SOAP, WSDL, and UDDI standards. Each business logic component in the process-centric architecture is implemented as a web service. SOAP is used as the application communication protocol and HTTP is used as the transport protocol between the process layer and the business logic element. The process layer also exposes its services to the external systems and processes as web services that are invoked using SOAP over HTTP. In the case of asynchronous invocations, SOAP is still preferred as the application protocol and some intra-technology standards such as JMS are used for the transport.

User interface applications supporting the user activities can also be implemented based on standards. The standards popularly used in this are the web application related ones such as HTML, HTTP, and SOAP. Typically, the users perform the user activities through web UI applications. The web UI application interacts with the process layer using the web services exposed by the process layer implementation.

10.7 Technologies and Tools

There are various tools and technologies that can be used and applied in the implementation of process-centric architecture. They apply for different aspects of the architecture. Let us glance through some of the popular ones.

10.7.1 Process Component and Process Layer

BPMS is a technology that directly applies for realizing the process layer and the process component. The process layer is realized as a process server or a process execution engine (or simple process engine) that is part of a typical BPMS. The process execution engine is a runtime component and a key part of the BPMS. It concerns itself with execution of processes. There are various products (called BPM products) that provide this technology. Some of them are Appian™, IBM Websphere business process suite (WebSphere, FileNet, Ilog, and MQ), Intalio, Oracle (with Fusion, Collaxa, BEA Weblogic, and Aqualogic, combined), Pegasystems, Metastorm, Microsoft (BizTalk), K2, SAP Netweaver (XI/PI), Savvion, Lombardi, Sterling Commerce, and TIBCO-staffware. This is not necessarily in any specific order. Some prefer to call these products BPM suites.

10.7.2 Adapter Layer or Collaboration Layer

This can be implemented using enterprise service bus (ESB) technologies. Examples of products are Mule™, OpenESB, etc. Since this layer is part of the process layer in the architecture, this layer is also part of many BPMS products. They can do the job that EAI tools used to do previously. Activity-services that the process needs to invoke are invoked through the ESB, where the product performs service lookup, service selection, data transformation, and service invocation on behalf of the process layer. If the activity-services are implemented by other technologies such as a mainframe component, for example, then the process engine connects to the mainframe using appropriate technologies (e.g., CICS gateways) and invokes the mainframe component and gets the result back and transforms the data to the process' format.

10.7.3 Implementation of Business Logic

The activity-services are implemented by the BLEs. The BLE can be realized as business components in a specific technology platform. One example is implementing them as EJBs in the JEE (JAVA technology) platform. Either the process engine may call this component natively using JAVA invocation mechanisms (RMI and EJB) or use XML, SOAP, HTTP web services for the communication between the process layer and the component, that is, the web service implementation for the BLE actually invokes the EJB component to realize the service. Another example is implementing them as .NET business components in Microsoft .NET platform. The process engine may natively invoke this in the .NET environment or can use web services mechanism. While designing and programming the BLEs, an application framework such as Spring, for example, can be used to handle system/infrastructural services in a common way across multiple BLEs and save effort. For addressing specific concerns such as data access (that includes object-relational table mapping), for example, a framework such as Hibernate can be looked at.

10.7.4 Server Components

The components in the architecture that are server-style can be realized through appropriate technologies. We saw about the process engine.

A rule engine realizes the rules layer of the architecture. It implements all the rules functionality and houses the business rule for execution. Some examples are rule engine products such as Drools™ and Ilog. The rule engines provide interfaces that can be invoked by the process engine. Some BPMSs support business rules very natively with their own rule engine; an example is Pega®. In such cases, the rule engine provided by the BPMS is used for housing the rules.

Application servers such as a JEE server or Microsoft Biz Talk server realize the infrastructure part for the business logic components. The business logic components are housed in these servers. They make sure that the EJB component or the .Net component gets all the required infrastructure support including support for quality of system attributes such as reliability, performance, security, and transaction support.

Web servers realize the user interface application layer. Examples are Apache Tomcat™, IIS™, etc. When using the web servers, the UI applications are implemented as web UI applications using a language platform such as Java (JSP™/Servlets™/HTML). The taskflow within a user activity can further be realized using a technology such as Struts that lets the taskflow be defined in the form of actions and the order for the actions. Techniques such as Ajax and frameworks such as JSF™, for example, can be used to make the UI more richer and effective for the individual screens for taskflows within the user activities.

A document management system (DMS) or content management system (CMS) may be used for managing documents that are involved as key entities in a process. Example, as part of a credit card application process, the credit card application form paper version can be scanned and put into a DMS such as FileNet for maintaining and managing the document. The process typically uses a reference to the document (a document id) as a process parameter that can be used to refer to the document any time in the activities instead of carrying the entire document in the process as a value.

10.7.5 Design-Time Component

During design-time, the process modeler tool of a BPMS product can be used for the process modeling. Unified modeling language (UML) and UML tools can be used for the detailed design of the business logic components. For programming of the BLE, an Integrated Development Environment (IDE) such as Eclipse or Microsoft Visual Studio™ (VSTS) can be used.

10.7.6 Operations and Administration

At run-time, the system administrators would need to monitor the health and needs of the system. BPMS products provide tools (configurators, consoles) to allow the administrator to configure the system (process servers) for various quality aspects such as scalability, performance, and reliability. For the process administrators, the objective is to manage the operations with respect to the business process such as deploying processes into BPMS to make them go live, taking actions on processes including terminating them forcefully, restarting processes as part of error/exception handling, and undeploying processes. All these are supported by BPMS products through specific tools with appropriate user interfaces. Typically, they provide administration portals for this purpose. Process managers also use these portals to monitor execution of processes as part of their business activity monitoring (BAM) work. During error situations, debugging is a critical activity for the administrator and IT support team. PCA based systems require debugging to start at the process-level itself. Identifying which process instance failed and tracing the execution trail of the process including the branches taken in the process flow, to check if the prior steps in the sequence have completed properly, is part of process-level debugging. Also, process-level debugging involves, the person debugging needing to figure out which prior activity in the sequence caused this error—the activity that has failed with error could be different from the activity that actually caused it. Troubleshooting utilities provided by the BPMS help in process-level debugging—they provide visibility into what has happened with the process in its execution.

10.8 Implementation Options

A process-centric architecture can be implemented in various ways. Some of the options for designing the process layer include the following:

- The process layer is realized as a stand-alone process server. In this case it exists independently in physically separate hardware (machines) and supports different business processes and IT systems related to those processes.
- The process layer is designed as a software component (process engine) that can be embedded in the application realizing the business process. The

process engine is really lightweight in this option and will live within the physical confines of the application embedding it, by sharing the run-time memory (RAM/virtual memory) of the application and with a low memory footprint. It will become just another component of the embedding application. Examples are applications where using a full scale process server (BPMS) might not be feasible—the application might be one that has been developed in traditional approach as a single system. Here, cost of changes, resource consumption, etc., can work against going for a full scale BPMS. Thus, embedding the process layer as an application component inside the application is more feasible.

- A software component that implements the process layer and the process model can be auto-generated in the native language (programming language) of the application that realizes the business process, from the process definition in a standard execution language such as WS-BPEL. This process component then becomes a component of the application. This is especially relevant when we are looking at a legacy application (with its own system environment) that is not easy to change, but in which we still want to gain the benefits of process-centricity. For example, a mainframe COBOL application (AR) that takes care of an account reconciliation process can have this process logic defined in WS-BPEL. Now, instead of having to use technologies from a different environment (say JAVA) for the process layer, the code for the process can be generated from the WS-BPEL definition automatically in COBOL language which is native to the AR application and specifically for the target Mainframe platform. This COBOL process component will reside with the native AR application executing the process logic, and all the process step invocations would become native subroutine calls in COBOL. This can also be done in the case of a platform neutral programming language such as Java to create process layer implementations that can work irrespective of the operating system.

Though there are a host of different ways by which activity invocations may be implemented, the most popular way is the use of the web services standard for all the activity-services invocation and client-to-process layer interactions. This means, all the activity services (and the services that the process layer provides to clients such as initiation of the process) are designed as web services. Here, the activity web services could be standard web services that are SOAP-based (we call them SOAP Web Services) or they could be RESTful (REpresentational State Transfer) web services. In the case of SOAP web services, the service implementations use a SOAP engine, which, after parsing the SOAP message (XML), invokes the business logic implementing component for this service such as an EJB. In the case of RESTful web services, web services are implemented in a simpler manner—using principles of REST and thereby see the service as providing basic HTTP method-based operations (get, put, post, delete) on resources (e.g., customer or other business entities in the enterprise). RESTful web services use only HTTP and do not use XML. Wherever their use is applicable, they might give a performance benefit over SOAP web services due to avoidance of the SOAP/XML processing overload. However, RESTful web services do not have any official standard yet. In the case of RESTful web service for an activity service, the implementation code in the web service would invoke the business logic implementing component directly or would itself implement the business logic required. When it comes to the applications that implement the services, services can be implemented in various ways with trade-offs. We can have one big application providing interfaces for and supporting each service as a specific functionality. Or, a set of applications can come together exposing their functionalities as these services. Yet another way is to have all the services implemented by components on purely one technology such as Java EJB or mainframe—this is relevant in situations where the enterprise predominantly uses a particular technology environment.

In the case of some business processes, performance could be an important concern to be met by the system. This is seen in transaction-oriented processes, such as banking and trading, and processes where invocation of activity services or other processes are synchronous. When such activity services are implemented, options such as web services or even an adapter based invocation (e.g., ESB) may not work well for performance. XML processing (parsing, marshaling, unmarshaling), SOAP processing (handling SOAP specific elements), transportation protocol related processing, processing related to data (or message) transformations done by the adapters, and processing for routing and version resolution, all become significant performance overheads. In such cases, giving performance concerns a high priority, the service is implemented as a plain remote call in the native run-time environment (or if feasible as a local call in the run-time environment itself). For example, say the activity service "Credit amount to account" can be implemented as a Java RMI (remote method invocation) method that is invoked natively from the process in the process layer, assuming that the process layer is implemented in the Java run-time environment. This gives a better performance due to minimal processing overheads, this being just a native Java call. However, in situations where web services or other XML-based invocation options have to be chosen due to various reasons, using accelerators such as XML accelerators to speed up the processing may help reduce the performance overheads.

10.9 Exercise Questions

1. Are these standards exhaustively helpful for the PCA IT system realization in your view?
2. What are other implementation technology options that you can think of? List their pros and cons.

Chapter 11

Case Study—Architectural Design Applying PCA

11.1 Objectives

- To understand how to apply PCA
- To learn how to design the architecture of an IT system using PCA
- To learn how to design the components of IT system
- To learn how to implement the IT system, the PCA way

11.2 Case Study I

As the first case study let us consider the case of a fictitious product company named "Sysinfo electronics" that manufactures and sells electronic goods. This case study is a purely hypothetical one, though it is closer to what typically happens in a real-life process.

Let us take the sales order processing in Sysinfo electronics as our example here. The objective of this case study is to demonstrate the application of process-centric architecture style in architecting an IT system. Here, we specifically architect the IT system ("sales order processing system") that supports the sales order process in Sysinfo electronics. The assumption here is that this is a totally new system, so the entire system is architected and would be built from scratch.

11.2.1 Modeling of the Business Process

First the business analyst in Sysinfo electronics models the high-level process model of the process. This is shown in Figure 11.1. The process goes as follows:

- It begins when a customer enquires about items the customer wishes to buy. This is through a phone call to the sales representative of Sysinfo electronics. A sales representative takes the call, and collects the details from the customer such as the products and their quantity. Examples of products sold by Sysinfo electronics are cell phones, cordless phone sets, television sets, and DVD players. The sales representative also indicates whether the customer is a new one or an existing customer. A quotation is then initiated.
- The system automatically computes the price of the items and generates a quotation for the customer. A new quotation number is generated, the price for each item is computed based on the defined rates, applicable discounts are applied, and shipping charges are computed and included in the quotation. The quotation price also includes the applicable taxes such as the sales tax and VAT based on the geographic location. For the rates of items, any surcharges that are applicable are also included in the quotation price.
- The sales representative provides the generated quotation to the customer.
- The customer then places an order through phone and provides the quotation number for the quotation the customer received as reference. The sales representative handles the call and initiates the order in the system. The call is then transferred to an order clerk who does the order entry.
- If the customer is a new customer for Sysinfo electronics, that is, the customer has not transacted with Sysinfo electronics at all previously, then a customer account needs to be created in the system.
- The order clerk enters the customer details in the system to create an account for the new customer. Details such as customer name, billing address, preferred delivery address, phone numbers, and e-mail addresses are entered in the customer account details and a customer account is created in the system.
- The order clerk then enters the order details and submits the order. He enters all the required information for the order in the system such as items ordered and quantity, billing address, delivery address (if different from that in the customer account details), and phone number. Some customer details may require modification in the order details. The order is then submitted by the order clerk for further processing.
- If the total amount calculated for the order is above $1000, the group manager needs to review the order. The manager reviews the details of the order, the correctness of the rates, applied discounts, applied surcharges, etc. The manager also corrects the order details if required.
- The order clerk then confirms the order after discussing with the customer. The status of the order becomes “confirmed.”

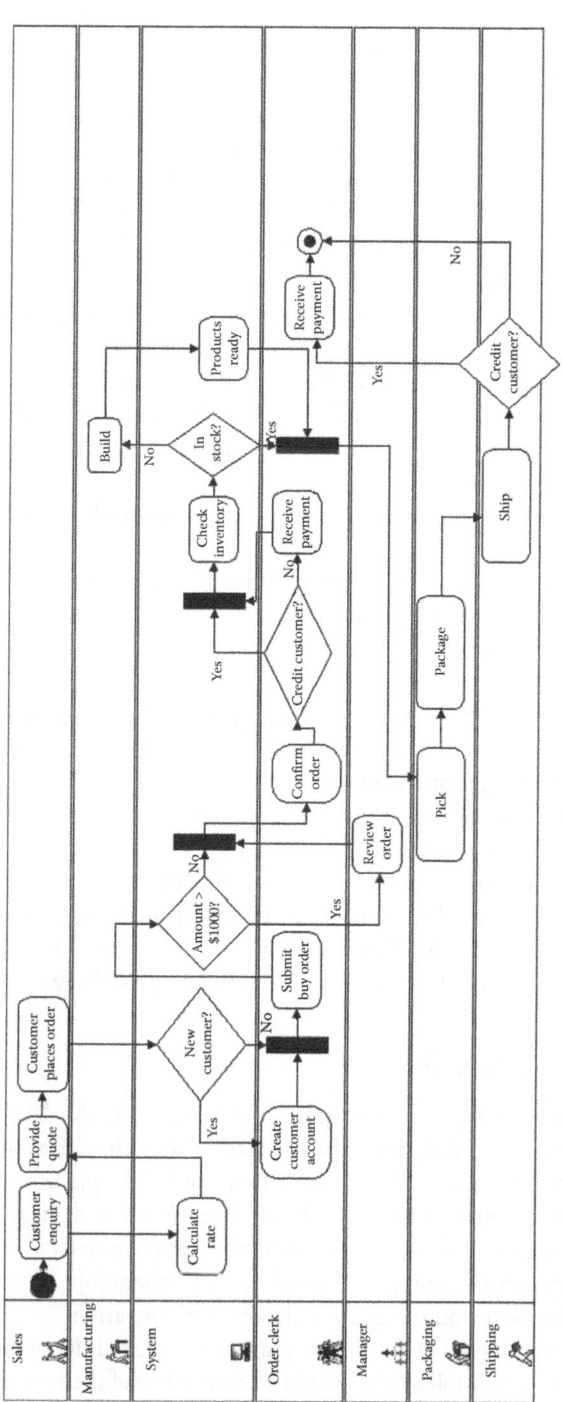

Figure 11.1 High-level process model.

- If the customer is not a credit customer (i.e., cash customer), he is expected to pay the full amount for the products ordered before the order is processed. The order clerk receives the payment for the order from the customer. He then enters the payment details such as check number, check date, bank details, and amount paid, and records these in the system.
- Credit customers can pay the amount after the delivery of the items.
- The system checks if the items ordered are available or not. If they are not, build is initiated in the manufacturing department. This is another system that takes care of the build activity.
- The process then waits for the products to be built and are ready for picking. Once they are ready, the processing moves on to the packaging department.
- The packaging department picks the items from the warehouse. They package the products for shipping specifying the delivery address of the customer.
- The shipping department then ships the package with the products to the customer's delivery address.
- If the customer is a credit customer, the process waits until it receives the payment from the customer.
- The order clerk collects the payment from the customer and records the details of the payment into the system.
- The process then ends.

This process has been designed as composing the activities shown in Figure 11.1. The activities "calculate rate," "check inventory," and "build" are system activities. They are performed by the system automatically.

Others are user activities. "Customer enquiry," "provide quote," and "customer places order" are activities performed by the sales representative. The order clerk performs the "create customer account," "submit buy order," "confirm order," and "receive payment" activities. The manager in the order-processing group performs the "review order" activity. "Pick" and "package" activities are carried out by the packaging department. The "ship" activity is performed by the shipping department.

11.2.1.1 Design Rationale

Each activity in the process, as can be seen, is at a high granular level and this is appropriate for the process definition. Just to help clarify this: If we had the two activities "enter order details" followed by "submit order" in place of the "submit buy order" activity, the granularity would have been lower and inappropriate for this process. Entering the order details in the order entry screens and then submitting the order is actually one complete logical business operation. Doing just order entry and not submission would make it only a partial operation.

Some of the thoughts that have driven granularity-related decisions are scope, ownership, potential applicability contexts, and reusability of the business function being performed. For example, the calculate rate activity could very well have been part of the customer enquiry activity since it could be seen as the response part of the enquiry in the UI application supporting the customer enquiry function. However, when we look at applicability, the calculate rate business function has a wider applicability—it is also applicable in contexts other than where a sales representative requests a rate calculation on behalf of the customer; for example, one such context would be when a customer goes online and does a direct enquiry. In yet another context, the customer's enquiry could also be received offline through an e-mail and the sales representative may not need to respond to it instantly. Instead, the rate calculation could be performed by the system as a physically separate system action and then the sales representative could get back to the customer with the quote as the next activity named "provide quote," which is a physically separate action. Also, depending on the amount of time involved in the rate calculation, it is possible that a different sales representative perform the provide quote action—sales representative availability and their load can also be factors in this—leading us to define the scope of these actions clearly and separately from each other. So, the ownership of the calculate rate activity could be seen as with the system and not the sales representative or the customer, and the scope of the activity is strictly limited only to the calculation of the rate given a set of inputs such as item, quantity, and where the delivery is to be made. And, the calculate rate activity can be reused as is in those processes easily. Thus, the scope of the specific business function of the sales representative, as part of the enquiry activity, ends as soon as the enquiry details are collected and submitted to the process for subsequent processing.

The rule "amount >$1000" is a business rule that affects the flow of the process. Thus, it is defined in the conditional branch. The same is the case with the "new customer?," "credit customer?," and "in stock?" conditions in the conditional branches. They are explicitly defined here and could be changed in the future if the business so demands.

The "check inventory" system activity can potentially be reused in another process, say the periodic inventory monitoring process or a routing stock check process. Its reuse is at a business process level and not at a technical function level.

11.2.2 Detail-Level Business Process Modeling

Now we create the executable process model from the high-level process model. For this, we come up with the detailed process model shown in Figure 11.2.

In this example, the technical architect supports each manual activity by a web UI application. The calculate rate system activity is specified as a service provided by an EJB component housed in the application server. This component is part of the pricing application and it has to do job-costing as part of the business logic for rate calculation. The check inventory and build activities are services invoked as web services by the process. These web services are supported by business components of the order application and the manufacturing application, respectively. "Products ready" is a system activity that is a receive-type activity. This is exposed as a web

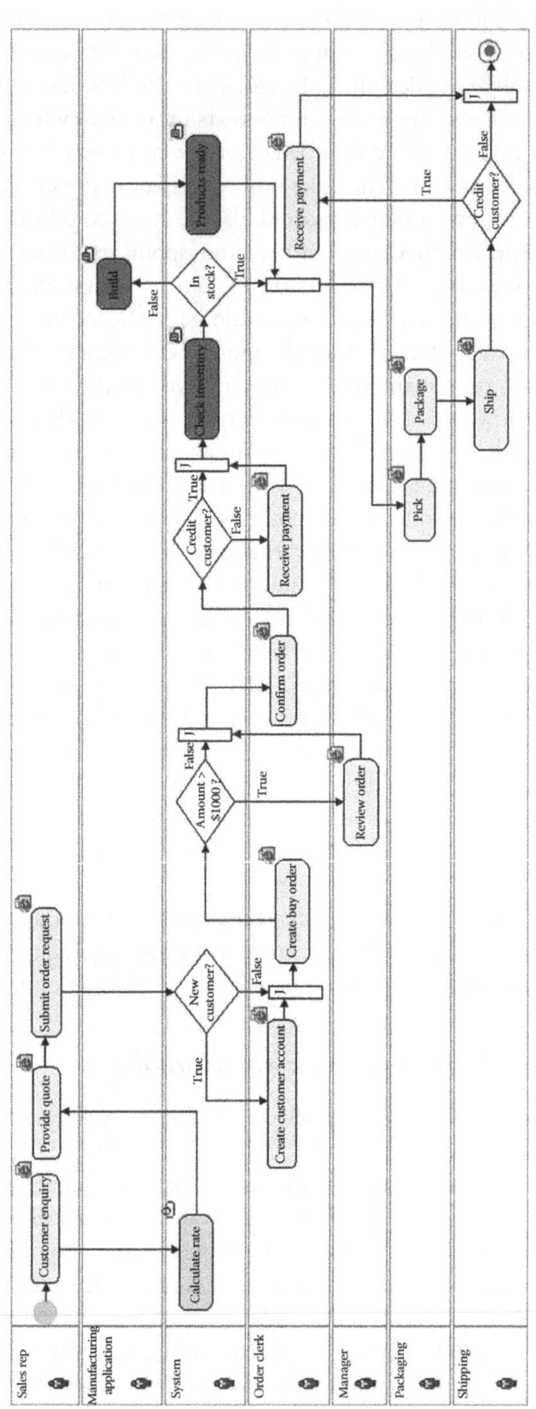

Figure 11.2 Detailed process model.

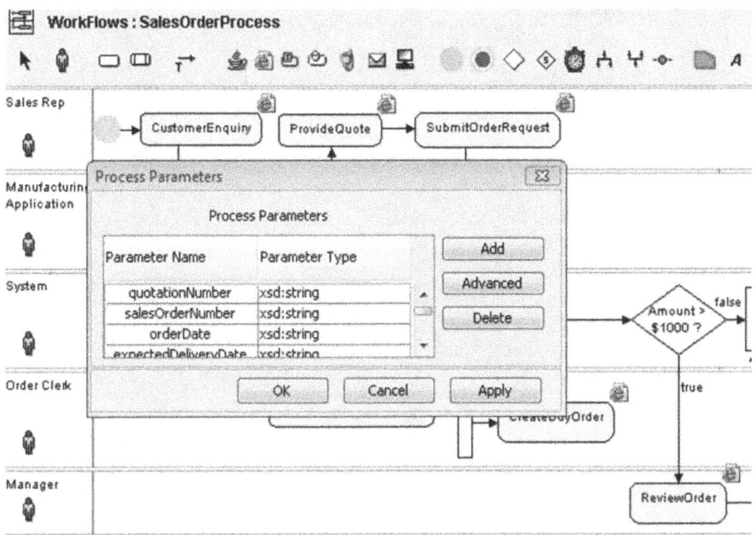

Figure 11.3 Process parameters.

service by the process so that the manufacturing application can invoke it when the products are ready after the build. This process definition is a block-structured one.

Parameters are specified for the process at the process level. Some of these are "quotationNumber," "salesOrderNumber," "orderDate," "expectedDelivery date," "orderAmount," "customer ID," "customerName," "creditCustomerFlag," and "orderStatus." This is shown in Figure 11.3. These are the business data that are relevant to most of the activities in the process.

For each system activity, the service interface and details are supplied. (See Figure 11.4 for the calculate rate activity and Figure 11.5 for the check inventory activity.) The first one is an EJB component that implements the activity service, so its invocation details are specified. The input parameters to the EJB and output parameters from the EJB are specified here. The second one, check inventory, is a web service. The service details such as the port type, and input and output parameters are specified in this.

Figure 11.6 shows the product ready activity's service specifications. This is a receive activity and is of the notification interaction type as far as the client of this activity is concerned. It is an asynchronous receive operation. This activity service is invoked by the manufacturing application after completing the manufacturing of the products. Since this is an asynchronous activity, the transport chosen is Java messaging service (JMS). This service is exposed by the order processing system at run-time when the process instance is in execution. Sales order number parameter is used as the correlation parameter to correlate the invocation to the process instance corresponding to the order number for which the manufacturing has been completed. This parameter is chosen because it is unique for each order

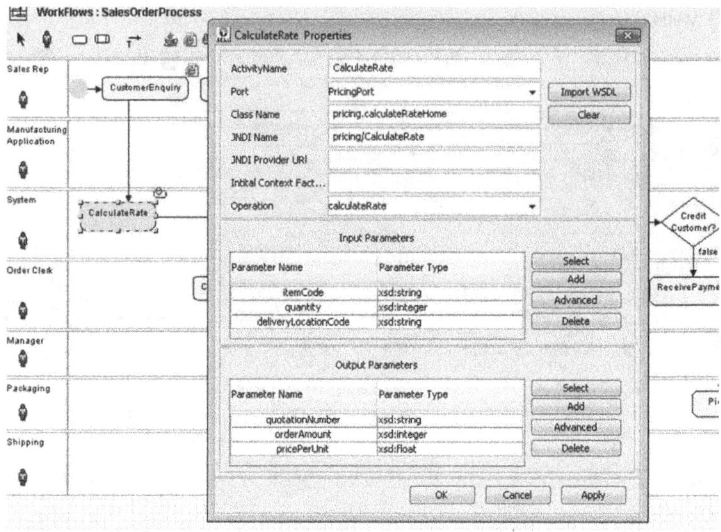

Figure 11.4 Calculate rate user activity.

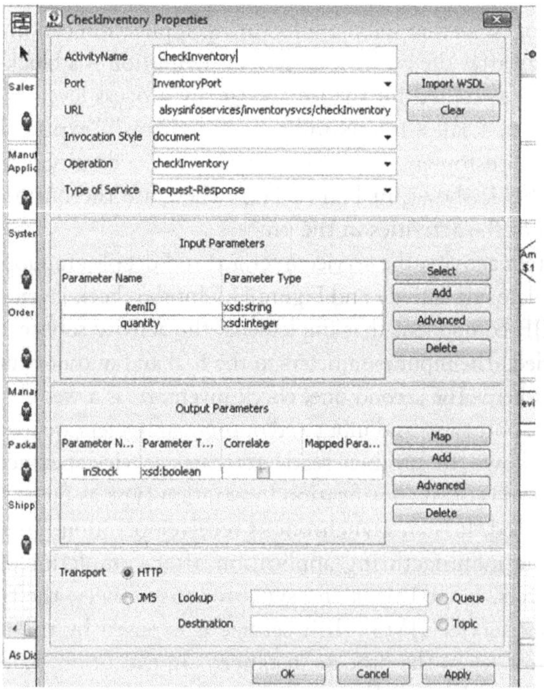

Figure 11.5 Check inventory activity.

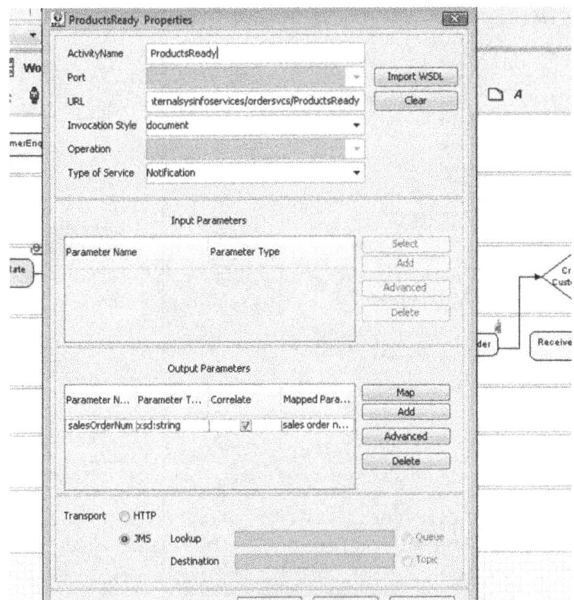

Figure 11.6 Products ready activity.

process instance and thus can help the system or humans identify the matching process instance correctly.

Similarly Figure 11.7 shows the build activity details. This is a web service that is a one-way invocation and is asynchronous. The transport used is thus JMS.

Figure 11.8 shows the details of the customer places order user activity. This is designed as a web UI activity (i.e., it is supported by a web application with the user using the Internet browser) and the URL value is used to construct the actual and full URL at run-time. The display and submit parameters represent the parameters sent to (or pulled by) the web UI application and received by the process from the web UI application, respectively. It is specified that the sales representative would perform the activity. Other user activities in the process also follow a similar convention in the details—they are also designed as user interfaces provided through the Internet browser by the web application.

For this process, the executable process definition is created in the WS-BPEL language. An important point to note here is that though it provides a number of standard constructs, WS-BPEL, at the moment, does not explicitly support some aspects of a business process such as user activities (or activities that involve user interaction). WS-BPEL specification allows the implementations of the language to support such aspects by allowing them to extend WS-BPEL. This allows the implementation to introduce elements and attributes that are needed to support aspects not explicitly supported by WS-BPEL—they are introduced as extension elements

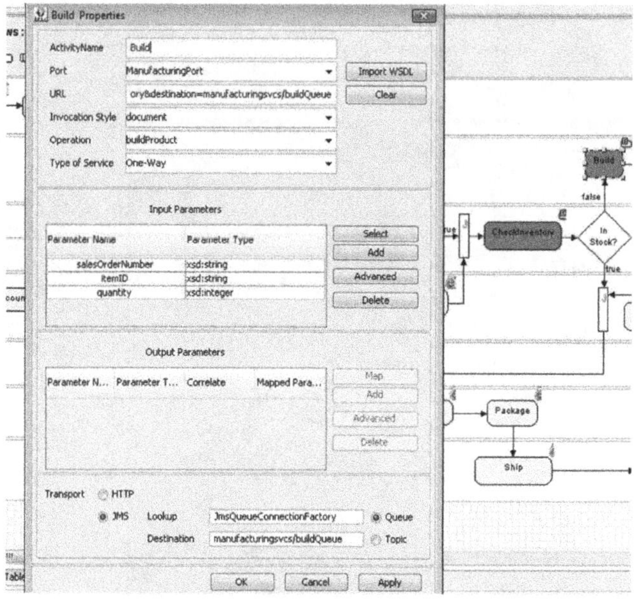

Figure 11.7 Build activity.

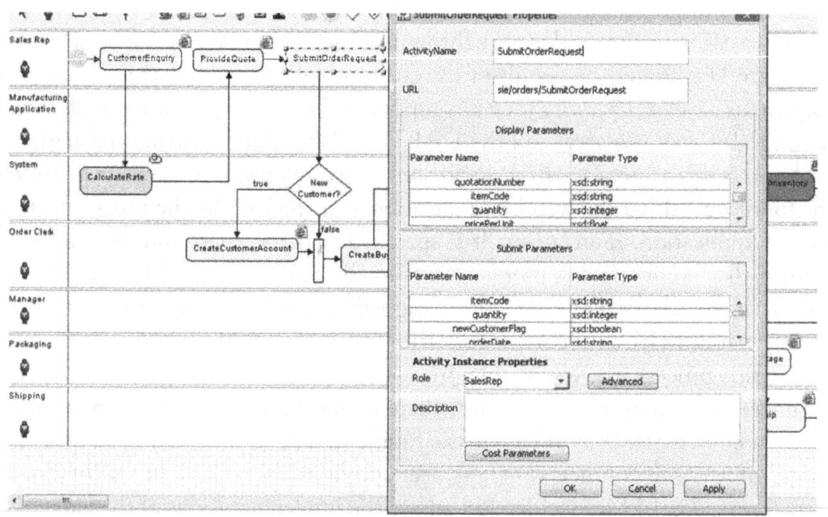

Figure 11.8 Submit order request activity.

and attributes. In our example here, we have used some extensions such as "mode," "role," "actType," "allocationScheme," "locate," "wsdlfilename," and so on.

The executable process definition in WS-BPEL for this detailed process model is as follows:

```
<?xml version="1.0" encoding="UTF-8"?>
<process abstractProcess="no" enableInstanceCompensation="no"
  expressionLanguage="http://www.w3.org/TR/1999/
  REC-xpath-19991116"
  name="SalesOrderProcess" sie:appName="SalesOrder" sie:
    sie:queryLanguage="http://www.w3.org/TR/1999/
    REC-xpath-19991116"
  supressJoinFailure="no"
  targetNamespace="http://www.onlinesieservices.com/BPEL/
  ordertocash"
  xmlns="http://docs.oasis-open.org/wsbpel/2.0/process/
  executable"
  xmlns:bpws="http://docs.oasis-open.org/wsbpel/2.0/process/
  executable"
  xmlns:inst="http://www.onlinesieservices.com/BPEL/
  extensions/inst"
  xmlns:java="http://www.onlinesieservices.com/java"
  xmlns:sie="http://www.onlinesieservices.com/BPEL/extensions"
  xmlns:wsdl="http://schemas.xmlsoap.org/wsdl/"
  xmlns:xsd="http://www.w3.org/2001/XMLSchema"
xmlns:xsi="http://www.w3.org/2001/XMLSchema-instance">
  <extensions>
    <extension
namespace="http://www.onlinesieservices.com/BPEL/extensions/
inst" mustUnderstand="yes" />
    <extension
namespace="http://www.onlinesieservices.com/BPEL/extensions"
mustUnderstand="no" />
  </extensions>
  <correlationSets/>
  <variables>
    <variable name="inst:endprocess" type="xsd:boolean"/>
    <variable name="quotationNumber" type="xsd:string"/>
    <variable name="salesOrderNumber" type="xsd:string"/>
    <variable name="orderDate" type="xsd:string"/>
    <variable name="expectedDeliveryDate" type="xsd:string"/>
    <variable name="orderAmount" type="xsd:integer"/>
    <variable name="customerID" type="xsd:string"/>
    <variable name="customerName" type="xsd:string"/>
    <variable name="creditCustomerFlag" type="xsd:boolean"/>
    <variable name="orderStatus" type="xsd:string"/>
  </variables>
  <scope>
```

```
  <variables>
     <variable messageType="CustomerEnquiryOutParams"
name="CustomerEnquiry.OutParam"/>
     <variable messageType="ProvideQuoteInParams"
name="ProvideQuote.InParam"/>
     <variable messageType="SubmitOrderRequestInParams"
name="SubmitOrderRequest.InParam"/>
     <variable messageType="SubmitOrderRequestOutParams"
name="SubmitOrderRequest.OutParam"/>
     <variable messageType="calculateRateRequest"
name="CalculateRate.InParam"/>
     <variable messageType="calculateRateResponse"
name="CalculateRate.OutParam"/>
     <variable messageType="CreateCustomerAccountInParams"
name="CreateCustomerAccount.InParam"/>
     <variable messageType="CreateCustomerAccountOutParams"
name="CreateCustomerAccount.OutParam"/>
     <variable messageType="CreateBuyOrderInParams"
name="CreateBuyOrder.InParam"/>
     <variable messageType="CreateBuyOrderOutParams"
name="CreateBuyOrder.OutParam"/>
     <variable messageType="ReviewOrderInParams"
name="ReviewOrder.InParam"/>
     <variable messageType="ReviewOrderOutParams"
name="ReviewOrder.OutParam"/>
     <variable messageType="ConfirmOrderInParams"
name="ConfirmOrder.InParam"/>
     <variable messageType="ConfirmOrderOutParams"
name="ConfirmOrder.OutParam"/>
     <variable messageType="ReceivePaymentInParams"
name="ReceivePayment.InParam"/>
     <variable messageType="ReceivePaymentOutParams"
name="ReceivePayment.OutParam"/>
     <variable messageType="checkInventoryRequest"
name="CheckInventory.InParam"/>
     <variable messageType="checkInventoryResponse"
name="CheckInventory.OutParam"/>
     <variable messageType="buildProductRequest"
name="Build.InParam"/>
     <variable messageType="ProductsReadyOutParams"
name="ProductsReady.OutParam"/>
     <variable messageType="PickInParams"
name="Pick.InParam"/>
     <variable messageType="PickOutParams"
name="Pick.OutParam"/>
     <variable messageType="PackageInParams"
name="Package.InParam"/>
     <variable messageType="PackageOutParams"
name="Package.OutParam"/>
```

```
    <variable messageType="ShipInParams" name="Ship.InParam"/>
    <variable messageType="ShipOutParams" name="Ship.OutParam"/>
  </variables>
  <correlationSets>
    <correlationSet name="ProductsReady"
properties="salesOrderNumber"/>
  </correlationSets>
  <sequence>
    <receive createInstance="yes" name="start_
    SalesOrderProcess"
      operation="start_SalesOrderProcess"
portType="start_SalesOrderProcessPT" />
    <assign>
      <copy>
        <from>false</from>
        <to part="inst:endprocess" variable="inst:endprocess"/>
      </copy>
    </assign>
    <assign>
      <copy>
        <from variable="inst:processidentifier"/>
        <to part="processid"
variable="SalesOrderProcess.response"/>
      </copy>
    </assign>
    <reply name="start_SalesOrderProcess"
            operation="start_SalesOrderProcess"
portType="start_SalesOrderProcessPT"
variable="SalesOrderProcess.response"/>

    <invoke locate="sie/orders/Cust_Enq"
      sie:mode="Manual" name="CustomerEnquiry"
operation="customerEnquiry"
      outputVariable="CustomerEnquiry.OutParam"
        sei:acttype="webUI:Activity"
      sie:userAllocationScheme=""
      portType="OrdersUserActionsPT">
      <sie:roles sie:allocationScheme="default">
        <sie:role>SalesRep</sie:role>
      </sie:roles>
    </invoke>
    <assign>
      <copy>
        <from part="item" variable="CustomerEnquiry.OutParam"/>
        <to part="itemCode" variable="CalculateRate.InParam"/>
      </copy>
    </assign>
    <assign>
      <copy>
```

```
        <from part="quantity"
variable="CustomerEnquiry.OutParam"/>
        <to part="quantity" variable="CalculateRate.InParam"/>
      </copy>
    </assign>
    <assign>
      <copy>
        <from part="deliveryLocationCode"
variable="CustomerEnquiry.OutParam"/>
        <to part="deliveryLocationCode"
variable="CalculateRate.InParam"/>
      </copy>
    </assign>
    <invoke inputVariable="CalculateRate.InParam"
locate="ejb:/className=pricing.calculateRateHome&amp;jndiName=
pricing/CalculateRate"
      name="CalculateRate"
      operation="calculateRate"
      outputVariable="CalculateRate.OutParam"
      sie:portname="PricingPort"
      sie:wsdlfilename="CalculateRate.wsdl"
      sei:acttype="EJB:Activity"
      portType="PricingPT" />
    <assign>
      <copy>
        <from part="quotationNumber"
variable="CalculateRate.OutParam"/>
        <to variable="quotationNumber"/>
      </copy>
    </assign>
    <assign>
      <copy>
        <from part="orderAmount"
variable="CalculateRate.OutParam"/> <to variable="orderAmount"/>
      </copy>
    </assign>
    <assign>
      <copy>
        <from part="pricePerUnit"
        variable="CalculateRate.OutParam"/>
        <to part="price" variable="ProvideQuote.InParam"/>
      </copy>
    </assign>
    <assign>
      <copy>
        <from part="item" variable="CustomerEnquiry.OutParam"/>
        <to part="itemCode" variable="ProvideQuote.InParam"/>
      </copy>
    </assign>
```

```
      <assign>
        <copy>
          <from part="quantity"
variable="CustomerEnquiry.OutParam"/>
          <to part="quantity" variable="ProvideQuote.InParam"/>
        </copy>
      </assign>
      <assign>
        <copy>
          <from variable="quotationNumber"/>
          <to part="quotationNumber"
variable="ProvideQuote.InParam"/>
        </copy>
      </assign>
      <assign>
        <copy>
          <from variable="orderAmount"/>
         <to part="orderAmount" variable="ProvideQuote.InParam"/>
        </copy>
      </assign>
      <invoke inputVariable="ProvideQuote.InParam"
        locate="sie/orders/Quote" sie:mode="Manual"
        name="ProvideQuote" operation="provideQuote"
                sei:acttype="webUI:Activity"
        sie:userAllocationScheme=""
        portType="OrdersUserActionsPT">
        <sie:roles sie:allocationScheme="default">
          <sie:role>SalesRep</sie:role>
        </sie:roles>
      </invoke>
      <assign>
        <copy>
          <from part="item" variable="CustomerEnquiry.
          OutParam"/>
          <to part="itemCode"
variable="SubmitOrderRequest.InParam"/>
        </copy>
      </assign>
      <assign>
        <copy>
          <from part="quantity"
variable="CustomerEnquiry.OutParam"/>
          <to part="quantity"
variable="SubmitOrderRequest.InParam"/>
        </copy>
      </assign>
      <assign>
        <copy>
          <from part="pricePerUnit"
```

```
variable="CalculateRate.OutParam"/>
        <to part="pricePerUnit"
variable="SubmitOrderRequest.InParam"/>
      </copy>
    </assign>
    <assign>
      <copy>
        <from part="deliveryLocationCode"
variable="CustomerEnquiry.OutParam"/>
        <to part="deliveryLocation"
variable="SubmitOrderRequest.InParam"/>
      </copy>
    </assign>
    <assign>
      <copy>
        <from variable="quotationNumber"/>
        <to part="quotationNumber"
variable="SubmitOrderRequest.InParam"/>
      </copy>
    </assign>
    <assign>
      <copy>
        <from variable="orderAmount"/>
        <to part="orderAmount"
variable="SubmitOrderRequest.InParam"/>
      </copy>
    </assign>
    <invoke
      inputVariable="SubmitOrderRequest.InParam"
      locate="sie/orders/SubmitOrderRequest" sie:mode="Manual"
      name="SubmitOrderRequest" operation="submitOrderRequest"
      outputVariable="SubmitOrderRequest.OutParam"
              sei:acttype="webUI:Activity"
      sie:userAllocationScheme="" portType="OrdersUserActionsPT">
      <sie:roles sie:allocationScheme="default">
        <sie:role>SalesRep</sie:role>
      </sie:roles>
    </invoke>
    <assign>
      <copy>
        <from part="orderDate"
variable="SubmitOrderRequest.OutParam"/>
        <to variable="orderDate"/>
      </copy>
    </assign>
    <assign>
      <copy>
        <from part="orderStatus"
variable="SubmitOrderRequest.OutParam"/>
```

```
        <to variable="orderStatus"/>
      </copy>
    </assign>
    <assign>
      <copy>
        <from part="orderAmount"
variable="SubmitOrderRequest.OutParam"/>
        <to variable="orderAmount"/>
      </copy>
    </assign>
    <assign>
      <copy>
        <from part="customerID"
variable="SubmitOrderRequest.OutParam"/>
        <to variable="customerID"/>
      </copy>
    </assign>
    <assign>
      <copy>
        <from part="customerName"
variable="SubmitOrderRequest.OutParam"/>
        <to variable="customerName"/>
      </copy>
    </assign>
    <switch name="New Customer?">
      <case
sie:conditionExpression="java:((sievar:(SubmitOrderRequest.
OutParam.newCustomerFlag)) == true)">
        <assign>
          <copy>
            <from variable="customerName"/>
            <to part="customerName"
variable="CreateCustomerAccount.InParam"/>
          </copy>
        </assign>
        <assign>
          <copy>
            <from part="deliveryAddress"
variable="SubmitOrderRequest.OutParam"/>
            <to part="delivery address"
variable="CreateCustomerAccount.InParam"/>
          </copy>
        </assign>
        <invoke
          inputVariable="CreateCustomerAccount.InParam"
          locate="sie/orders/CreateCustomer"
          sie:mode="Manual"
          name="CreateCustomerAccount"
operation="createCustomerAccount"
```

```
          outputVariable="CreateCustomerAccount.OutParam"
                      sei:acttype="webUI:Activity"
          sie:userAllocationScheme=""
portType="OrdersUserActionsPT">
          <sie:roles sie:allocationScheme="default">
            <sie:role>Order Clerk</sie:role>
          </sie:roles>
        </invoke>
        <assign>
          <copy>
            <from part="customerID"
variable="CreateCustomerAccount.OutParam"/>
            <to variable="customerID"/>
          </copy>
        </assign>
      </case>
      <case
sie:conditionExpression="java:((sievar:(SubmitOrderRequest.
OutParam.newCustomerFlag)) == false)"/>
    </switch>
    <assign>
      <copy>
        <from variable="quotationNumber"/>
        <to part="quotationNumber"
variable="CreateBuyOrder.InParam"/>
      </copy>
    </assign>
    <assign>
      <copy>
        <from variable="customerID"/>
        <to part="customerID" variable="CreateBuyOrder.InParam"/>
      </copy>
    </assign>
    <assign>
      <copy>
        <from variable="orderStatus"/>
        <to part="orderStatus"
variable="CreateBuyOrder.InParam"/>
      </copy>
    </assign>
    <invoke inputVariable="CreateBuyOrder.InParam"
        locate="sie/orders/CreateBuyOrder" sie:mode="Manual"
        name="CreateBuyOrder" operation="createBuyOrder"
        outputVariable="CreateBuyOrder.OutParam"
                sei:acttype="webUI:Activity"
        sie:userAllocationScheme=""
        portType="OrdersUserActionsPT">
        <sie:roles sie:allocationScheme="default">
          <sie:role>OrderClerk</sie:role>
```

```
        </sie:roles>
        <correlations>
          <correlation initiate="yes" pattern="in"
set="ProductsReady"/>
        </correlations>
      </invoke>
      <assign>
        <copy>
          <from part="salesOrderNumber"
variable="CreateBuyOrder.OutParam"/>
  <to variable="salesOrderNumber"/>
        </copy>
      </assign>
  <assign>
        <copy>
          <from part="orderStatus"
variable="CreateBuyOrder.OutParam"/>
          <to variable="orderStatus"/>
        </copy>
      </assign>
      <assign>
        <copy>
          <from part="orderAmount"
variable="CreateBuyOrder.OutParam"/>
          <to variable="orderAmount"/>
        </copy>
      </assign>
      <assign>
        <copy>
          <from part="orderDate"
variable="CreateBuyOrder.OutParam"/>
          <to variable="orderDate"/>
        </copy>
      </assign>
      <assign>
        <copy>
          <from part="creditCustomerFlag"
variable="CreateBuyOrder.OutParam"/>
          <to variable="creditCustomerFlag"/>
        </copy>
      </assign>
      <assign>
        <copy>
          <from part="expectedDeliveryDate"
variable="CreateBuyOrder.OutParam"/>
          <to variable="expectedDeliveryDate"/>
        </copy>
      </assign>
      <switch name="Amount &gt; $1000 ?">
```

```
        <case
sie:conditionExpression="java:((sievar:(orderAmount)&gt;1000)
== false)"/>
        <case
sie:conditionExpression="java:((sievar:(orderAmount)&gt;1000)
== true)">
          <assign>
            <copy>
              <from variable="salesOrderNumber"/>
              <to part="salesOrderNumber"
variable="ReviewOrder.InParam"/>
            </copy>
          </assign>
          <invoke
            inputVariable="ReviewOrder.InParam"
            locate="sie/orders/ReviewOrder" sie:mode="Manual"
            name="ReviewOrder" operation="reviewOrder"
            outputVariable="ReviewOrder.OutParam"
                        sei:acttype="webUI:Activity"
            sie:userAllocationScheme=""
portType="OrdersUserActionsPT">
            <sie:roles sie:allocationScheme="default">
              <sie:role>Manager</sie:role>
            </sie:roles>
          </invoke>
          <assign>
            <copy>
              <from part="orderStatus"
variable="ReviewOrder.OutParam"/>
              <to variable="orderStatus"/>
            </copy>
          </assign>
        </case>
      </switch>
      <assign>
        <copy>
          <from variable="salesOrderNumber"/>
          <to part="salesOrderNumber"
variable="ConfirmOrder.InParam"/>
        </copy>
      </assign>
      <invoke inputVariable="ConfirmOrder.InParam"
        locate="sie/orders/ConfirmOrder" sie:mode="Manual"
        name="ConfirmOrder" operation="confirmOrder"
        outputVariable="ConfirmOrder.OutParam"
                sei:acttype="webUI:Activity"
        sie:userAllocationScheme=""
        portType="OrdersUserActionsPT">
        <sie:roles sie:allocationScheme="default">
```

```
          <sie:role>OrderClerk</sie:role>
        </sie:roles>
      </invoke>
      <assign>
        <copy>
          <from part="orderStatus"
variable="ConfirmOrder.OutParam"/>
          <to variable="orderStatus"/>
        </copy>
      </assign>
      <switch name="Credit Customer?">
        <case
sie:conditionExpression="java:((sievar:(creditCustomerFlag))
== false)">
          <assign>
          <copy>
            <from variable="salesOrderNumber"/>
            <to part="salesOrderNumber"
variable="ReceivePayment.InParam"/>
          </copy>
        </assign>
        <invoke
          inputVariable="ReceivePayment.InParam"
          locate="sie/orders/ReceivePayment" sie:mode="Manual"
          name="ReceivePayment" operation="receivePayment"
          outputVariable="ReceivePayment.OutParam"
                      sei:acttype="webUI:Activity"
          sie:userAllocationScheme=""
portType="OrdersUserActionsPT">
          <sie:roles sie:allocationScheme="default">
            <sie:role>OrderClerk</sie:role>
          </sie:roles>
        </invoke>
        <assign>
          <copy>
            <from part="orderStatus"
variable="ReceivePayment.OutParam"/>
            <to variable="orderStatus"/>
          </copy>
        </assign>
      </case>
      <case
sie:conditionExpression="java:((sievar:(creditCustomerFlag))
== true)"/>
    </switch>
    <assign>
      <copy>
        <from part="itemCode"
variable="SubmitOrderRequest.OutParam"/>
```

```
        <to part="itemID" variable="CheckInventory.InParam"/>
      </copy>
    </assign>
    <assign>
      <copy>
        <from part="quantity"
variable="SubmitOrderRequest.OutParam"/>
        <to part="quantity" variable="CheckInventory.InParam"/>
      </copy>
    </assign>
    <invoke inputVariable="CheckInventory.InParam"
locate="http://internalsysinfoservices/inventorysvcs/
checkInventory"
      name="CheckInventory"
      operation="checkInventory"
      outputVariable="CheckInventory.OutParam"
      sie:portname="InventoryPort"
      sie:wsdlfilename="CheckInventory.wsdl"
              sei:acttype="SOAPHTTPDOC:Activity"
      portType="InventoryPT" />
    <switch name="In Stock?">
      <case
sie:conditionExpression="java:((sievar:(CheckInventory.
OutParam.inStock)) == false)">
        <assign>
          <copy>
            <from part="itemCode"
variable="SubmitOrderRequest.OutParam"/>
            <to part="itemID" variable="Build.InParam"/>
          </copy>
        </assign>
        <assign>
          <copy>
            <from part="quantity"
variable="SubmitOrderRequest.OutParam"/>
            <to part="quantity" variable="Build.InParam"/>
          </copy>
        </assign>
        <assign>
          <copy>
            <from variable="salesOrderNumber"/>
            <to part="salesOrderNumber"
variable="Build.InParam"/>
          </copy>
        </assign>
        <invoke inputVariable="Build.InParam"
locate="jms:/queue?connectionFactory=JmsQueueConnectionFactory
&amp;destination=manufacturingsvcs/buildQueue"
          name="Build"
```

```
          operation="buildProduct"
          sie:portname="ManufacturingPort"
          sie:wsdlfilename="Build.wsdl"
                      sei:acttype="SOAPJMSDOC:Activity"
          portType="ManufacturingPT" />
        <receive createInstance="no"
          name="ProductsReady"
          operation="ProductsReady"
                      sei:acttype="SOAPJMSDOC:Receive"
          portType="OrdersPT"
variable="ProductsReady.OutParam">
          <correlations>
            <correlation initiate="no" set="ProductsReady"/>
          </correlations>
        </receive>
      </case>
      <case
sie:conditionExpression="java:((sievar:(CheckInventory.
OutParam.inStock)) == true)"/>
    </switch>
    <assign>
      <copy>
        <from variable="salesOrderNumber"/>
        <to part="salesOrderNumber" variable="Pick.InParam"/>
      </copy>
    </assign>
    <invoke inputVariable="Pick.InParam"
        locate="sie/orders/Pick" sie:mode="Manual" name="Pick"
        operation="pick" outputVariable="Pick.OutParam"
               sei:acttype="webUI:Activity"
        sie:userAllocationScheme=""
        portType="OrdersUserActionsPT">
        <sie:roles sie:allocationScheme="default">
          <sie:role>Packaging</sie:role>
        </sie:roles>
      </invoke>
      <assign>
        <copy>
          <from part="orderStatus" variable="Pick.OutParam"/>
          <to variable="orderStatus"/>
        </copy>
      </assign>
      <assign>
        <copy>
          <from part="deliveryLocation"
variable="SubmitOrderRequest.OutParam"/>
         <to part="deliveryLocation" variable="Package.InParam"/>
        </copy>
      </assign>
```

```
      <assign>
        <copy>
          <from part="deliveryAddress"
variable="SubmitOrderRequest.OutParam"/>
         <to part="deliveryAddress" variable="Package.InParam"/>
        </copy>
      </assign>
      <assign>
        <copy>
          <from variable="salesOrderNumber"/>
         <to part="salesOrderNumber" variable="Package.InParam"/>
        </copy>
      </assign>
      <assign>
        <copy>
          <from variable="customerName"/>
          <to part="customerName" variable="Package.InParam"/>
        </copy>
      </assign>
      <assign>
        <copy>
          <from variable="expectedDeliveryDate"/>
          <to part="expectedDeliveryDate"
variable="Package.InParam"/>
        </copy>
      </assign>
      <invoke inputVariable="Package.InParam"
        locate="sie/orders/Package" sie:mode="Manual"
        name="Package"
      operation="package" outputVariable="Package.OutParam"
              sei:acttype="webUI:Activity"
      sie:userAllocationScheme="" portType="OrdersUserActionsPT">
      <sie:roles sie:allocationScheme="default">
        <sie:role>Packaging</sie:role>
      </sie:roles>
     </invoke>
     <assign>
       <copy>
         <from part="orderStatus" variable="Package.OutParam"/>
         <to variable="orderStatus"/>
       </copy>
     </assign>
     <assign>
       <copy>
         <from part="deliveryAddress"
variable="SubmitOrderRequest.OutParam"/>
         <to part="deliveryAddress" variable="Ship.InParam"/>
       </copy>
     </assign>
```

```
      <assign>
        <copy>
          <from variable="salesOrderNumber"/>
          <to part="salesOrderNumber" variable="Ship.InParam"/>
        </copy>
      </assign>
      <assign>
        <copy>
          <from variable="customerName"/>
          <to part="customerName" variable="Ship.InParam"/>
        </copy>
      </assign>
      <assign>
        <copy>
          <from variable="expectedDeliveryDate"/>
         <to part="expectedDeliveryDate" variable="Ship.InParam"/>
        </copy>
      </assign>
      <invoke inputVariable="Ship.InParam"
        locate="sie/orders/Ship" sie:mode="Manual" name="Ship"
        operation="ship" outputVariable="Ship.OutParam"
                sei:acttype="webUI:Activity"
       sie:userAllocationScheme="" portType="OrdersUserActionsPT">
        <sie:roles sie:allocationScheme="default">
          <sie:role>Shipping</sie:role>
        </sie:roles>
      </invoke>
      <assign>
        <copy>
          <from part="orderStatus" variable="Ship.OutParam"/>
          <to variable="orderStatus"/>
        </copy>
      </assign>
      <switch name="Credit Customer?">
        <case
sie:conditionExpression="java:((sievar:(creditCustomerFlag))
  == true)">
          <assign>
            <copy>
              <from variable="salesOrderNumber"/>
              <to part="salesOrderNumber"
variable="ReceivePayment.InParam"/>
            </copy>
          </assign>
          <invoke
            inputVariable="ReceivePayment.InParam"
            locate="sie/orders/ReceivePayment" sie:mode="Manual"
            name="ReceivePayment" operation="receivePayment"
            outputVariable="ReceivePayment.OutParam"
```

```
                        sei:acttype="webUI:Activity"
            sie:userAllocationScheme=""
portType="OrdersUserActionsPT">
            <sie:roles sie:allocationScheme="default">
              <sie:role>OrderClerk</sie:role>
            </sie:roles>
          </invoke>
          <assign>
            <copy>
              <from part="orderStatus"
variable="ReceivePayment.OutParam"/>
              <to variable="orderStatus"/>
            </copy>
          </assign>
        </case>
        <case
sie:conditionExpression="java:((sievar:(creditCustomerFlag))
  == false)"/>
      </switch>
      <assign>
        <copy>
          <from>true</from>
          <to part="inst:endprocess" variable="inst:endprocess"/>
        </copy>
      </assign>
    </sequence>
  </scope>
</process>
```

The WSDL definition for the entire process is given in the below listing: UserActions.wsdl:

```
<?xml version="1.0" encoding="UTF-8"?>
<wsdl:definitions
  targetNamespace="http://www.onlinesieservices.com/BPEL/
  salesorder"
  xmlns="http://www.onlinesieservices.com/BPEL/extensions"
  xmlns:bpws="http://docs.oasis-open.org/wsbpel/2.0/process/
  executable"
  xmlns:wsdl="http://schemas.xmlsoap.org/wsdl/"
  xmlns:xsd="http://www.w3.org/2001/XMLSchema"
  xmlns:xsi="http://www.w3.org/2001/XMLSchema-instance"
xsi:schemaLocation="http://schemas.xmlsoap.org/wsdl/wsdl.xml">
  <bpws:property name="sales order number" type="xsd:string"/>
  <bpws:propertyAlias messageType="CreateBuyOrderOutParams"
    part="sales order number" propertyName="sales order number"/>
  <bpws:propertyAlias messageType="ProductsReadyOutParams"
    part="salesOrderNum" propertyName="sales order number"/>
  <wsdl:message name="CustomerEnquiryInParams"/>
```

```
<wsdl:message name="CustomerEnquiryOutParams">
  <wsdl:part name="item" type="xsd:string"/>
  <wsdl:part name="quantity" type="xsd:integer"/>
  <wsdl:part name="deliveryLocationCode" type="xsd:string"/>
</wsdl:message>
<wsdl:message name="ProvideQuoteInParams">
  <wsdl:part name="price" type="xsd:float"/>
  <wsdl:part name="itemCode" type="xsd:string"/>
  <wsdl:part name="quotatioNumber" type="xsd:string"/>
  <wsdl:part name="orderAmount" type="xsd:integer"/>
  <wsdl:part name="quantity" type="xsd:integer"/>
</wsdl:message>
<wsdl:message name="ProvideQuoteOutParams"/>
<wsdl:message name="SubmitOrderRequestInParams">
  <wsdl:part name="quotationNumber" type="xsd:string"/>
  <wsdl:part name="itemCode" type="xsd:string"/>
  <wsdl:part name="quantity" type="xsd:integer"/>
  <wsdl:part name="pricePerUnit" type="xsd:float"/>
  <wsdl:part name="orderAmount" type="xsd:integer"/>
  <wsdl:part name="deliveryLocation" type="xsd:string"/>
</wsdl:message>
<wsdl:message name="SubmitOrderRequestOutParams">
  <wsdl:part name="itemCode" type="xsd:string"/>
  <wsdl:part name="quantity" type="xsd:integer"/>
  <wsdl:part name="newCustomerFlag" type="xsd:boolean"/>
  <wsdl:part name="orderDate" type="xsd:string"/>
  <wsdl:part name="orderStatus" type="xsd:string"/>
  <wsdl:part name="orderAmount" type="xsd:integer"/>
  <wsdl:part name="customerID" type="xsd:string"/>
  <wsdl:part name="deliveryLocation" type="xsd:string"/>
  <wsdl:part name="customerName" type="xsd:string"/>
  <wsdl:part name="deliveryAddress" type="xsd:string"/>
</wsdl:message>
<wsdl:message name="CreateCustomerAccountInParams">
  <wsdl:part name="customerName" type="xsd:string"/>
  <wsdl:part name="billingAddress" type="xsd:string"/>
  <wsdl:part name="deliveryAddress" type="xsd:string"/>
</wsdl:message>
<wsdl:message name="CreateCustomerAccountOutParams">
  <wsdl:part name="customerID" type="xsd:string"/>
</wsdl:message>
<wsdl:message name="CreateBuyOrderInParams">
  <wsdl:part name="quotationNumber" type="xsd:string"/>
  <wsdl:part name="customerID" type="xsd:string"/>
  <wsdl:part name="orderStatus" type="xsd:string"/>
</wsdl:message>
<wsdl:message name="CreateBuyOrderOutParams">
  <wsdl:part name="salesOrderNumber" type="xsd:string"/>
  <wsdl:part name="orderStatus" type="xsd:string"/>
```

```
  <wsdl:part name="orderAmount" type="xsd:integer"/>
  <wsdl:part name="orderDate" type="xsd:string"/>
  <wsdl:part name="creditCustomerFlag" type="xsd:boolean"/>
  <wsdl:part name="expectedDeliveryDate" type="xsd:string"/>
</wsdl:message>
<wsdl:message name="ReviewOrderInParams">
  <wsdl:part name="salesOrderNumber" type="xsd:string"/>
</wsdl:message>
<wsdl:message name="ReviewOrderOutParams">
  <wsdl:part name="orderStatus" type="xsd:string"/>
</wsdl:message>
<wsdl:message name="ConfirmOrderInParams">
  <wsdl:part name="salesOrderNumber" type="xsd:string"/>
</wsdl:message>
<wsdl:message name="ConfirmOrderOutParams">
  <wsdl:part name=" orderStatus " type="xsd:string"/>
</wsdl:message>
<wsdl:message name="ReceivePaymentInParams">
  <wsdl:part name="salesOrderNumber " type="xsd:string"/>
</wsdl:message>
<wsdl:message name="ReceivePaymentOutParams">
  <wsdl:part name="paymentType" type="xsd:string"/>
  <wsdl:part name="paymentDetail" type="xsd:string"/>
  <wsdl:part name="paymentAmount" type="xsd:float"/>
  <wsdl:part name="orderStatus" type="xsd:string"/>
</wsdl:message>
<wsdl:message name="PickInParams">
  <wsdl:part name="salesOrderNumber" type="xsd:string"/>
</wsdl:message>
<wsdl:message name="PickOutParams">
  <wsdl:part name="orderStatus" type="xsd:string"/>
</wsdl:message>
<wsdl:message name="PackageInParams">
  <wsdl:part name="deliveryLocation" type="xsd:string"/>
  <wsdl:part name="deliveryAddress" type="xsd:string"/>
  <wsdl:part name="salesOrderNumber" type="xsd:string"/>
  <wsdl:part name="customerName" type="xsd:string"/>
  <wsdl:part name="expectedDeliveryDate" type="xsd:string"/>
</wsdl:message>
<wsdl:message name="PackageOutParams">
  <wsdl:part name="orderStatus" type="xsd:string"/>
</wsdl:message>
<wsdl:message name="ShipInParams">
  <wsdl:part name="salesOrderNumber" type="xsd:string"/>
  <wsdl:part name="customerName" type="xsd:string"/>
  <wsdl:part name="deliveryAddress" type="xsd:string"/>
  <wsdl:part name="expectedDeliveryDate" type="xsd:string"/>
</wsdl:message>
<wsdl:message name="ShipOutParams">
```

```
    <wsdl:part name="orderStatus" type="xsd:string"/>
  </wsdl:message>
  <wsdl:portType name="OrdersUserActionsPT">
    <wsdl:operation name="CustomerEnquiry">
      <wsdl:input message="CustomerEnquiryInParams"/>
      <wsdl:output message="CustomerEnquiryOutParams"/>
    </wsdl:operation>
    <wsdl:operation name="ProvideQuote">
      <wsdl:input message="ProvideQuoteInParams"/>
      <wsdl:output message="ProvideQuoteOutParams"/>
    </wsdl:operation>
    <wsdl:operation name="SubmitOrderRequest">
      <wsdl:input message="SubmitOrderRequestInParams"/>
      <wsdl:output message="SubmitOrderRequestOutParams"/>
    </wsdl:operation>
    <wsdl:operation name="CreateCustomerAccount">
      <wsdl:input message="CreateCustomerAccountInParams"/>
      <wsdl:output message="CreateCustomerAccountOutParams"/>
    </wsdl:operation>
    <wsdl:operation name="CreateBuyOrder">
      <wsdl:input message="CreateBuyOrderInParams"/>
      <wsdl:output message="CreateBuyOrderOutParams"/>
    </wsdl:operation>
    <wsdl:operation name="ReviewOrder">
      <wsdl:input message="ReviewOrderInParams"/>
      <wsdl:output message="ReviewOrderOutParams"/>
    </wsdl:operation>
    <wsdl:operation name="ConfirmOrder">
      <wsdl:input message="ConfirmOrderInParams"/>
      <wsdl:output message="ConfirmOrderOutParams"/>
    </wsdl:operation>
    <wsdl:operation name="ReceivePayment">
      <wsdl:input message="ReceivePaymentInParams"/>
      <wsdl:output message="ReceivePaymentOutParams"/>
    </wsdl:operation>
    <wsdl:operation name="Pick">
      <wsdl:input message="PickInParams"/>
      <wsdl:output message="PickOutParams"/>
    </wsdl:operation>
    <wsdl:operation name="Package">
      <wsdl:input message="PackageInParams"/>
      <wsdl:output message="PackageOutParams"/>
    </wsdl:operation>
    <wsdl:operation name="Ship">
      <wsdl:input message="ShipInParams"/>
      <wsdl:output message="ShipOutParams"/>
    </wsdl:operation>
  </wsdl:portType>
</wsdl:definitions>
```

CalculateRate.wsdl:

```
<?xml version="1.0" encoding="UTF-8"?>
<wsdl:definitions name="PricingPort"
targetNamespace="http://www.onlinesieservices.com/BPEL/
salesorder"
xmlns:soapenc="http://schemas.xmlsoap.org/soap/encoding/"
xmlns:xsd="http://www.w3.org/2001/XMLSchema"
xmlns:soap="http://schemas.xmlsoap.org/wsdl/soap/"
xmlns:wsdl="http://schemas.xmlsoap.org/wsdl/"
xmlns="http://www.onlinesieservices.com/BPEL/extensions"
xmlns:jms="http://schemas.xmlsoap.org/wsdl/jms/"
xmlns:ejb="http://schemas.xmlsoap.org/wsdl/ejb/"
xmlns:format="http://schemas.xmlsoap.org/wsdl/formatbinding/" >
  <wsdl:message name="calculateRateResponse">
    <wsdl:part name="quotationNumber" type="xsd:string"/>
    <wsdl:part name="orderAmount" type="xsd:integer"/>
    <wsdl:part name="pricePerUnit" type="xsd:float"/>
  </wsdl:message>
  <wsdl:message name="calculateRateRequest">
    <wsdl:part name="itemCode" type="xsd:string"/>
    <wsdl:part name="quantity" type="xsd:integer"/>
    <wsdl:part name="deliveryLocationCode" type="xsd:string"/>
  </wsdl:message>
  <wsdl:portType name="PricingPT">
    <wsdl:operation name="calculateRate"
      parameterOrder="itemCode quantity deliveryLocationCode">
      <wsdl:input name="calculateRateRequest"
message="calculateRateRequest"/>
      <wsdl:output name="calculateRateResponse"
message="calculateRateResponse"/>
    </wsdl:operation>
  </wsdl:portType>
  <wsdl:binding name="PricingPortBinding" type="PricingPT">
      <ejb:binding/>
        <format:typeMapping style="Java" encoding="Java">
          <format:typeMap typeName="xsd:string"
formatType="java.lang.String"/>
        </format:typeMapping>
  <wsdl:operation name="calculateRate">
    <ejb:operation methodName="calculateRate"
interface="remote"
  parameterOrder="itemCode quantity deliveryLocationCode"/>
    <wsdl:input name="calculateRateRequest">
    </wsdl:input>
    <wsdl:output name="calculateRateResponse">
    </wsdl:output>
    </wsdl:operation>
    </wsdl:binding>
```

```
    <wsdl:service name="CalculateRate">
    <wsdl:port name="PricingPort" binding="PricingPortBinding">
      <ejb:address className="pricing.calculateRateHome"
jndiName="pricing/CalculateRate"/>
    </wsdl:port>
  </wsdl:service>
</wsdl:definitions>
```

CheckInventory.wsdl:

```
<?xml version="1.0" encoding="UTF-8"?>
<wsdl:definitions name="InventoryPort"
targetNamespace="http://www.onlinesieservices.com/BPEL/
salesorder"
xmlns:soapenc="http://schemas.xmlsoap.org/soap/encoding/"
xmlns:xsd="http://www.w3.org/2001/XMLSchema"
xmlns:soap="http://schemas.xmlsoap.org/wsdl/soap/"
xmlns:wsdl="http://schemas.xmlsoap.org/wsdl/"
xmlns="http://www.onlinesieservices.com/BPEL/extensions"
xmlns:jms="http://schemas.xmlsoap.org/wsdl/jms/">
  <wsdl:message name="checkInventoryResponse">
    <wsdl:part name="inStock" type="xsd:boolean"/>
  </wsdl:message>
  <wsdl:message name="checkInventoryRequest">
    <wsdl:part name="itemID" type="xsd:string"/>
    <wsdl:part name="quantity" type="xsd:integer"/>
  </wsdl:message>
  <wsdl:portType name="InventoryPT">
    <wsdl:operation name="checkInventory">
      <wsdl:input name="checkInventoryRequest"
message="checkInventoryRequest"/>
      <wsdl:output name="checkInventoryResponse"
message="checkInventoryResponse"/>
    </wsdl:operation>
  </wsdl:portType>
  <wsdl:binding name="InventoryPortBinding"
    type="InventoryPT">
  <soap:binding style="document"
transport="http://schemas.xmlsoap.org/soap/http"/>
  <wsdl:operation name="checkInventory">
    <soap:operation soapAction=""/>
    <wsdl:input name="checkInventoryRequest">
    <soap:body use="literal"/>
    </wsdl:input>
    <wsdl:output name="checkInventoryResponse">
      <soap:body use="literal"/>
    </wsdl:output>
  </wsdl:operation>
  </wsdl:binding>
```

```
  <wsdl:service name="CheckInventory">
    <wsdl:port name="InventoryPort"
    binding="InventoryPortBinding">
    <soap:address
location="http://internalsysinfoservices/inventorysvcs/
checkInventory"/>
    </wsdl:port>
  </wsdl:service>
</wsdl:definitions>
```

Build.wsdl:

```
<?xml version="1.0" encoding="UTF-8"?>
<wsdl:definitions name="ManufacturingPort"
targetNamespace="http://www.onlinesieservices.com/BPEL/salesorder"
xmlns:soapenc="http://schemas.xmlsoap.org/soap/encoding/"
xmlns:xsd="http://www.w3.org/2001/XMLSchema"
xmlns:soap="http://schemas.xmlsoap.org/wsdl/soap/"
xmlns:wsdl="http://schemas.xmlsoap.org/wsdl/"
xmlns="http://www.onlinesieservices.com/BPEL/extensions"
xmlns:jms="http://schemas.xmlsoap.org/wsdl/jms/">
  <wsdl:message name="buildProductRequest">
    <wsdl:part name="salesOrderNumber" type="xsd:string"/>
    <wsdl:part name="itemID" type="xsd:string"/>
    <wsdl:part name="quantity" type="xsd:integer"/>
  </wsdl:message>
  <wsdl:portType name="ManufacturingPT">
    <wsdl:operation name="buildProduct">
      <wsdl:input name="buildProductRequest"
        message="buildProductRequest"/>
    </wsdl:operation>
  </wsdl:portType>
  <wsdl:binding name="ManufacturingPortBinding"
  type="ManufacturingPT">
    <soap:binding style="document"
transport="http://schemas.xmlsoap.org/soap/jms"/>
    <wsdl:operation name="buildProduct">
      <soap:operation soapAction=""/>
      <wsdl:input name="buildProductRequest">
        <soap:body use="literal"/>
      </wsdl:input>
    </wsdl:operation>
  </wsdl:binding>
  <wsdl:service name="Build">
    <wsdl:port name="ManufacturingPort"
    binding="ManufacturingPortBinding">
      <jms:address destinationStyle="queue"
jndiConnectionFactoryName="JmsQueueConnectionFactory"
jndiDestinationName="manufacturingsvcs/buildQueue">
```

```
</jms:address>
    </wsdl:port>
  </wsdl:service>
</wsdl:definitions>
```

ReceiveActions.wsdl:

```
<?xml version="1.0" encoding="UTF-8"?>
<wsdl:definitions name="SalesOrderProcess"
targetNamespace="http://www.onlinesieservices.com/BPEL/
salesorder"
xmlns:soapenc="http://schemas.xmlsoap.org/soap/encoding/"
xmlns:xsd="http://www.w3.org/2001/XMLSchema"
xmlns:prefix="http://www.w3.org/2001/XMLSchema"
xmlns:soap="http://schemas.xmlsoap.org/wsdl/soap/"
xmlns:jms="http://schemas.xmlsoap.org/wsdl/jms/"
xmlns:wsdl="http://schemas.xmlsoap.org/wsdl/"
xmlns="http://www.onlinesieservices.com/BPEL/extensions" >
  <wsdl:message name="start_SalesOrderProcessRequest">
  </wsdl:message>
  <wsdl:message name="ProductsReadyRequest">
    <wsdl:part name="salesOrderNum" type="xsd:string"/>
  </wsdl:message>
  <wsdl:message name="start_SalesOrderProcessResponse">
    <wsdl:part name="processid" type="xsd:string"/>
  </wsdl:message>
  <wsdl:portType name="start_SalesOrderProcessPT">
    <wsdl:operation name="start_SalesOrderProcess">
      <wsdl:output name="start_SalesOrderProcessResponse"
message="start_SalesOrderProcessResponse"/>
    </wsdl:operation>
  </wsdl:portType>
  <wsdl:portType name="OrdersPT">
    <wsdl:operation name="ProductsReady">
      <wsdl:input name="ProductsReadyRequest"
message="ProductsReadyRequest"/>
    </wsdl:operation>
  </wsdl:portType>
  <wsdl:binding name="start_SalesOrderProcessBinding"
type="start_SalesOrderProcessPT">
    <soap:binding style="document"
transport="http://schemas.xmlsoap.org/soap/http"/>
    <wsdl:operation name="start_SalesOrderProcess">
      <soap:operation soapAction=""/>
      <wsdl:input name="start_SalesOrderProcessRequest">
        <soap:body use="literal"/>
      </wsdl:input>
      <wsdl:output name="start_SalesOrderProcessResponse">
        <soap:body use="literal"/>
```

```
      </wsdl:output>
    </wsdl:operation>
  </wsdl:binding>
  <wsdl:binding name="ProductsReadyBinding" type="OrdersPT">
    <soap:binding style="document"
transport="http://schemas.xmlsoap.org/soap/jms"/>
    <wsdl:operation name="ProductsReady">
      <soap:operation soapAction=""/>
      <wsdl:input name="ProductsReadyRequest">
        <soap:body use="literal"/>
      </wsdl:input>
      <wsdl:output name="ProductsReadyResponse">
        <soap:body use="literal"/>
      </wsdl:output>
    </wsdl:operation>
  </wsdl:binding>
  <wsdl:service name="start_SalesOrderProcess">
    <wsdl:port name="start_SalesOrderProcess"
binding="start_SalesOrderProcessBinding">
      <soap:address
location="http://internalsysinfoservices/ordersvcs/
SalesOrderProcess"/>
    </wsdl:port>
  </wsdl:service>
  <wsdl:service name="ProductsReady">
    <wsdl:port name="ProductsReady"
      binding="ProductsReadyBinding">
      <jms:address destinationStyle="queue"
jndiConnectionFactoryName="JmsQueueConnectionFactory"
jndiDestinationName="ordersvcs/productsReadyQueue">
</jms:address>
    </wsdl:port>
  </wsdl:service>
</wsdl:definitions>
```

The logical expression for the condition defined for the amount check branch is shown in Figure 11.9, while that for "in stock?" check branch is shown in Figure 11.10. The other branch conditions are also defined in the same way.

Figures 11.11 and 11.12 show the specifications for the user activities "receive payment" and "pick," respectively. These are performed by different roles as can be seen in the specification and the process definition.

11.2.3 Logical Architecture

Let us now look at the logical architecture for this system, as shown in Figure 11.13. As per the process design, the activities can be broadly grouped into the following business function categories—this is a logical grouping. Each category is referred

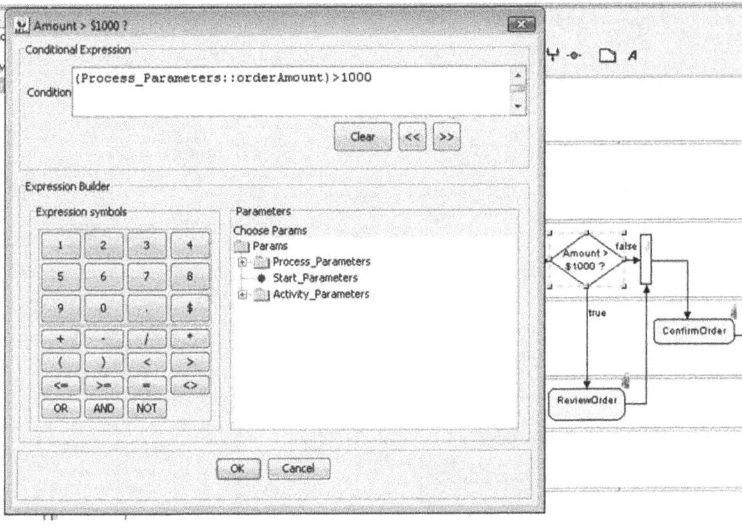

Figure 11.9 Conditional expression.

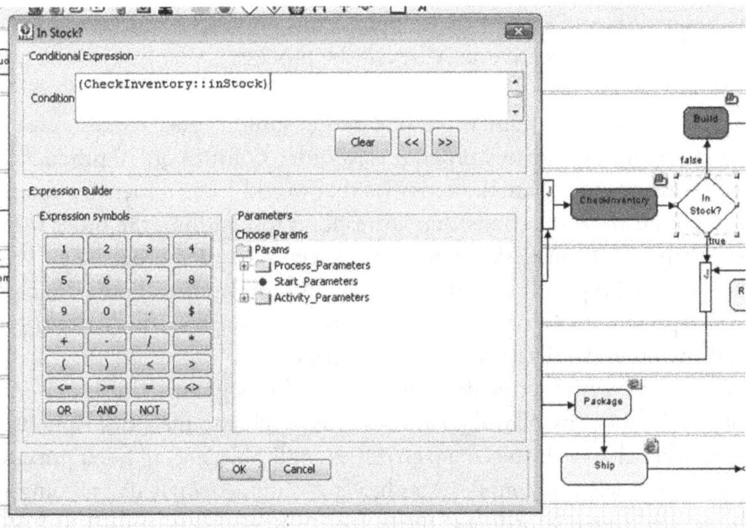

Figure 11.10 Conditional expression—instock.

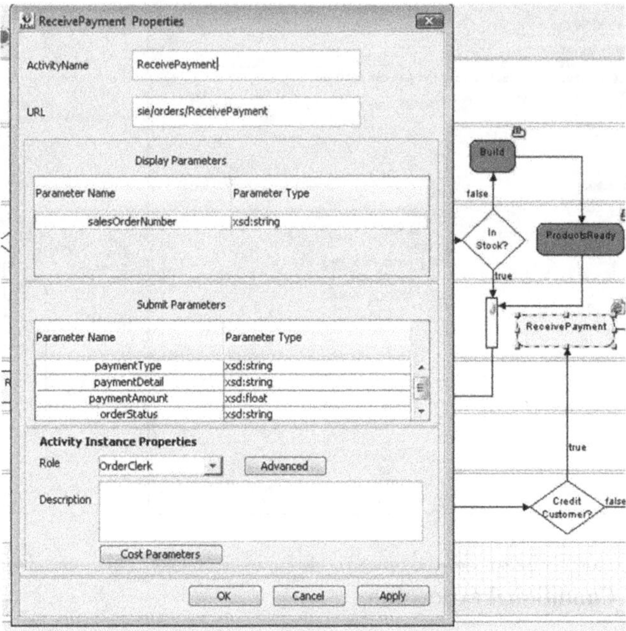

Figure 11.11 Receive payment—user activity.

to as an application, and each of these applications provides a collection of business services that support respective activities in the process:

- Orders—customer enquiry, provide quote, submit order request, create customer account, create buy order, review order, confirm order, products ready, and receive payment are the activities that would come under this category as they are business functions that correspond to handling the order life cycle, especially the front-desk (front-end) aspects of order processing. They are thus handled typically by a team that focuses on front-end orders such as the sales representatives, order clerks, and their managers. This category would hold the order details data for all the orders.
- Pricing—the activity calculate rate is part of this group. This group includes data and functions related to the various products, their descriptions, their rates, other charges involved, taxes, duties applicable, and all other price-related information (e.g., discounts). Another factor influencing this grouping is that the pricing team comprising of raters, credit assessment personnel, and contract negotiators/managers, take care of these business functions as focused work.
- Inventory—the activity check inventory is part of this category. This category is responsible for the inventory data and related functions such as stock levels replenishment, checking, periodic reporting, etc.

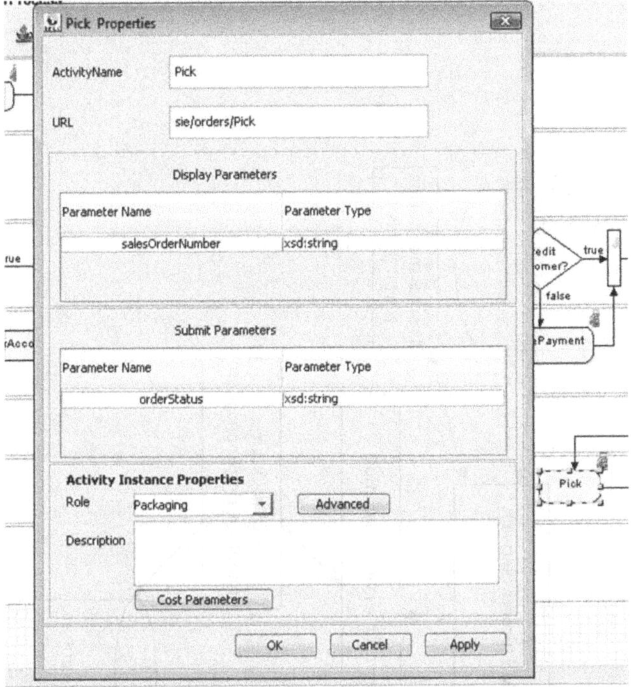

Figure 11.12 Pick—user activity.

- Manufacturing—build activity is in this group. All the business operations and functions associated with making the products that would be sold as part of future orders or the products sold for the current order, as requested, are included in this group. The data relevant to manufacturing is kept and maintained by this group.
- Dispatch—pick, package, and ship are activities related to order processing that are back-end facing. These are part of dispatching the products ordered to the customer. These operations are performed by the packaging and shipping teams, which deal with physically carrying out the order.

Thus, we have multiple applications that work together in this IT system—inventory application, the manufacturing application, order management application, pricing application, and the dispatch application. All these components make the business logic elements (BLEs) of the order-processing system.

Apart from providing invocable services that perform specific business functions, some of them also provide a web-based UI application so that they can support user activities too—order management application and dispatch application provides web-based UI.

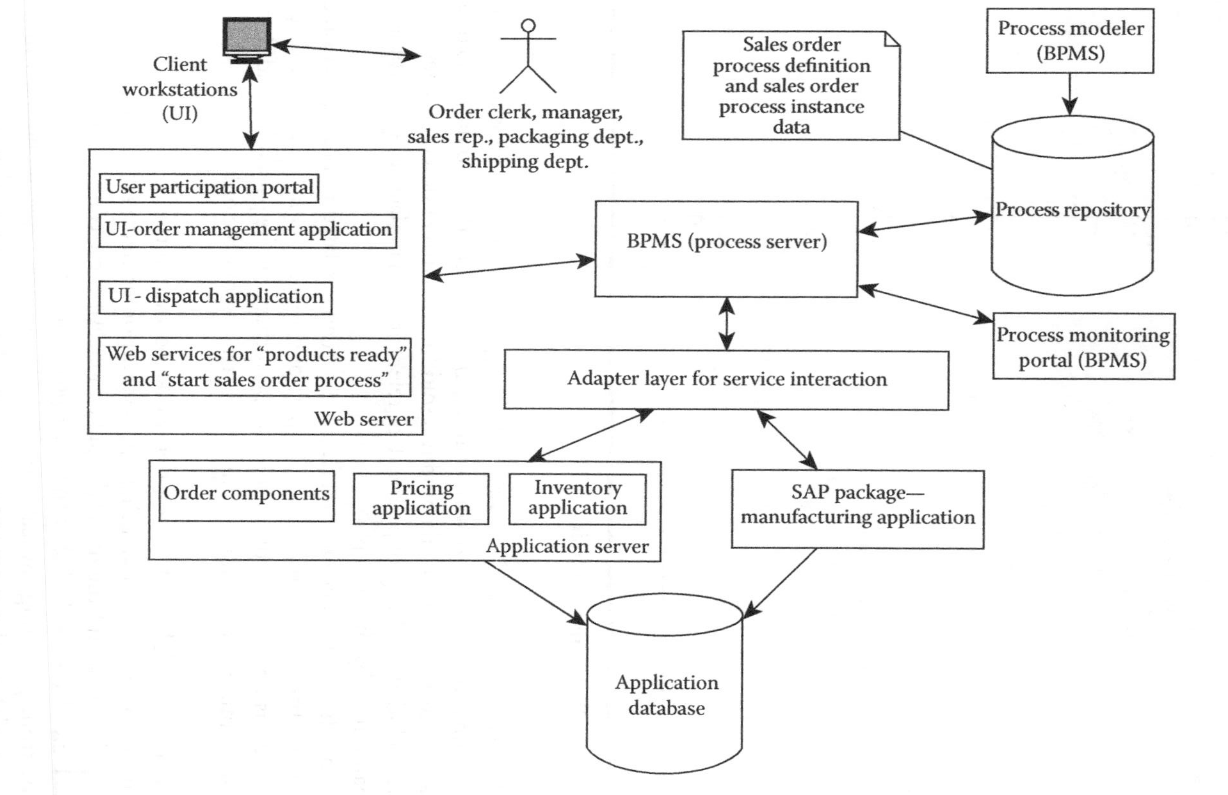

Figure 11.13 Logical view.

The process layer is realized in the form of a run-time process engine (process server) provided by a BPMS. It provides the implementation of the entire process layer. Sales order process instances are created and managed in the process engine. The design-level component for creating process definition is realized through the process modeler provided by a BPMS. Sales order process definitions thus created are housed in the process repository and managed by the process server once they are deployed onto the process server.

Components for order management, pricing application, and inventory application are housed as business components in an application container. These are invoked from the process layer. The services that the process offers, the receive activity "products ready" and the process triggering itself are services exposed as web services. These web services are implemented by the process in the web layer, which then invokes the process layer to pass on the message received in the process ready activity service.

Manufacturing application is an application package. It exposes a service (as web service) that other components can invoke to trigger manufacturing of the products.

The order management web application supports the user activities involving front-desk processing for orders that include customer enquiry, provide quote, submit order request, create customer account, create buy order, review order, confirm order, and receive payment.

The pick, package, and ship user activities are supported by the dispatch web application and this will be used by the packaging and shipping departments while carrying out the backend processing.

There are two separate logical databases in this system. One is the process repository and the other is the application database. The process repository houses all the process-related data—run-time data as well as design-time data. All the process-state data for the sales order process instances and data relevant to the execution of the process instances go here including the process parameters (such as order status, sales order number), process execution time details, and process execution history. This database is used only by the process server and the process modeler, which are the manifestations of the process layer.

The application database is used by the applications that perform the activity-specific business operations. Example data in the application database include inventory data, full order detail, manufacturing/production data, and pricing information. This database is not referred to by the process layer explicitly and the data here is owned and managed by the respective application—pricing data is accessed and maintained by the pricing application, for example.

The adapter layer brides the connection gap between the process layer and the BLEs by enabling the process layer to invoke different types of services, such as HTTP/SOAP-based web services, exposed by the BLEs and vice versa. It is responsible for performing necessary data format transformations, service provider lookups, and concrete invocations. Practically, it is part of the BPMS process server.

11.2.4 Services

Each activity in the sales order process is designed as a business service and this is how the services are primarily identified for the system to be exposed by the BLEs in the sales order processing system. SOA is applied at this level in the architectural design. At this level, the process is seen as an interplay of the business services in a predefined order. Services required for this process are defined as per the principles of SOA as self-contained stateless services that clearly separate their service interface from the service implementation. The process would depend on the well-defined service interfaces for these services and not on their implementations. Implementations of the services are hidden by the applications involved and made transparent to the process.

The business services corresponding to the user activities are performed by users playing the appropriate role—for example, the submit order request activity is performed by a sales representative speaking to the customer. Service implementation is purely dependent on how the user performs the set of tasks as part of the business function concerned, say submit order. Service definitions for them are created in WSDL as shown in the code listing above under the name “process_Sales order process.wsdl.”

The following business services are identified for the system activities in the process:

Check inventory, calculate rate, build, and products ready. As we can see their granularity is decided top-down from the process definition. Their service interfaces are defined next as given in WSDL definitions shown above in the code listing: “Build.wsdl,” “Calculate rate.wsdl,” and “Check Inventory.wsdl.”

The check inventory service corresponds to the check inventory activity in the process. As per the design, this service is a service provided by the inventory application—this application is responsible for the stock-control logic. Input and output parameters for this service are

```
<wsdl:message name="checkInventoryResponse">
  <wsdl:part name="inStock" type="xsd:boolean"/>
</wsdl:message>
<wsdl:message name="checkInventoryRequest">
  <wsdl:part name="itemID" type="xsd:string"/>
  <wsdl:part name="quantity" type="xsd:integer"/>
</wsdl:message>
```

The operation or the service it provides is “checkInventory”:

```
<wsdl:portType name="InventoryPT">
  <wsdl:operation name="checkInventory">
    <wsdl:input name="checkInventoryRequest"
message="checkInventoryRequest"/>
    <wsdl:output name="checkInventoryResponse"
message="checkInventoryResponse"/>
  </wsdl:operation>
</wsdl:portType>
```

They together make up the abstract part of the service definition. The operation is a request–response operation.

This service takes the item and quantity details as input and checks if the item is in stock or not. The service logic might have to go through a set of checks to finally confirm if the items are indeed available in the inventory. The business logic for this service is implemented in the inventory application in the form of a business component and this implementation is independent of the process. The concrete bindings for the service, that is, the wsdl:binding, wsdl:port, and wsdl:port specifications in the wsdl are figured out at run-time by the process layer. One possible set of values for these can be

```
  <wsdl:binding name="InventoryPortBinding" type="InventoryPT">
    <soap:binding style="document"
transport="http://schemas.xmlsoap.org/soap/http"/>
    <wsdl:operation name="checkInventory">
      <soap:operation soapAction=""/>
      <wsdl:input name="checkInventoryRequest">
        <soap:body use="literal"/>
      </wsdl:input>
      <wsdl:output name="checkInventoryResponse">
        <soap:body use="literal"/>
      </wsdl:output>
    </wsdl:operation>
  </wsdl:binding>
  <wsdl:service name="CheckInventory">
    <wsdl:port name="InventoryPort"
    binding="InventoryPortBinding">
    <soap:address
location="http://internalsysinfoservices/inventorysvcs/
checkInventory"/>
    </wsdl:port>
  </wsdl:service>
```

In this concrete binding the service is a web service, invoked using SOAP as the application protocol and http as the transport protocol. The location for the service is given in the soap:address element as http://internalsysinfoservices/inventorysvcs/checkInventory.

At run-time, the process engine connects to this location to invoke the check inventory service. The design of the component that is going to implement this service is taken care of only in the next stage, which is the design stage of the sales order processing system. The design stage involves the detailed design of all these components that are supposed to implement the services, the business logic for them, and the technology dependencies for them such as the run-time environment, programming language, and platforms.

In the case of the above service, one of the ways the web service can be implemented is by using a platform such as Java, and a SOAP engine such as Axis. The service URL above can be mapped to a Java Servlet in the web server. An EJB component can be defined and designed with the business logic for check inventory. It can then be deployed on to the JEE application server. The servlet in turn can invoke this EJB for carrying out the check inventory function when the web service is invoked.

In the case of the build service that corresponds to the build activity in the process, the service is asynchronous and the operation is a one-way operation—It has only a request message and no response message:

```
<wsdl:message name="buildProductRequest">
  <wsdl:part name="sales order number" type="xsd:string"/>
  <wsdl:part name="itemID" type="xsd:string"/>
  <wsdl:part name="quantity" type="xsd:integer"/>
</wsdl:message>
<wsdl:portType name="ManufacturingPT">
  <wsdl:operation name="buildProduct">
    <wsdl:input name="buildProductRequest"
    message="buildProductRequest"/>
  </wsdl:operation>
</wsdl:portType>
```

This is realized as a service invoked using the JMS transport protocol (that is asynchronous) and SOAP for the application protocol. We chose JMS here as the transport technology implementation option as opposed to SMTP or http because this service is an internal service as far as this enterprise is concerned and the manufacturing application package supports a JEE environment in place so this component can be invoked by other systems with maximum ease. Also, JMS provides better reliability for the request processing—we need to make sure that the manufacturing application reliably receives the request for build from the order process and initiates the production of products ordered.

```
<wsdl:binding name="ManufacturingPortBinding"
  type="ManufacturingPT">
  <soap:binding style="document"
transport="http://schemas.xmlsoap.org/soap/jms"/>
  <wsdl:operation name="buildProduct">
    <soap:operation soapAction=""/>
    <wsdl:input name="buildProductRequest">
      <soap:body use="literal"/>
    </wsdl:input>
  </wsdl:operation>
</wsdl:binding>
<wsdl:service name="Build">
  <wsdl:port name="ManufacturingPort"
```

```
     binding="ManufacturingPortBinding">
     <jms:address destinationStyle="queue"
jndiConnectionFactoryName="JmsQueueConnectionFactory"
jndiDestinationName="manufacturingsvcs/buildQueue">
</jms:address>
    </wsdl:port>
  </wsdl:service>
```

The EJB component that provides the calculate rate system activity needs to be designed in detail in the subsequent design stage. The algorithm for calculating the rate, the other business logic (e.g., job-costing) involved in the rate calculation operation are all specified or figured out only in the design stage of the EJB. This would be become part of the design of the pricing application. It needs to then be deployed onto the JEE application server. The choice of EJB as the implementation option for the service is just one of the many implementation options possible. One of the assumptions here is that JEE application server and the Java platform is already in use in this enterprise and thus it is an intuitive decision to go for implementing the component leveraging the quality of system features enabled by JEE. Also, this service is expected to be invoked primarily from within the enterprise, so we can minimize overheads associated with http/XML processing by opting not to implement it as a web service.

Similarly, products ready service is designed as a web service supported through JMS as the transport. It is a notification operation. This is a service exposed by the process and the process engine exposes it dynamically by defining the queue in the JMS provider and initiating a listener Java component on that queue. The listener component is generic and once the manufacturing application makes a call to the products ready service by sending a notification to the JMS queue, it hands over the message to the process instance in the process engine. Such features to support a receive activity are typically provided by the process engine itself. So, unlike the invoke type activities, receive activities might not need any further design beyond what we have done in the architecture stage.

For all the above services, the concrete bindings we have given (EJB, web services, JMS, etc.) are just some of the implementation options we have chosen. These can be dynamic by allowing the process engine to dynamically pick up a service implementation and associated binding at run-time from the options made available to it in non-code means such as selecting from a set of WSDLs for the same service, or specifying as a configuration entry to the process engine through file and other data-sharing means.

11.3 Case Study II

Let us now look at another case study. Here, let us consider the case of a fictitious shipping company named Best Express Shipping (BES) that provides services such as express delivery, courier services, and shipping services through multimodal transport including air, sea, rail, and road.

11.3.1 The Process

The example we shall take here is the case of order-to-cash process where the customer places a shipping order with BES, which then carries out the shipping, delivers the shipment to the recipient (consignee), and collects the cash for the shipment thus completing the process.

This involves the following steps:

- Customer enquiry—the customer (shipper) enquires with BES about the rate for shipping customer's package and BES provides a quotation in return
- Booking—the shipper places a shipping order with BES, providing the package for shipment
- Documentation—the waybill (e.g., airwaybill) is prepared and other related documents are prepared
- Invoicing—the invoice for the shipment charges is prepared
- Payment—the invoice is paid by the customer
- Deliver package—the package is shipped and delivered to the recipient

11.3.2 Background Context

There is an existing set of applications and systems that jointly take care of this process currently. Some of these are custom-in-house-developed legacy applications that have been around for decades; some others are application packages (legacy as well as modern), and yet others are in-house-developed relatively modern applications involving the latest technologies.

There have been various issues with these current IT systems with regard to the flexibility and agility that is constantly being demanded of them by the business process. It has motivated the decision makers to decide that, for supporting this process better, the system (as a whole) needs a re-architecture based on the PCA style.*

11.3.3 The Current System

Let us look at some of the salient features of the architecture of the current system (the set of applications) that supports the order-to-cash business process. This is shown in Figure 11.14.

* Here, we chose not to go into too much detail into the problems with the existing setup and the related justifications for taking the decision to re-architect this system for the sake of sticking to the focus of this chapter, which is the re-architecting work. We have discussed in the earlier chapters the motivation for arriving at decisions related to re-architecting an existing IT system to the PCA style considering the business justifications.

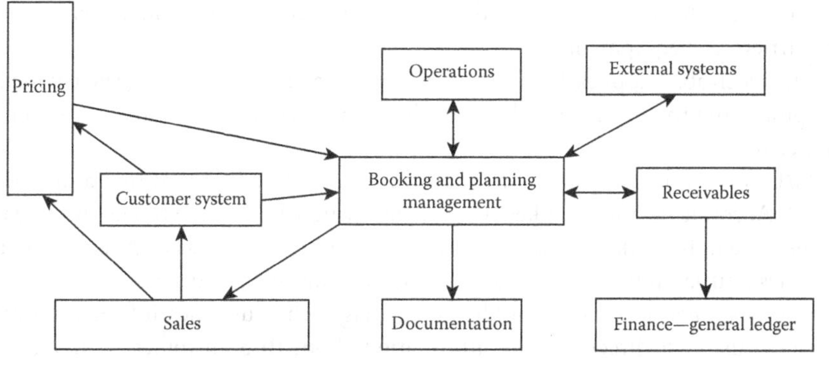

Figure 11.14 Architecture of the existing system.

Each arrow in the diagram indicates the direction of information flow in the interaction between the respective systems involved. As we can see, the following applications are involved in supporting the process: Sales, pricing, customer system, booking and planning management (BAP), documentation, operations, receivables, general ledger (G/L), and the external systems. These applications have been conceived, modeled, and created based on the various functions (departments or groups) in the organization and how those departments do their specific business work.

11.3.3.1 Applications

The BAP system has a major role in the architecture since it takes the shipment request and creates the shipment booking (or the shipment order). It is also in charge of planning the transport and delivery of the shipment. It maintains all shipment booking–related information such as the shipper/consignee details, commodity details, package details, origin/destination details, schedule details for this shipment, waybill details, and location-related data for BES.

Pricing system supports rate enquiry and quotation for the shipment. It maintains all the transportation-related rates, surcharges, policies, and rules governing the applicability of charges, taxes, customs, duties, and legal costs—these are what BES would charge the customer. These also include the rates agreed upon with the customer and then signed as contracts.

The documentation system assists with preparing the necessary documents for the shipment such as the airwaybill, commercial invoice, documents related to compliance with laws/regulations/rules, and exportation documents.

The operations system takes care of the actual physical transportation of the package from the origin to the destination, including the final delivery, through various modes such as air, rail, and road using equipment such as trucks, aircrafts, and containers. It maintains all data related to carriers, equipments, cargo, ports, terminals, etc. It also keeps all schedule, route, and cost information involving various carriers and equipment.

The receivables application is concerned with invoicing, receiving the payment, and processing the payment. It handles the entire accounts receivables function of finance in BES.

G/L is the finance system where all the financial data is captured and maintained. Accounting and bookkeeping for the entire BES is done based on the data in this system. It would have ledgers and various journals such as cash receipts journal, sales journal, purchase journal, and cash disbursement journal.

The customer application holds and manages the customer information and provides customer directory. The information about BES customers—they could be shippers or forwarders or consignees—is kept here. This information includes profiles, customer account information, specific requirements, and directory information (customer detail codes).

11.3.3.2 Flow Support

Currently, the process is supported in a disorganized way and the process looks disjointed. Quoting part is separately done for the customer. The quotation number and details are not integrated with the booking. While doing the actual booking, it might involve a fresh lookup of the rates from the pricing application.

There is a lot of batch data transfer and processing involved in the flow and the integration has been designed primarily based on batch-driven data-flows. The BAP system periodically (several times a day) sends the booking data (order data) for multiple shipments (batched up) to the receivables system. Subsequently, invoices are created in the receivables system based on this data, again in batch processing. When payments are received from the customer for the shipments, the receivables application informs the BAP system so that the package is cleared for delivery to the recipient.

As part of quotation and booking, the customer data from the customer application of BES is received by pricing and BAP applications. The documentation system also gets all the order data that is relevant for creating waybills and other documentation in a mix of batch/online data-sharing modes—batch is the dominant mode, however. The planned delivery date, planned schedules, package/freight to carriage equipments mappings data, and legs planned for the shipments are sent by BAP to the operations application in batches. The operations application then uses this to carry out the transportation and freight handling, from the origin to the destination.

The BAP system periodically sends the shipment order data to the sales system for data analysis as part of warehousing. For all the shipments, receivables application sends the invoice data and payment received data periodically in batches to the G/L for further accounting. BAP also sends shipment data to external systems such as customs for those systems to issue clearances for the shipments. This is also done in batches. Also, the external systems such as customs send batch data to BAP for actions such as shipments-hold or shipments-release. External systems also include customer systems (systems belonging to customers of BES) for actions such as delivery/arrival notifications.

Whenever new customers are on-boarded, that is, via sales, the sales system provides the customer-specific data to the customer application for adding the customer to BES and to the pricing for capturing the rates for the customer based on contract.

11.3.3.3 Issues

Briefly, the key issues with the existing system architecture are

- Disjointed process flow.
- Flow is not real-time as far a specific shipment order is concerned.
- For the customers, visibility to the shipment through this process is poor and is supported largely manually.
- Control of the process is manual and there is a lot of scope for automation here to improve the efficiencies.
- There is much paperwork involved.
- Customer sales representatives (CSR) presently spend significant time on regular, repetitive, and low-value actions that could ideally be done by systems automatically. It leaves them with less time to focus on work such as exception handling.
- There is significant rework involved.
- Integrity of information is an issue. There are multiple applications involved, redundant data and heavy data flows, especially in batch mode, that leads to this.
- For the management and CSR team, there is little visibility to what is happening with specific customer's shipments, reducing their effectiveness in assisting customers.

11.3.4 The New System

Our goal is to architect the new IT system that would support this order-to-cash process end-to-end from the customer's perspective. That is, the process scope is defined thus—it begins when BES engages with the customer for a specific shipment request of the customer's and it ends when BES disengages with the customer.

11.3.4.1 The Business Process Model

First, we model the order-to-cash business process. The high-level business process model for this process is given in Figure 11.15 and the subprocess for the payment is detailed out in Figure 11.16 as the high-level process model.

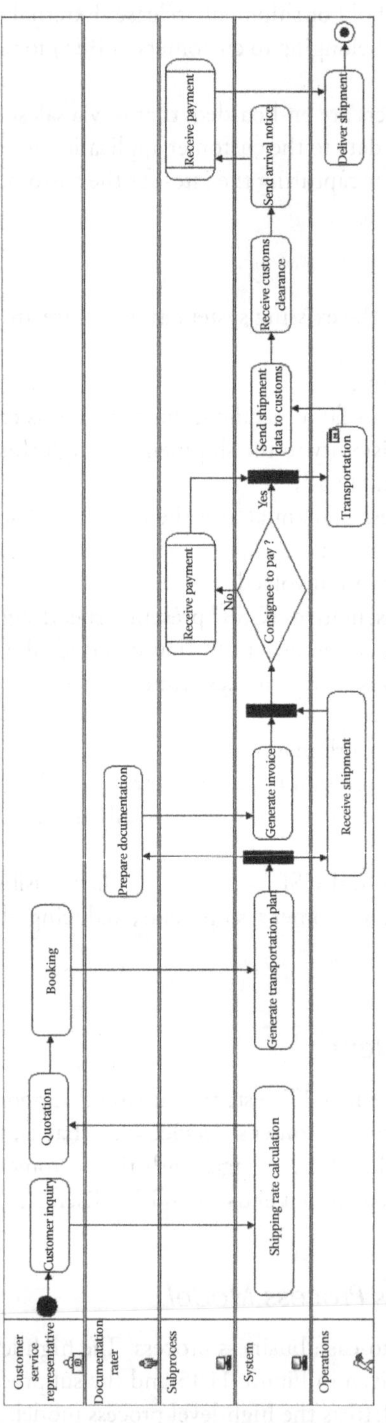

Figure 11.15 Order-to-cash high-level process model.

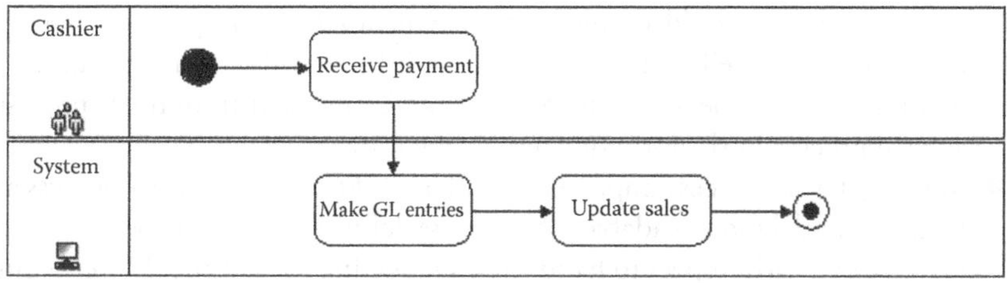

Figure 11.16 Receive payment high-level process model.

While doing this process design, it is important not to get influenced by the functionalities currently being provided by the existing applications. It is best to design the process as if it is a new one—from scratch. We identify the following user activities: customer enquiry, quotation, booking, prepare documentation, receive shipment, transportation, receive payment, and deliver shipment. We also identify the roles performing them: customer service representative, documentation rater, cashier, and operations. To identify the user activities, we follow the same approach as that was taken in the first case study.

We come up with the following system activities: shipment rate calculation, generate transportation plan, generate invoice, send shipment data to customs, receive customs clearance, send arrival notice, make GL entries, and update sales.

The activity names for all the activities in the process are self-explanatory and thus give an idea of the business function/operation that is performed as part of carrying out the activity.

Receiving payment from the customer involves a set of activities and this has been made a subprocess and it is being invoked from the order-to-call process at appropriate points. The philosophy behind this decision is as follows:

- Payment is not a single activity since it involves multiple distinct business functions such as collecting the payment, and accounting/bookkeeping activities associated with the transaction. Also, in this enterprise, sales would like to be appraised of and capture the details from the perspective of that specific customer. Therefore, this is also part of the payment procedure. It can technically thus be a process on its own.
- Payment is a procedure that is relevant to not just the order-to-cash process alone. It can very well apply or be used in other processes that involve any kind of collection work. For example, there could be a periodic process to collect amounts related to open items (outstanding amounts) from customers. As part of such a process, one step could be this payment procedure. BES may have other services that it provides to customers, such as "collect export item value from consignee on delivery," "logistics services for retailers," and "container leasing services" to name a few. Each of them is ideally a separate

process and they would all involve the payment step. Thus, payment is a separate process by itself and we are enabling it be reused by other processes by making it an independent process that can be invoked from other processes as a subprocess in the form of a service invocation.

- Making it a subprocess improves modularity of the order to cash process and make its model more readable. The process definition therefore becomes more manageable with respect to handling its modeling complexity. More so, since the payment step occurs in the process at multiple points and repeating the entire set of steps belonging to payment at each of these points would make the process model cluttered.

The process involves a rule check that determines the flow of the process. If the shipment charges are to be collected from the consignee and not from the shipper, then the package is shipped and delivered to the consignee before the payment is collected from the consignee. Instead, if the shipper pays the shipping charges, then the charges are collected by BES before the package is transported.

After sending the information on the shipment to the customs, the process flow will wait at the receive activity named receive customs clearance to receive the clearance from customs for the goods in this package. This activity completes only when the notification arrives from the customs system allowing the goods/package to be released for final delivery to the consignee.

This process also involves parallelization of activity executions at some points. After generating the transportation plan, the process flow can be split into two paths that can be executed in parallel (simultaneously)—these are the prepare documentation and the receive shipment steps. This is possible in the design because the two activities have no dependencies on each other and at that point their dependencies on the prior activities have already been satisfied so that they are ready to run. While the documentation rater prepares documentation, the operations team can go ahead with physically collecting the package (either pickup or receive) for shipment from the shipper. Operations need not wait for the documentation work to get over before picking up the package—both can be done concurrently. Generation of invoice step also belongs to the first of the parallel paths (the path that starts with prepare documentation) because it is also independent of the receive shipment activity.

11.3.4.2 Detailed Process Model

Figures 11.17 and 11.18 give the detailed level process model for the order-to-cash process. For each of the activities we define the corresponding business service that would perform the business function associated with the activity, specifying the input and output parameters for the service and the invocation pattern (invoke or receive) applicable for that activity. At this time too, we do not consider the existence of the current applications and the functions and services that they currently provide.

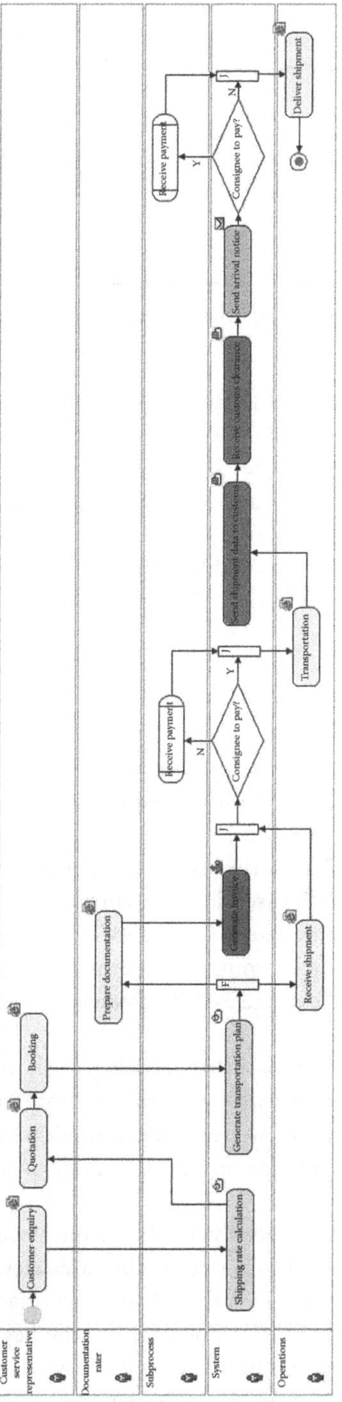

Figure 11.17 Order-to-cash detailed-level process model.

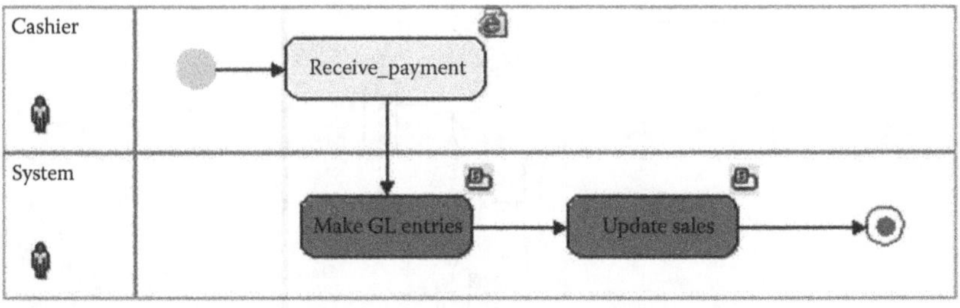

Figure 11.18 Receive payment detailed-level process model.

We define the process parameters. The shipment tracking number will be the unique business parameter that would identify each order-to-cash process instance uniquely. Each time a shipment order is made by the customer, a new process instance is created in the system and a new shipment tracking number is generated and associated with this process instance.

We define the expressions for the conditional branches. We define the subprocess invocation activity parameters and map this activity to the payment process definition.

11.3.4.3 Services Design

The business services required by the process are identified through the system activities in the detailed process definition. Through that we list the following services: shipment rate calculation service, transportation plan generation service, customs service for shipment data, customs clearance receipt service, arrival notice sending service, invoice generation service, GL entry service, and sales updating service. We apply SOA principles here for each service design by explicitly specifying the service interface separately from the implementation details. The guiding principle in this example is to leverage existing system assets (read applications) to the maximum extent possible.

For each of the services, we look in the existing applications such as pricing, sales, and others to see if they already provide, in some form, the business function associated with the service. That is, we see if those applications already expose the same service or, if not, at least similar services that perform similar business function that matches our service.

Another principle followed, especially for service interface definition, is to only specify those parameters as input and output that are relevant to the particular service's particular business function rather than providing all the data required by the function as input and, as far as possible, use the key business data of the process (such as shipment tracking number) that are available as process parameters as input to the service operation. The service implementation logic can get all the other related business data related to this specific business function from the application database. Parameters that are relevant to the specific business function and that are really data items can come only from other activities in the process (since they are mapped to application or business functions belonging to a different function group) should be defined as input parameters to the service. For example, origin and destination, which are business data coming from the customer enquiry activity, are defined as input parameters for the shipping rate calculation activity. This is because these two are separate business functions and thus share data through only the process. Whereas on the other hand, the receive payment user activity needs only the invoice number (a key process parameter) as input parameter and not all the invoice details such as the amount due or due date, because the activity is part of the receivables function and the activity that generated the invoice is also part of the receivables function group, and therefore all the details related to the invoice is available (for access) to the receive payment activity from the receivables data in the application database. The process need not be used as a conduit for data sharing here.

11.3.4.3.1 Shipping Rate Calculation Service

Since calculate rate is a pricing-related business function, we look at the pricing system. We find that it already exposes this function through an EJB component for the use of a web application, though the pricing system is basically a legacy application. We simply map the shipping rate calculation service in the process to this calculateRate EJB component (class name pricing.CalculateRateHome) belonging to the pricing application and its method named calculateRate (so the operation we associate with this service is calculateRate) after matching the input and output parameters of the service in the process with that of the EJB. The calculate rate operation takes in the origin, destination, commodity to be shipped, its weight, and the customer ID as the parameters and performs the rate calculation utilizing the data (such as rates, surcharges, and contracts) available in the pricing application database and also generates a quotation number for this since this is a quote request. These inputs will be supplied by the activity in the process. The operation then returns the price data as output through the parameters, transportation charge, other charges, quotation number, and the total amount to be paid. This is mentioned in the wsdl, ShippingRateCalculation.wsdl in Listing 11.1.

Listing 11.1

```
<?xml version="1.0" encoding="UTF-8"?>
<wsdl:definitions name="PricingPort"
xmlns:ejb="http://schemas.xmlsoap.org/wsdl/ejb/"
xmlns:format="http://schemas.xmlsoap.org/wsdl/formatbinding/"
targetNamespace="http://www.onlinebesservices.com/BPEL/
ordertocash"
```

```
xmlns:soapenc="http://schemas.xmlsoap.org/soap/encoding/"
xmlns:xsd="http://www.w3.org/2001/XMLSchema"
xmlns:soap="http://schemas.xmlsoap.org/wsdl/soap/"
xmlns:wsdl="http://schemas.xmlsoap.org/wsdl/"
xmlns="http://www.onlinebesservices.com/BPEL/extensions">
  <wsdl:message name="calculateRateResponse">
    <wsdl:part name="transportationCharge" type="xsd:float"/>
    <wsdl:part name="otherCharges" type="xsd:float"/>
    <wsdl:part name="quotationNumber" type="xsd:string"/>
    <wsdl:part name="totalAmount" type="xsd:float"/>
  </wsdl:message>
  <wsdl:message name="calculateRateRequest">
    <wsdl:part name="origin" type="xsd:string"/>
    <wsdl:part name="destination" type="xsd:string"/>
    <wsdl:part name="commodity" type="xsd:string"/>
    <wsdl:part name="weight" type="xsd:integer"/>
    <wsdl:part name="customerID" type="xsd:string"/>
  </wsdl:message>
  <wsdl:portType name="PricingPortPT">
    <wsdl:operation name="calculateRate" parameterOrder="origin
    destination commodity weight customerID">
      <wsdl:input name="calculateRateRequest"
message="calculateRateRequest"/>
      <wsdl:output name="calculateRateResponse"
message="calculateRateResponse"/>
    </wsdl:operation>
  </wsdl:portType>
  <wsdl:binding name="PricingPortBinding" type="PricingPortPT">
      <ejb:binding/>
        <format:typeMapping style="Java" encoding="Java">
          <format:typeMap typeName="xsd:string"
formatType="java.lang.String"/>
        </format:typeMapping>
    <wsdl:operation name="calculateRate">
      <ejb:operation methodName="calculateRate" interface="remote"
parameterOrder="origin destination commodity weight customerID"/>
      <wsdl:input name="calculateRateRequest">
      </wsdl:input>
      <wsdl:output name="calculateRateResponse">
      </wsdl:output>
    </wsdl:operation>
  </wsdl:binding>
  <wsdl:service name="ShippingRateCalculation">
    <wsdl:port name="PricingPort" binding="PricingPortBinding">
      <ejb:address className="pricing.CalculateRateHome"
jndiName="pricing/CalculateRate"/>
    </wsdl:port>
  </wsdl:service>
</wsdl:definitions>
```

11.3.4.3.2 Generate Transportation Plan Service

This service is expected to execute logic that would come up with a transportation plan for the package after considering the equipment (carriers) data such as trucks, cargo trains, containers, aircrafts, ships data, the available/defined routes, equipment schedules, costs related to the routes and equipments, and data about points such as ports and terminals. It takes in just the shipment tracking number, which would help it uniquely identify a shipment order and get the relevant details from it such as the origin, destination, and item as input and returns the plan for transportation including the number of legs, planned delivery date (estimated), routing information, and package to carrier mapping. Another way would have been to expect origin, destination, package size, weight, and shipment item as input for the service operation and define it that way. Here, we go with the tracking number input instead, because this service is in the context of booking functionality and so with this number all other details related to the shipment can be got by the service implementation from the application database.

This is a booking-related business function and so we look in the BAP system for this service since this system has been responsible for bookings management. It is a legacy system based on mainframe. We find that it indeed supports this business function; however, it is accessed internally from the legacy screen and the logic is coupled to the legacy screens. Thus, it is not exposed to other applications right now. We decide to define this as a new service and implement it as a component (EJB) since the enterprise already has a JEE environment in place, which is being made use of by the current web application. This booking EJB component for generating the transportation plan would make use of Java Connector Architecture (JCA) for integrating with the mainframe BAP application. On the mainframe side of BAP, we design a new program that would hold the logic for using all the relevant data and compute the transportation plan. As part of implementation, this mainframe program would be a new program that will involve development; however, we can reuse a good amount of code (though in pieces as the logic is currently intertwined in different programs) from the existing BAP programs that support this function. It needs to be made sure that we explicitly remove or avoid adding any code that takes care of process logic—for example, sending data to another application or a different business function through any means, or relinquishing control to other systems (of other departments especially), say receivables or coordinating function calls to multiple applications for multiple business functions.

The WSDL for the service is given in Listing 11.2.

Listing 11.2

```
<?xml version="1.0" encoding="UTF-8"?>
<wsdl:definitions name="BookingPort"
xmlns:ejb="http://schemas.xmlsoap.org/wsdl/ejb/"
xmlns:format="http://schemas.xmlsoap.org/wsdl/formatbinding/"
targetNamespace="http://www.onlinebesservices.com/BPEL/
ordertocash"
```

```
xmlns:soapenc="http://schemas.xmlsoap.org/soap/encoding/"
xmlns:xsd="http://www.w3.org/2001/XMLSchema"
xmlns:soap="http://schemas.xmlsoap.org/wsdl/soap/"
xmlns:wsdl="http://schemas.xmlsoap.org/wsdl/"
xmlns="http://www.onlinebesservices.com/BPEL/extensions">
  <wsdl:message name="generateTransportPlanResponse">
    <wsdl:part name="numOfLegs" type="xsd:integer"/>
    <wsdl:part name="plannedDeliveryDate" type="xsd:string"/>
    <wsdl:part name="routing" type="xsd:string"/>
    <wsdl:part name="packageToCarriageMappings"
      type="xsd:string"/>
  </wsdl:message>
  <wsdl:message name="generateTransportPlanRequest">
    <wsdl:part name="shipmentTrackingNumber"
      type="xsd:string"/>
  </wsdl:message>
  <wsdl:portType name="BookingPortPT">
    <wsdl:operation name="generateTransportPlan"
parameterOrder="shipmentTrackingNumber">
      <wsdl:input name="generateTransportPlanRequest"
message="generateTransportPlanRequest"/>
      <wsdl:output name="generateTransportPlanResponse"
message="generateTransportPlanResponse"/>
    </wsdl:operation>
  </wsdl:portType>
  <wsdl:binding name="BookingPortBinding" type="BookingPortPT">
      <ejb:binding/>
        <format:typeMapping style="Java" encoding="Java">
          <format:typeMap typeName="xsd:string"
formatType="java.lang.String"/>
        </format:typeMapping>
    <wsdl:operation name="generateTransportPlan">
      <ejb:operation methodName="generateTransportPlan"
        interface="remote"
parameterOrder="shipmentTrackingNumber"/>
      <wsdl:input name="generateTransportPlanRequest">
      </wsdl:input>
      <wsdl:output name="generateTransportPlanResponse">
      </wsdl:output>
    </wsdl:operation>
  </wsdl:binding>
  <wsdl:service name="GenerateTransportationPlan">
    <wsdl:port name="BookingPort" binding="BookingPortBinding">
      <ejb:address className="booking.GenerateTransportPlanHome"
jndiName="booking/generateTransportPlan"/>
    </wsdl:port>
  </wsdl:service>
</wsdl:definitions>
```

11.3.4.3.3 Send Shipment Data to Customs Service

This involves an external service—the service provided by the customs department. So here, we pick up the service that is exposed by the customs department for the purpose of informing customs of arrival of the shipment package to the destination country entry port.

The WSDL for the service is given in Listing 11.3 as imagined to be provided by customs (this WSDL is only a hypothetical one just to serve as an example in the case study and is not to be taken as the real WSDL for customs operations). We then make the input/output activity parameters aligned to the input/output parameters defined for the inform Customs operation in the service definition.

Listing 11.3

```
<?xml version="1.0" encoding="UTF-8"?>
<wsdl:definitions name="CustomsPort"
targetNamespace="http://www.onlinebesservices.com/BPEL/
ordertocash"
xmlns:soapenc="http://schemas.xmlsoap.org/soap/encoding/"
xmlns:xsd="http://www.w3.org/2001/XMLSchema"
xmlns:soap="http://schemas.xmlsoap.org/wsdl/soap/"
xmlns:wsdl="http://schemas.xmlsoap.org/wsdl/"
xmlns="http://www.onlinebesservices.com/BPEL/extensions">
  <wsdl:message name="informCustomsRequest">
    <wsdl:part name="shipper" type="xsd:string"/>
    <wsdl:part name="consignee" type="xsd:string"/>
    <wsdl:part name="totalShipmentValueForCustoms"
    type="xsd:float"/>
    <wsdl:part name="shipmentInfo" type="xsd:string"/>
    <wsdl:part name="mainfest" type="xsd:string"/>
    <wsdl:part name="shipmentRefereneForCustoms"
    type="xsd:string"/>
  </wsdl:message>
  <wsdl:portType name="CustomsPortPT">
    <wsdl:operation name="informCustoms">
      <wsdl:input name="informCustomsRequest"
message="informCustomsRequest"/>
    </wsdl:operation>
  </wsdl:portType>
  <wsdl:binding name="CustomsPortBinding"
  type="CustomsPortPT">
    <soap:binding style="document"
  transport="http://schemas.xmlsoap.org/soap/http"/>
    <wsdl:operation name="informCustoms">
      <soap:operation soapAction=""/>
```

```
    <wsdl:input name="informCustomsRequest">
      <soap:body use="literal"/>
    </wsdl:input>
   </wsdl:operation>
  </wsdl:binding>
  <wsdl:service name="SendShipmentDataToCustoms">
   <wsdl:port name="CustomsPort" binding="CustomsPortBinding">
    <soap:address
location="http://www.onlinecustomsservices.com/
InformCustoms"/>
    </wsdl:port>
  </wsdl:service>
</wsdl:definitions>
```

This service operation is a one-way invocation pattern (asynchronous)—the activity invokes the service by passing the informCustomsRequest input parameter data that includes shipper/consignee names, total declared shipment value for customs purposes, information about the shipment/package/cargo, the manifest prepared for the customs perusal, and the reference data (e.g., shipment tracking number) that is associated with the shipment that the customs system can later use to send back in response for identifying this particular shipment. As we can see, this service is exposed as a web service by the customs department system. An easily understandable decision since multiple systems from different transportation service providers such as BES would be expected to invoke this service and they may all be in disparate technologies. Therefore, web services, which is a standard, better fits here.

11.3.4.3.4 Receive Customs Clearance Service

This is a service the process (read our new order-to-cash system) provides to the external systems (the customs department system in this case) to notify it in case of customs clearance for the package. It is a receive type activity and follows the notification pattern of integration. The moment the control comes to this activity in the process, the activity just waits for the notification message to come from the customs. It would take as input the reference number (which is actually the same shipment tracking number that was sent to customs in the send shipment data to customs activity of this process instance) and customs cleared flag that indicates that customs has cleared the shipment. This reference number parameter is used by the order-to-cash system to correlate the notification message to the process instance that has the same shipment tracking number value as that in the reference number parameter. The activity hands over this input data to the process and gets completed right away with no further function. The process flow then proceeds to the next activity in the order. This service does not return any parameter to the invoker (the customs system). The WSDL for the service is given in Listing 11.4.

Listing 11.4

```
<?xml version="1.0" encoding="UTF-8"?>
<wsdl:definitions name="OrderToCash"
targetNamespace="http://www.onlinebesservices.com/BPEL/
ordertocash"
xmlns:soapenc="http://schemas.xmlsoap.org/soap/encoding/"
xmlns:xsd="http://www.w3.org/2001/XMLSchema"
xmlns:prefix="http://www.w3.org/2001/XMLSchema"
xmlns:soap="http://schemas.xmlsoap.org/wsdl/soap/"
xmlns:jms="http://schemas.xmlsoap.org/wsdl/jms/"
xmlns:wsdl="http://schemas.xmlsoap.org/wsdl/"
xmlns="http://www.onlinebesservices.com/BPEL/extensions">
  <wsdl:message name="start_OrderToCashRequest">
  </wsdl:message>
  <wsdl:message name="ReceiveCustomsClearanceRequest">
    <wsdl:part name="customsCleared" type="xsd:boolean"/>
    <wsdl:part name="shipmentTrackingNum" type="xsd:string"/>
  </wsdl:message>
  <wsdl:message name="start_OrderToCashResponse">
    <wsdl:part name="processid" type="xsd:string"/>
  </wsdl:message>
  <wsdl:portType name="ReceiveCustomsClearancePT">
    <wsdl:operation name="ReceiveCustomsClearance">
        <wsdl:input name="ReceiveCustomsClearanceRequest"
message="ReceiveCustomsClearanceRequest"/>
    </wsdl:operation>
  </wsdl:portType>
  <wsdl:portType name="start_OrderToCashPT">
    <wsdl:operation name="start_OrderToCash">
      <wsdl:output name="start_OrderToCashResponse"
message="start_OrderToCashResponse"/>
    </wsdl:operation>
  </wsdl:portType>
  <wsdl:binding name="start_OrderToCashBinding"
  type="start_OrderToCashPT">
    <soap:binding style="document"
transport="http://schemas.xmlsoap.org/soap/http"/>
    <wsdl:operation name="start_OrderToCash">
      <soap:operation soapAction=""/>
      <wsdl:input name="start_OrderToCashRequest">
        <soap:body use="literal"/>
      </wsdl:input>
      <wsdl:output name="start_OrderToCashResponse">
        <soap:body use="literal"/>
      </wsdl:output>
      </wsdl:operation>
  </wsdl:binding>
  <wsdl:binding name="ReceiveCustomsClearanceBinding"
```

```
type="ReceiveCustomsClearancePT">
    <soap:binding style="document"
transport="http://schemas.xmlsoap.org/soap/http"/>
    <wsdl:operation name="ReceiveCustomsClearance">
      <soap:operation soapAction=""/>
      <wsdl:input name="ReceiveCustomsClearanceRequest">
        <soap:body use="literal"/>
      </wsdl:input>
    </wsdl:operation>
  </wsdl:binding>
  <wsdl:service name="start_OrderToCash">
    <wsdl:port name="start_OrderToCash"
    binding="start_OrderToCashBinding">
      <soap:address
location="http://internalbesservices/shipmentsvcs/
start_OrderToCash"/>
    </wsdl:port>
  </wsdl:service>
  <wsdl:service name="ReceiveCustomsClearance">
    <wsdl:port name="ReceiveCustomsClearance"
binding="ReceiveCustomsClearanceBinding">
      <soap:address
location="http://www.onlinebesservices.com/shipmentsvcs/
ReceiveCustomsClearance"/>
    </wsdl:port>
  </wsdl:service>
</wsdl:definitions>
```

This service is implemented by the order-to-cash system as an http/SOAP-based web service since this is invoked by external systems and we do not have any control over the technology platform used by those systems. Thus, a standard protocol in the form of web services suits the invocation better with good isolation from technology changes on both sides.

11.3.4.3.5 Make GL Entries Service

This service is a finance bookkeeping-related service. Thus, it is part of the finance function group. It updates the general ledger with the entries for the payment transaction for this shipment. The service is a generic service that the finance G/L system provides for capturing any financial transaction in BES for accounting. Order-to-cash is just one of the processes in BES that would invoke this service. The operation takes as input transaction details such as transaction number, date, amount, and the type (e.g., "payment" since this transaction is a payment transaction) and records this in the G/L with appropriate entries and enables further accounting. It is a one-way type invocation pattern operation (asynchronous) and so there are no parameters returned by the service to the caller.

The WSDL is shown in Listing 11.5.

Listing 11.5

```
<?xml version="1.0" encoding="UTF-8"?>
<wsdl:definitions name="GLPort"
targetNamespace="http://www.onlinebesservices.com/BPEL/
ordertocash"
xmlns:soapenc="http://schemas.xmlsoap.org/soap/encoding/"
xmlns:xsd="http://www.w3.org/2001/XMLSchema"
xmlns:soap="http://schemas.xmlsoap.org/wsdl/soap/"
xmlns:wsdl="http://schemas.xmlsoap.org/wsdl/"
xmlns="http://www.onlinebesservices.com/BPEL/extensions">
  <wsdl:message name="makeGLEntryRequest">
    <wsdl:part name="transactionNumber" type="xsd:string"/>
    <wsdl:part name="transactionDate" type="xsd:string"/>
    <wsdl:part name="transactionAmount" type="xsd:string"/>
    <wsdl:part name="transactionType" type="xsd:string"/>
    <wsdl:part name="customerID" type="xsd:string"/>
    <wsdl:part name="reference" type="xsd:string"/>
  </wsdl:message>
  <wsdl:portType name="GLPortPT">
    <wsdl:operation name="makeGLEntry">
      <wsdl:input name="makeGLEntryRequest"
      message="makeGLEntryRequest"/>
    </wsdl:operation>
  </wsdl:portType>
  <wsdl:binding name="GLPortBinding" type="GLPortPT">
    <soap:binding style="document"
transport="http://schemas.xmlsoap.org/soap/http"/>
    <wsdl:operation name="makeGLEntry">
      <soap:operation soapAction=""/>
      <wsdl:input name="makeGLEntryRequest">
        <soap:body use="literal"/>
      </wsdl:input>
    </wsdl:operation>
  </wsdl:binding>
  <wsdl:service name="MakeGLEntries">
    <wsdl:port name="GLPort" binding="GLPortBinding">
      <soap:address location="http://internalbesservices/GL/
        MakeGLEntries"/>
    </wsdl:port>
  </wsdl:service>
</wsdl:definitions>
```

This being a finance function, we expect this service to be provided by the G/L system. The G/L system in BES is an application package that is based on its own technology platform. It currently provides a native API that performs the G/L entry functionality. Also, the parameters it uses do not directly match fully with the service definition we have come up with above (which is a generic definition that can apply in other contexts also), data format wise as well as quantum of information wise. We design a new service component to service-enable this API and it should be also one that accepts these parameters so that the service is reusable in different processes of BES. We implement it as a web service for better interoperability with other systems/processes and use HTTP as transport protocol and SOAP as the message protocol. The new component is built on top of the G/L system by extending it and using its existing APIs. The component (G/L comp) can be designed as a program implemented in the same technology as the package using the package's own extension mechanisms. It would have the necessary business logic coded to invoke the appropriate APIs of the G/L in the required order and transform parameter data into the formats expected by the package. We can implement the web service in the form of a JAVA servlet running in the web server and the servlet can be made to invoke the new G/L comp for the service execution.

11.3.4.3.6 Update Sales Service

This sales service involves the business function of capturing the sales information for the customer placing the shipping order and for further sales-related processing that is involved. The operation here is enter sales data and it takes sales data such as customer id, amount of sales (shipping charges paid), date, shipment tracking number, and payment date as input. This is also a one-way operation (asynchronous)—does not return any parameters. The WSDL is given in Listing 11.6.

Listing 11.6

```
<?xml version="1.0" encoding="UTF-8"?>
<wsdl:definitions name="SalesPort"
targetNamespace="http://www.onlinebesservices.com/BPEL/
ordertocash"
xmlns:soapenc="http://schemas.xmlsoap.org/soap/encoding/"
xmlns:xsd="http://www.w3.org/2001/XMLSchema"
xmlns:soap="http://schemas.xmlsoap.org/wsdl/soap/"
xmlns:wsdl="http://schemas.xmlsoap.org/wsdl/"
xmlns="http://www.onlinebesservices.com/BPEL/extensions">
  <wsdl:message name="enterSalesDataRequest">
    <wsdl:part name="customerID" type="xsd:string"/>
    <wsdl:part name="salesAmount" type="xsd:string"/>
    <wsdl:part name="salesDate" type="xsd:string"/>
    <wsdl:part name="shipmentNumber" type="xsd:string"/>
    <wsdl:part name="paymentReceivedDate" type="xsd:string"/>
  </wsdl:message>
  <wsdl:portType name="SalesPT">
    <wsdl:operation name="enterSalesData">
      <wsdl:input name="enterSalesDataRequest"
```

```
message="enterSalesDataRequest"/>
    </wsdl:operation>
  </wsdl:portType>
  <wsdl:binding name="SalesPortBinding" type="SalesPT">
    <soap:binding style="document"
transport="http://schemas.xmlsoap.org/soap/http"/>
    <wsdl:operation name="enterSalesData">
      <soap:operation soapAction=""/>
      <wsdl:input name="enterSalesDataRequest">
        <soap:body use="literal"/>
      </wsdl:input>
    </wsdl:operation>
  </wsdl:binding>
  <wsdl:service name="UpdateSales">
    <wsdl:port name="SalesPort" binding="SalesPortBinding">
      <soap:address location="http://internalbesservices/Sales/
        UpdateSales"/>
    </wsdl:port>
  </wsdl:service>
</wsdl:definitions>
```

We look in the sales application to see if such a service is available. It is a legacy system built in-house on top of Oracle and PowerBuilder. We find that it already provides the function through a legacy API. To make it more interoperable, we decide to service-enable this legacy system and thereby expose the API as a new service. Since the technology involved is different, we rely on standards to ease the invocation and loose-couple it by exposing the new service as a web service on HTTP/SOAP protocols. We implement the web service as a Java servlet, design a service wrapper to wrap the legacy API, and expose it as an invocable service using XML for the data interchange. The only development effort involved here would be to write the minimal code for the servlet and to write a small Java component that would act as a wrapper for the legacy API. The business functionality would still continue to be provided by the sales system's legacy API.

11.3.4.3.7 Generate Invoice Service

This service automatically generates invoice for the shipment booking made. It is designed to take as input shipment tracking number and details such as whom to be billed, waybill number, amount to be paid, and different charges included in the amount as input to generate the invoice. It outputs the invoice generated with a unique invoice number. This is a receivables function and so we look in the receivables system to see if such a service exists. The receivables application is an in-house developed application based on Java. It has a web application (as JSPs, Java Servlets, and plain Java code) part that is client–server based. There are, currently, batch programs that perform a major portion of invoicing function. So, we decide to design a POJO (Plain Old Java Object) kind of Java class bes.receivables.Invoicing that would perform the invoicing function as a java service. We get the existing code from the batch programs and the web application Java code extracted and reuse it in the new POJO service object to quickly create it. This service is associated with the generate invoice activity in the process.

The WSDL for the service is shown as part of Listing 11.7. The operation name is GenerateInvoice.

Listing 11.7

```
<?xml version="1.0" encoding="UTF-8"?>
<wsdl:definitions
  targetNamespace="http://www.onlinebesservices.com/BPEL/
  ordertocash"
  xmlns="http://www.onlinebesservices.com/BPEL/extensions"
  xmlns:bpws="http://docs.oasis-open.org/wsbpel/2.0/process/
  executable"
  xmlns:wsdl="http://schemas.xmlsoap.org/wsdl/"
  xmlns:xsd="http://www.w3.org/2001/XMLSchema"
  xmlns:xsi="http://www.w3.org/2001/XMLSchema-instance"
xsi:schemaLocation="http://schemas.xmlsoap.org/wsdl/wsdl.xml">
  <bpws:property name="shipmentTrackingNumber" type="xsd:string"/>
  <bpws:propertyAlias messageType="BookingOutParams"
    part="shipmentTrackingNumber"
    propertyName="shipmentTrackingNumber"/>
  <bpws:propertyAlias messageType="ReceiveCustomsClearanceOut
    Params"
    part="shipmentTrackingNum"
    propertyName="shipmentTrackingNumber"/>
  <wsdl:message name="ReceivePaymentInParams">
    <wsdl:part name="invoiceNumber" type="xsd:string"/>
  </wsdl:message>
  <wsdl:message name="ReceivePaymentOutParams">
    <wsdl:part name="paymentReceived" type="xsd:boolean"/>
  </wsdl:message>
  <wsdl:message name="CustomerEnquiryOutParams">
    <wsdl:part name="origin" type="xsd:string"/>
    <wsdl:part name="destination" type="xsd:string"/>
    <wsdl:part name="commodity" type="xsd:string"/>
    <wsdl:part name="weight" type="xsd:integer"/>
  <wsdl:part name="customerID" type="xsd:string"/>
  </wsdl:message>
  <wsdl:message name="QuotationInParams">
    <wsdl:part name="quotationNumber" type="xsd:string"/>
    <wsdl:part name="totalAmount" type="xsd:float"/>
  </wsdl:message>
  <wsdl:message name="QuotationOutParams"/>
  <wsdl:message name="BookingInParams">
```

```
    <wsdl:part name="customerID" type="xsd:string"/>
    <wsdl:part name="quotationNumber" type="xsd:string"/>
  </wsdl:message>
  <wsdl:message name="BookingOutParams">
    <wsdl:part name="shipper" type="xsd:string"/>
    <wsdl:part name="recipient" type="xsd:string"/>
    <wsdl:part name="billTherecipient" type="xsd:boolean"/>
    <wsdl:part name="shipmentInfo" type="xsd:string"/>
    <wsdl:part name="valueForCustoms" type="xsd:float"/>
    <wsdl:part name="shippersReference" type="xsd:string"/>
    <wsdl:part name="customersInternalBillingReference"
type="xsd:string"/>
    <wsdl:part name="shipmentTrackingNumber"
    type="xsd:string"/>
    <wsdl:part name="shipperAddress" type="xsd:string"/>
    <wsdl:part name="recipientAddress" type="xsd:string"/>
    <wsdl:part name="shipperEmail" type="xsd:string"/>
    <wsdl:part name="recipientEmail" type="xsd:string"/>
  </wsdl:message>
  <wsdl:message name="PrepareDocumentationInParams">
    <wsdl:part name="shipmentTrackingNumber" type="xsd:string"/>
    <wsdl:part name="customerID" type="xsd:string"/>
    <wsdl:part name="shipper" type="xsd:string"/>
    <wsdl:part name="recipient" type="xsd:string"/>
    <wsdl:part name="shipmentDetails" type="xsd:string"/>
    <wsdl:part name="billTherecipient" type="xsd:boolean"/>
    <wsdl:part name="shippersReference" type="xsd:string"/>
    <wsdl:part name="shippersInternalReference"
    type="xsd:string"/>
    <wsdl:part name="origin" type="xsd:string"/>
    <wsdl:part name="destination" type="xsd:string"/>
    <wsdl:part name="routing" type="xsd:string"/>
    <wsdl:part name="shipperAddress" type="xsd:string"/>
    <wsdl:part name="recipientAddress" type="xsd:string"/>
  </wsdl:message>
  <wsdl:message name="PrepareDocumentationOutParams">
    <wsdl:part name="wayBillNumber" type="xsd:string"/>
    <wsdl:part name="wayBillDate" type="xsd:string"/>
    <wsdl:part name="otherDocumentationAttached"
    type="xsd:string"/>
    <wsdl:part name="customsManifestData" type="xsd:string"/>
  </wsdl:message>
  <wsdl:message name="GenerateInvoiceInParams">
    <wsdl:part name="shipmentTrackingNumber"
    type="xsd:string"/>
    <wsdl:part name="billTherecipient" type="xsd:boolean"/>
    <wsdl:part name="wayBillNumber" type="xsd:string"/>
    <wsdl:part name="plannedDeliveryDate" type="xsd:string"/>
```

```
  <wsdl:part name="totalAmount" type="xsd:float"/>
  <wsdl:part name="transportationCharge" type="xsd:float"/>
  <wsdl:part name="otherCharges" type="xsd:float"/>
  <wsdl:part name="customerID" type="xsd:string"/>
</wsdl:message>
<wsdl:message name="GenerateInvoiceOutParams">
  <wsdl:part name="invoiceNumber" type="xsd:string"/>
</wsdl:message>
<wsdl:message name="ReceiveShipmentInParams">
  <wsdl:part name="shipmentTrackingNumber"
  type="xsd:string"/>
  <wsdl:part name="shipmentInfo" type="xsd:string"/>
</wsdl:message>
<wsdl:message name="ReceiveShipmentOutParams">
  <wsdl:part name="packageReceivedForShipping"
  type="xsd:boolean"/>
</wsdl:message>
<wsdl:message name="TransportationInParams">
  <wsdl:part name="shipmentTrackingNumber"
  type="xsd:string"/>
  <wsdl:part name="customerID" type="xsd:string"/>
  <wsdl:part name="recipientAddress" type="xsd:string"/>
  <wsdl:part name="legs" type="xsd:integer"/>
  <wsdl:part name="routing" type="xsd:string"/>
  <wsdl:part name="plannedDeliveryDate" type="xsd:string"/>
  <wsdl:part name="packageToCarriageMappings"
  type="xsd:string"/>
</wsdl:message>
<wsdl:message name="TransportationOutParams"/>
<wsdl:message name="SendMailInParams">
  <wsdl:part name="To" type="xsd:string"/>
  <wsdl:part name="Cc" type="xsd:string"/>
  <wsdl:part name="Bcc" type="xsd:string"/>
  <wsdl:part name="Subject" type="xsd:string"/>
  <wsdl:part name="Body" type="xsd:string"/>
</wsdl:message>
<wsdl:message name="DeliverShipmentInParams">
  <wsdl:part name="shipmentTrackingNumber"
  type="xsd:string"/>
</wsdl:message>
<wsdl:portType name="OrderToCashUserActionsPT">
  <wsdl:operation name="customerEnquiry">
    <wsdl:input message="CustomerEnquiryInParams"/>
    <wsdl:output message="CustomerEnquiryOutParams"/>
  </wsdl:operation>
  <wsdl:operation name="shippingRateCalculation">
    <wsdl:input message="ShippingRateCalculationInParams"/>
    <wsdl:output message="ShippingRateCalculationOutParams"/>
  </wsdl:operation>
```

```
    <wsdl:operation name="quotation">
      <wsdl:input message="QuotationInParams"/>
      <wsdl:output message="QuotationOutParams"/>
    </wsdl:operation>
    <wsdl:operation name="booking">
      <wsdl:input message="BookingInParams"/>
      <wsdl:output message="BookingOutParams"/>
    </wsdl:operation>
    <wsdl:operation name="PrepareDocumentation">
      <wsdl:input message="PrepareDocumentationInParams"/>
      <wsdl:output message="PrepareDocumentationOutParams"/>
    </wsdl:operation>
    <wsdl:operation name="ReceiveShipment">
      <wsdl:input message="ReceiveShipmentInParams"/>
      <wsdl:output message="ReceiveShipmentOutParams"/>
    </wsdl:operation>
    <wsdl:operation name="Transportation">
      <wsdl:input message="TransportationInParams"/>
      <wsdl:output message="TransportationOutParams"/>
    </wsdl:operation>
    <wsdl:operation name="DeliverShipment">
      <wsdl:input message="DeliverShipmentInParams"/>
      <wsdl:output message="DeliverShipmentOutParams"/>
    </wsdl:operation>
  </wsdl:portType>
    <wsdl:portType name="ReceivablesPT">
      <wsdl:operation name="GenerateInvoice">
        <wsdl:input message="GenerateInvoiceInParams"/>
        <wsdl:output message="GenerateInvoiceOutParams"/>
      </wsdl:operation>
    </wsdl:portType>
    <wsdl:portType name="EmailPortPT">
        <wsdl:operation name="sendMail">
                <wsdl:input message="SendMailInParams"/>
        </wsdl:operation>
    </wsdl:portType>
</wsdl:definitions>
<?xml version="1.0" encoding="UTF-8"?>
<wsdl:definitions
  targetNamespace="http://www.onlinebesservices.com/BPEL/
  ordertocash"
  xmlns="http://www.onlinebesservices.com/BPEL/extensions"
  xmlns:bpws="http://docs.oasis-open.org/wsbpel/2.0/process/
  executable"
  xmlns:wsdl="http://schemas.xmlsoap.org/wsdl/"
  xmlns:xsd="http://www.w3.org/2001/XMLSchema"
  xmlns:xsi="http://www.w3.org/2001/XMLSchema-instance"
xsi:schemaLocation="http://schemas.xmlsoap.org/wsdl/wsdl.xml">
  <wsdl:message name="Receive_PaymentInParams">
```

```
    <wsdl:part name="invoiceNumber" type="xsd:string"/>
  </wsdl:message>
  <wsdl:message name="Receive_PaymentOutParams">
    <wsdl:part name="totalPymtAmount" type="xsd:string"/>
    <wsdl:part name="payorName" type="xsd:string"/>
    <wsdl:part name="paymentDate" type="xsd:string"/>
    <wsdl:part name="paymentNumber" type="xsd:string"/>
    <wsdl:part name="customerID" type="xsd:string"/>
    <wsdl:part name="shipmentTrackingNumber"
    type="xsd:string"/>
    <wsdl:part name="shippingOrderDate" type="xsd:string"/>
  </wsdl:message>
  <wsdl:portType name="ReceivePaymentUserActionsPT">
    <wsdl:operation name="Receive_Payment">
      <wsdl:input message="Receive_PaymentInParams"/>
      <wsdl:output message="Receive_PaymentOutParams"/>
    </wsdl:operation>
  </wsdl:portType>
</wsdl:definitions>
```

11.3.4.3.8 Send Arrival Notice Service

Sending arrival notice is a one-way operation (asynchronous) that involves sending mail to the consignee alerting them of the arrival of the shipped package. The service is a generic e-mail service that is reusable in any process context where e-mails have to be sent automatically. It takes the recipient e-mail address, cc e-mail address, bcc e-mail address, subject of mail, and body of mail as input and sends the mail. In this activity, we map the consignee e-mail address to the recipient address, shipper e-mail address to the cc, and put arrival-related text in the subject and the body. Since this is a generic service, it would exist as part of the infrastructure layer of the architecture.

The WSDL is shown in Listing 11.7, the operation is sendMail.

11.3.4.3.9 Receive Payment Subprocess Call

The subprocess activity named "receive payment," in the order-to-cash process invokes the subprocess as a service just like any other service. The WSDL for the receive payment process service is given in Listing 11.8. The operation is start_ReceivePayment.

Listing 11.8

```
<?xml version="1.0" encoding="UTF-8"?>
<wsdl:definitions name="ReceivePayment"
   targetNamespace="http://www.onlinebesservices.com/BPEL/
   ordertocash"
```

```
xmlns:soapenc="http://schemas.xmlsoap.org/soap/encoding/"
   xmlns:xsd="http://www.w3.org/2001/XMLSchema"
xmlns:prefix="http://www.w3.org/2001/XMLSchema"
   xmlns:soap="http://schemas.xmlsoap.org/wsdl/soap/"
xmlns:jms="http://schemas.xmlsoap.org/wsdl/jms/"
   xmlns:wsdl="http://schemas.xmlsoap.org/wsdl/"
xmlns="http://www.onlinebesservices.com/BPEL/extensions">
  <wsdl:message name="start_ReceivePaymentRequest">
    <wsdl:part name="invoiceNumber" type="xsd:string"/>
  </wsdl:message>
  <wsdl:message name="start_ReceivePaymentResponse">
    <wsdl:part name="paymentReceived" type="xsd:boolean"/>
  </wsdl:message>
  <wsdl:portType name="ReceivablesPT">
    <wsdl:operation name="start_ReceivePayment"
parameterOrder="invoiceNumber">
      <wsdl:input message="start_ReceivePaymentRequest"/>
      <wsdl:output message="start_ReceivePaymentResponse"/>
    </wsdl:operation>
  </wsdl:portType>
  <wsdl:binding name="start_ReceivePaymentBinding"
  type="ReceivablesPT">
    <soap:binding style="document"
transport="http://schemas.xmlsoap.org/soap/http"/>
    <wsdl:operation name="start_ReceivePayment">
      <soap:operation soapAction=""/>
      <wsdl:input name="start_ReceivePaymentRequest">
        <soap:body use="literal"/>
      </wsdl:input>
      <wsdl:output name="start_ReceivePaymentResponse">
        <soap:body use="literal"/>
      </wsdl:output>
    </wsdl:operation>
  </wsdl:binding>
  <wsdl:service name="start_ReceivePayment">
    <wsdl:port name="start_ReceivePayment"
binding="start_ReceivePaymentBinding">
        <soap:address
location="http://internalbesservices/receivablessvcs/
start_ReceivePayment"/>
    </wsdl:port>
  </wsdl:service>
</wsdl:definitions>
```

11.3.4.4 User Activities

User activities for the process are defined in the form of WSDL-based services. It is listed in WSDL code Listing 11.7.

To some extent similar to the architecture philosophy used above for system activity-services, we see which existing applications already provide or can support these business functions. Given that the future direction as far as the technology environment is concerned in BES is Java and web, we decide to let all the user activities be supported by web-based UI applications. In some cases, with existing applications such as receivables, there is not much effort involved in mapping these activities in the process to the respective UI screens, since those applications are already web-based UI applications. So, receive payment and quotation user activities can be easily mapped to existing web UI applications' URLs provided by receivables and pricing applications, respectively.

With the other user activities, the applications being legacy their user interfaces are also based on legacy screens that are not best suited to the new process-centric order-to-cash system that is based on web. Therefore, for supporting these user activities, we take the decision to create new web screens and thus new web applications based on JSP/Java Servlets deployed on web servers and EJB business components (if there is a business logic that needs to be performed for the user activity) for those web applications on the JEE application server. Those web applications would have only minimal code just to display a set of data relevant to the activity and allow the user to perform actions. Once the user clicks on the submission button on the last web page associated with a particular user activity such as booking, the associated Java servlet needs to have a line of code to invoke an API of the process layer to indicate completion of this user activity along with providing the output parameters required of the activity-service. This invoke would result in the process instance that has been waiting at that user activity to receive control and move forward with the process execution. The API for this is provided by the implementation of the process layer (in our case, it would be the BPMS process server). For example, the business logic for the booking user activity, would have an EJB to create the shipment booking in the system and generate (and associate with it) the shipment tracking number. The logic in the EJB would store the entire shipment data for the booking in the application database. We might not need to write the business logic code for this EJB from scratch—we can leverage the existing application code.

The prepare documentation activity is supported by the web UI application, documentation application. It is a distinct business function performed by the documentation rater and it expects inputs such as tracking number, customer id, shipper details, recipient details, shipment details (package contents/good description, weight, etc.), whether to bill the recipient or not, reference number from the shipper, internal reference number from the shipper to be put in the invoice, origin, destination, and routing information (which ports are touched). These inputs need to come from the process since these are parameters coming from the previous activities and the documentation application would not ideally have the data in its database nor would it be a good design to get it from other applications such as booking by making calls (that would mean conventional integration approach and not process-centricity). So, we map these input parameters from the parameters of prior activities. The UI application helps the documentation rater in generating the documentation such as waybill (airwaybill), commercial invoice, and customs manifest among others. The waybill number, date, and customs manifest data are output parameters from this activity that is for further use in the process.

11.3.4.5 Executable Process Definition

Finally, we get the executable process definition for the order-to-cash process in WS-BPEL as shown in Listing 11.9.

Listing 11.9

```
<?xml version="1.0" encoding="UTF-8"?>
<process abstractProcess="no" enableInstanceCompensation="no"
  expressionLanguage="http://www.w3.org/TR/1999/
  REC-xpath-19991116"
  name="OrderToCash" bes:appName="OrderToCash"
    bes:queryLanguage="http://www.w3.org/TR/1999/
    REC-xpath-19991116"
  supressJoinFailure="no"
  targetNamespace="http://www.onlinebesservices.com/BPEL/
  ordertocash"
  xmlns="http://docs.oasis-open.org/wsbpel/2.0/process/executable"
  xmlns:bpws="http://docs.oasis-open.org/wsbpel/2.0/process/
  executable"
  xmlns:inst="http://www.onlinebesservices.com/BPEL/
  extensions/inst"
  xmlns:java="http://www.onlinebesservices.com/java"
  xmlns:bes="http://www.onlinebesservices.com/BPEL/extensions"
  xmlns:wsdl="http://schemas.xmlsoap.org/wsdl/"
  xmlns:xsd="http://www.w3.org/2001/XMLSchema"
xmlns:xsi="http://www.w3.org/2001/XMLSchema-instance">
  <extensions>
          <extension
namespace="http://www.onlinebesservices.com/BPEL/extensions/
inst" mustUnderstand="yes" />
    <extension
namespace="http://www.onlinebesservices.com/BPEL/extensions"
mustUnderstand="no" />
    </extensions>
    <correlationSets/>
  <variables>
    <variable name="OrderToCash.response"
messageType="start_OrderToCashResponse"/>
    <variable name="inst:endprocess" type="xsd:boolean"/>
    <variable name="inst:processidentifier" type="xsd:string"/>
    <variable name="shipmentTrackingNumber" type="xsd:string"/>
```

```
    <variable name="billTherecipient" type="xsd:boolean"/>
    <variable name="totalAmount" type="xsd:float"/>
    <variable name="customerID" type="xsd:string"/>
    <variable name="shipperEmail" type="xsd:string"/>
    <variable name="recipientEmail" type="xsd:string"/>
  </variables>
  <scope>
    <variables>
      <variable messageType="start_ReceivePaymentRequest"
name="ReceivePayment.InParam"/>
      <variable messageType="start_ReceivePaymentResponse"
name="ReceivePayment.OutParam"/>
      <variable messageType="CustomerEnquiryOutParams"
name="CustomerEnquiry.OutParam"/>
      <variable messageType="calculateRateRequest"
name="ShippingRateCalculation.InParam"/>
      <variable messageType="calculateRateResponse"
name="ShippingRateCalculation.OutParam"/>
      <variable messageType="QuotationInParams"
name="Quotation.InParam"/>
      <variable messageType="BookingInParams" name="Booking.
      InParam"/>
      <variable messageType="BookingOutParams"
name="Booking.OutParam"/>
      <variable messageType="generateTransportPlanRequest"
name="GenerateTransportationPlan.InParam"/>
      <variable messageType="generateTransportPlanResponse"
name="GenerateTransportationPlan.OutParam"/>
      <variable messageType="PrepareDocumentationInParams"
name="PrepareDocumentation.InParam"/>
      <variable messageType="PrepareDocumentationOutParams"
name="PrepareDocumentation.OutParam"/>
      <variable messageType="GenerateInvoiceInParams"
name="GenerateInvoice.InParam"/>
      <variable messageType="GenerateInvoiceOutParams"
name="GenerateInvoice.OutParam"/>
      <variable messageType="ReceiveShipmentInParams"
name="ReceiveShipment.InParam"/>
      <variable messageType="ReceiveShipmentOutParams"
name="ReceiveShipment.OutParam"/>
      <variable messageType="TransportationInParams"
name="Transportation.InParam"/>
      <variable messageType="SendShipmentDataToCustomsInParams"
name="SendShipmentDataToCustoms.InParam"/>
      <variable messageType="ReceiveCustomsClearanceOutParams"
name="ReceiveCustomsClearance.OutParam"/>
      <variable messageType="SendMailInParams"
name="SendMail.InParam"/>
```

```
      <variable messageType="DeliverShipmentInParams"
name="DeliverShipment.InParam"/>
    </variables>
    <correlationSets>
      <correlationSet name="ReceiveCustomsClearance"
properties="shipmentTrackingNumber"/>
    </correlationSets>
    <sequence>
        <receive createInstance="yes" name="start_OrderToCash"
        operation="start_OrderToCash"
portType="start_OrderToCashPT"/>
      <assign>
        <copy>
          <from>false</from>
          <to variable="inst:endprocess"/>
        </copy>
      </assign>
      <assign>
        <copy>
          <from variable="inst:processidentifier"/>
          <to part="processid" variable="OrderToCash.response"/>
        </copy>
      </assign>
      <reply name="start_OrderToCash" operation="start_OrderToCash"
      portType="start_OrderToCashPT"
variable="OrderToCash.response"/>
      <invoke bes:locate="bes/CustomerEnquiry"
      bes:mode="Manual" name="CustomerEnquiry"
operation="customerEnquiry"
        outputVariable="CustomerEnquiry.OutParam"
                bes:acttype="webUI:Activity"
        bes:userAllocationScheme=""
portType="OrderToCashUserActionsPT">
        <bes:roles bes:allocationScheme="default">
          <bes:role>CustomerServiceRepresentative</bes:role>
        </bes:roles>
      </invoke>
      <assign>
        <copy>
          <from part="customerID"
variable="CustomerEnquiry.OutParam"/>
          <to variable="customerID"/>
        </copy>
      </assign>
      <assign>
        <copy>
          <from part="origin"
          variable="CustomerEnquiry.OutParam"/>
```

```
        <to part="origin"
variable="ShippingRateCalculation.InParam"/>
      </copy>
    </assign>
    <assign>
      <copy>
        <from part="destination"
variable="CustomerEnquiry.OutParam"/>
        <to part="destination"
variable="ShippingRateCalculation.InParam"/>
      </copy>
    </assign>
    <assign>
      <copy>
        <from part="commodity"
variable="CustomerEnquiry.OutParam"/>
        <to part="commodity"
variable="ShippingRateCalculation.InParam"/>
      </copy>
    </assign>
    <assign>
      <copy>
        <from part="weight" variable="CustomerEnquiry.OutParam"/>
        <to part="weight"
variable="ShippingRateCalculation.InParam"/>
      </copy>
    </assign>
    <assign>
      <copy>
        <from variable="customerID"/>
        <to part="customerID"
variable="ShippingRateCalculation.InParam"/>
      </copy>
    </assign>
    <invoke
      inputVariable="ShippingRateCalculation.InParam"
bes:locate="ejb:/className=pricing.CalculateRateHome&amp;
jndiName=pricing/CalculateRate"
      name="ShippingRateCalculation"
      operation="calculateRate"
      outputVariable="ShippingRateCalculation.OutParam"
      bes:portname="PricingPort"
      bes:wsdlfilename="ShippingRateCalculation.wsdl"
      bes:acttype="EJB:Activity"
      portType="PricingPortPT" />
    <assign>
      <copy>
         <from part="totalAmount"
variable="ShippingRateCalculation.OutParam"/>
```

```
          <to variable="totalAmount"/>
        </copy>
      </assign>
      <assign>
        <copy>
          <from part="quotationNumber"
variable="ShippingRateCalculation.OutParam"/>
          <to part="quotationNumber" variable="Quotation.InParam"/>
        </copy>
      </assign>
      <assign>
        <copy>
          <from variable="totalAmount"/>
          <to part="totalAmount" variable="Quotation.InParam"/>
        </copy>
      </assign>
      <invoke inputVariable="Quotation.InParam"
        bes:locate="bes/Quotation" bes:mode="Manual"
        name="Quotation"
                bes:acttype="webUI:Activity"
        operation="quotation" bes:userAllocationScheme=""
portType="OrderToCashUserActionsPT">
        <bes:roles bes:allocationScheme="default">
          <bes:role>CustomerServiceRepresentative</bes:role>
        </bes:roles>
      </invoke>
      <assign>
        <copy>
          <from variable="customerID"/>
          <to part="customerID" variable="Booking.InParam"/>
        </copy>
      </assign>
      <assign>
        <copy>
          <from part="quotationNumber"
variable="ShippingRateCalculation.OutParam"/>
          <to part="quotationNumber" variable="Booking.InParam"/>
        </copy>
      </assign>
      <invoke inputVariable="Booking.InParam"
        bes:locate="bes/Booking" bes:mode="Manual" name="Booking"
                bes:acttype="webUI:Activity"
        operation="booking" outputVariable="Booking.OutParam"
        bes:userAllocationScheme=""
portType="OrderToCashUserActionsPT">
        <bes:roles bes:allocationScheme="default">
          <bes:role>CustomerServiceRepresentative</bes:role>
        </bes:roles>
        <correlations>
```

```
        <correlation initiate="yes" pattern="in"
set="ReceiveCustomsClearance"/>
      </correlations>
    </invoke>
    <assign>
      <copy>
        <from part="shipmentTrackingNumber"
variable="Booking.OutParam"/>
        <to variable="shipmentTrackingNumber"/>
      </copy>
    </assign>
    <assign>
      <copy>
        <from part="shipperEmail" variable="Booking.OutParam"/>
        <to variable="shipperEmail"/>
      </copy>
    </assign>
    <assign>
      <copy>
        <from part="recipientEmail" variable="Booking.OutParam"/>
        <to variable="recipientEmail"/>
      </copy>
    </assign>
    <assign>
      <copy>
        <from variable="shipmentTrackingNumber"/>
        <to part="shipmentTrackingNumber"
variable="GenerateTransportationPlan.InParam"/>
      </copy>
    </assign>
    <invoke inputVariable="GenerateTransportationPlan.InParam"
      bes:locate="ejb:/className=booking.GenerateTransportPlan
      Home&amp;jndiName=booking/generateTransportPlan"
      name="GenerateTransportationPlan"
      operation="generateTransportPlan"
      outputVariable="GenerateTransportationPlan.OutParam"
      bes:portname="BookingPort"
      bes:wsdlfilename="GenerateTransportationPlan.wsdl"
      bes:acttype="EJB:Activity"
      portType="BookingPortPT" />
    <flow>
      <sequence>
        <assign>
          <copy>
            <from part="shipper"
variable="Booking.OutParam"/>
            <to part="shipper"
variable="PrepareDocumentation.InParam"/>
          </copy>
```

```
        </assign>
        <assign>
          <copy>
            <from part="recipient"
variable="Booking.OutParam"/>
            <to part="recipient"
variable="PrepareDocumentation.InParam"/>
          </copy>
        </assign>
        <assign>
          <copy>
            <from part="shipmentInfo"
variable="Booking.OutParam"/>
            <to part="shipmentDetails"
variable="PrepareDocumentation.InParam"/>
          </copy>
        </assign>
        <assign>
          <copy>
            <from part="shippersReference"
variable="Booking.OutParam"/>
            <to part="shippersReference"
variable="PrepareDocumentation.InParam"/>
          </copy>
        </assign>
        <assign>
          <copy>
            <from
            part="customersInternalBillingReference"
variable="Booking.OutParam"/>
            <to part="shippersInternalReference"
variable="PrepareDocumentation.InParam"/>
          </copy>
        </assign>
        <assign>
          <copy>
            <from part="origin"
variable="CustomerEnquiry.OutParam"/>
            <to part="origin"
variable="PrepareDocumentation.InParam"/>
          </copy>
        </assign>
        <assign>
          <copy>
            <from part="destination"
variable="CustomerEnquiry.OutParam"/>
            <to part="destination"
variable="PrepareDocumentation.InParam"/>
          </copy>
```

```
        </assign>
        <assign>
          <copy>
            <from part="routing"
variable="GenerateTransportationPlan.OutParam"/>
            <to part="routing"
variable="PrepareDocumentation.InParam"/>
          </copy>
        </assign>
        <assign>
          <copy>
            <from part="shipperAddress"
variable="Booking.OutParam"/>
            <to part="shipperAddress"
variable="PrepareDocumentation.InParam"/>
          </copy>
        </assign>
        <assign>
          <copy>
            <from part="recipientAddress"
variable="Booking.OutParam"/>
            <to part="recipientAddress"
variable="PrepareDocumentation.InParam"/>
          </copy>
        </assign>
        <assign>
          <copy>
            <from variable="shipmentTrackingNumber"/>
            <to part="shipmentTrackingNumber"
variable="PrepareDocumentation.InParam"/>
          </copy>
        </assign>
        <assign>
          <copy>
            <from variable="customerID"/>
            <to part="customerID"
variable="PrepareDocumentation.InParam"/>
          </copy>
        </assign>
        <assign>
          <copy>
            <from variable="billTherecipient"/>
            <to part="billTherecipient"
variable="PrepareDocumentation.InParam"/>
          </copy>
        </assign>
        <invoke
          inputVariable="PrepareDocumentation.InParam"
```

```
          bes:locate="bes/PrepareDocumentation"
bes:mode="Manual"
          name="PrepareDocumentation"
operation="prepareDocumentation"
          outputVariable="PrepareDocumentation.OutParam"
                      bes:acttype="webUI:Activity"
          bes:userAllocationScheme=""
portType="OrderToCashUserActionsPT">
          <bes:roles bes:allocationScheme="default">
            <bes:role>DocumentationRater</bes:role>
          </bes:roles>
        </invoke>
        <assign>
          <copy>
            <from part="wayBillNumber"
variable="PrepareDocumentation.OutParam"/>
            <to part="wayBillNumber"
variable="GenerateInvoice.InParam"/>
          </copy>
        </assign>
        <assign>
          <copy>
            <from part="plannedDeliveryDate"
variable="GenerateTransportationPlan.OutParam"/>
            <to part="plannedDeliveryDate"
variable="GenerateInvoice.InParam"/>
          </copy>
        </assign>
        <assign>
          <copy>
            <from part="transportationCharge"
variable="ShippingRateCalculation.OutParam"/>
            <to part="transportationCharge"
variable="GenerateInvoice.InParam"/>
          </copy>
        </assign>
        <assign>
          <copy>
            <from part="otherCharges"
variable="ShippingRateCalculation.OutParam"/>
            <to part="otherCharges"
variable="GenerateInvoice.InParam"/>
          </copy>
        </assign>
        <assign>
          <copy>
            <from variable="shipmentTrackingNumber"/>
            <to part="shipmentTrackingNumber"
variable="GenerateInvoice.InParam"/>
```

```
          </copy>
        </assign>
        <assign>
          <copy>
            <from variable="billTherecipient"/>
            <to part="billTherecipient"
variable="GenerateInvoice.InParam"/>
          </copy>
        </assign>
        <assign>
          <copy>
            <from variable="totalAmount"/>
            <to part="totalAmount"
variable="GenerateInvoice.InParam"/>
          </copy>
        </assign>
        <assign>
          <copy>
            <from variable="customerID"/>
            <to part="customerID"
variable="GenerateInvoice.InParam"/>
          </copy>
        </assign>
        <invoke inputVariable="GenerateInvoice.InParam"
          bes:locate="bes.receivables.invoicing"
          bes:acttype="java:invokeActivity"
          outputVariable="GenerateInvoice.OutParam"
          operation="generateInvoice"
                        portType="ReceivablesPT"/>
        </sequence>
        <sequence>
          <assign>
            <copy>
              <from part="shipmentInfo"
variable="Booking.OutParam"/>
              <to part="shipmentInfo"
variable="ReceiveShipment.InParam"/>
            </copy>
          </assign>
          <assign>
            <copy>
              <from variable="shipmentTrackingNumber"/>
              <to part="shipmentTrackingNumber"
variable="ReceiveShipment.InParam"/>
            </copy>
          </assign>
          <invoke
            inputVariable="ReceiveShipment.InParam"
            bes:locate="bes/ReceiveShipment" bes:mode="Manual"
```

```
            name="ReceiveShipment"
            operation="receiveShipment"
            outputVariable="ReceiveShipment.OutParam"
                        bes:acttype="webUI:Activity"
            bes:userAllocationScheme=""
portType="OrderToCashUserActionsPT">
            <bes:roles bes:allocationScheme="default">
              <bes:role>Operations</bes:role>
            </bes:roles>
          </invoke>
        </sequence>
      </flow>
      <switch name="ConsgineeToPay?">
        <case
bes:conditionExpression="java:((besvar:(billTherecipient)) ==
false)">
          <assign>
            <copy>
              <from part="invoiceNumber"
variable="GenerateInvoice.OutParam"/>
              <to part="invoiceNumber"
variable="ReceivePayment.InParam"/>
            </copy>
          </assign>
                  <invoke
                        inputVariable="ReceivePayment.InParam"
                        outputVariable="ReceivePayment.
OutParam"

      bes:locate="http://internalbesservices/receivablessvcs/
start_ReceivePayment"
                        name="ReceivePayment"
                        operation="informCustoms"
   bes:wsdlfilename="ReceivePayment_ReceiveActivities.wsdl"
                        portType="ReceivablesPT"
                        bes:portName="start_ReceivePayment"
                        bes:acttype="SOAPHTTPDOC:Activity" />
        </case>
        <case
bes:conditionExpression="java:((besvar:(billTherecipient)) ==
true)"/>
      </switch>
      <assign>
        <copy>
          <from part="recipientAddress"
variable="Booking.OutParam"/>
          <to part="recipientAddress"
variable="Transportation.InParam"/>
        </copy>
```

```
    </assign>
    <assign>
      <copy>
        <from part="numOfLegs"
variable="GenerateTransportationPlan.OutParam"/>
        <to part="legs" variable="Transportation.InParam"/>
      </copy>
    </assign>
    <assign>
      <copy>
        <from part="routing"
variable="GenerateTransportationPlan.OutParam"/>
        <to part="routing"
variable="Transportation.InParam"/>
      </copy>
    </assign>
    <assign>
      <copy>
        <from part="plannedDeliveryDate"
variable="GenerateTransportationPlan.OutParam"/>
        <to part="plannedDeliveryDate"
variable="Transportation.InParam"/>
      </copy>
    </assign>
    <assign>
      <copy>
        <from part="packageToCarriageMappings"
variable="GenerateTransportationPlan.OutParam"/>
        <to part="packageToCarriageMappings"
variable="Transportation.InParam"/>
      </copy>
    </assign>
    <assign>
      <copy>
        <from variable="shipmentTrackingNumber"/>
        <to part="shipmentTrackingNumber"
variable="Transportation.InParam"/>
      </copy>
    </assign>
    <assign>
      <copy>
        <from variable="customerID"/>
        <to part="customerID"
  variable="Transportation.InParam"/>
      </copy>
    </assign>
    <invoke inputVariable="Transportation.InParam"
      bes:locate="bes/Transportation" bes:mode="Manual"
```

```
        name="Transportation" operation="transportation"
                bes:acttype="webUI:Activity"
        bes:userAllocationScheme=""
portType="OrderToCashUserActionsPT">
        <bes:roles bes:allocationScheme="default">
          <bes:role>Operations</bes:role>
        </bes:roles>
      </invoke>
      <assign>
        <copy>
          <from part="shipper" variable="Booking.OutParam"/>
          <to part="shipper"
variable="SendShipmentDataToCustoms.InParam"/>
        </copy>
      </assign>
      <assign>
        <copy>
          <from part="recipient" variable="Booking.OutParam"/>
          <to part="consignee"
variable="SendShipmentDataToCustoms.InParam"/>
        </copy>
      </assign>
      <assign>
        <copy>
          <from part="valueForCustoms"
variable="Booking.OutParam"/>
          <to part="totalShipmentValueForCustoms"
variable="SendShipmentDataToCustoms.InParam"/>
        </copy>
      </assign>
      <assign>
        <copy>
          <from part="shipmentInfo" variable="Booking.OutParam"/>
          <to part="shipmentInfo"
          variable="SendShipmentDataToCustoms.InParam"/>
        </copy>
      </assign>
      <assign>
        <copy>
          <from part="customsManifestData"
variable="PrepareDocumentation.OutParam"/>
          <to part="mainfest"
variable="SendShipmentDataToCustoms.InParam"/>
        </copy>
      </assign>
      <assign>
        <copy>
          <from variable="shipmentTrackingNumber"/>
```

```
          <to part="shipmentRefereneForCustoms"
variable="SendShipmentDataToCustoms.InParam"/>
        </copy>
      </assign>
      <invoke
        inputVariable="SendShipmentDataToCustoms.InParam"
        bes:locate="http://www.onlinecustomsservices.com/
        InformCustoms"
        name="SendShipmentDataToCustoms"
        operation="informCustoms" bes:portname="CustomsPort"
        bes:wsdlfilename="SendShipmentDataToCustoms.wsdl"
        portType="CustomsPortPT"
        bes:acttype="SOAPHTTPDOC:Activity" />
  <receive createInstance="no"
        name="ReceiveCustomsClearance"
        operation="ReceiveCustomsClearance"
        portType="ReceiveCustomsClearancePT"
variable="ReceiveCustomsClearance.OutParam">
        bes:acttype="SOAPHTTPDOC:Receive">
        <correlations>
          <correlation initiate="no"
set="ReceiveCustomsClearance"/>
        </correlations>
      </receive>
      <assign>
        <copy>
          <from variable="recipientEmail"/>
          <to part="To" variable="SendMail.InParam"/>
        </copy>
      </assign>
      <assign>
        <copy>
          <from variable="shipperEmail"/>
          <to part="Cc" variable="SendMail.InParam"/>
        </copy>
      </assign>
      <assign>
        <copy>
          <from expression="concat(&quot;Shipment addressed to
you with shipment number &quot;,$shipmentTrackingNumber,&quot;
has arrived&quot;)"/>
          <to part="Subject" variable="SendMail.InParam"/>
        </copy>
      </assign>
      <assign>
        <copy>
          <from expression="The shipment addressed to you is
ready for delivery and will be delivered to you by the end of
today."/>
```

```
          <to part="Body" variable="SendMail.InParam"/>
        </copy>
      </assign>
      <invoke
        inputVariable="SendMail.InParam"
                bes:locate="bes.messagingservices.Email"
        name="SendArrivalNotice"
        operation="sendMail"
        portType="EmailPortPT"
        bes:acttype="mail:Activity" />
      <switch name="ConsigneeToPay?">
      <case
bes:conditionExpression="java:((besvar:(billTherecipient)) ==
true)">
           <assign>
             <copy>
               <from part="invoiceNumber"
variable="GenerateInvoice.OutParam"/>
               <to part="invoiceNumber"
variable="ReceivePayment.InParam"/>
             </copy>
           </assign>
                   <invoke
                      inputVariable="ReceivePayment.InParam"
                      outputVariable="ReceivePayment.OutParam"
   bes:locate="http://internalbesservices/receivablessvcs/
start_ReceivePayment"
                         name="ReceivePayment"
                         operation="informCustoms"
   bes:wsdlfilename="ReceivePayment_ReceiveActivities.wsdl"
                         portType="ReceivablesPT"
                         bes:portName="start_ReceivePayment"
   bes:acttype="SOAPHTTPDOC:Activity" />
          </case>
        <case
bes:conditionExpression="java:((besvar:(billTherecipient)) ==
  false)"/>
      </switch>
      <assign>
        <copy>
          <from variable="shipmentTrackingNumber"/>
          <to part="shipmentTrackingNumber"
variable="DeliverShipment.InParam"/>
        </copy>
      </assign>
      <invoke inputVariable="DeliverShipment.InParam"
        bes:locate="bes/DeliverShipment" bes:mode="Manual"
        name="DeliverShipment" operation="deliverShipment"
                bes:acttype="webUI:Activity"
```

```
        bes:userAllocationScheme=""
portType="OrderToCashUserActionsPT">
        <bes:roles bes:allocationScheme="default">
          <bes:role>Operations</bes:role>
        </bes:roles>
      </invoke>
      <assign>
        <copy>
          <from>true</from>
          <to variable="inst:endprocess"/>
        </copy>
      </assign>
    </sequence>
  </scope>
</process>
```

The executable process definition for the receive payment process in WS-BPEL as shown in Listing 11.10.

Listing 11.10

```
<?xml version="1.0" encoding="UTF-8"?>
<process abstractProcess="no" enableInstanceCompensation="no"
  expressionLanguage="http://www.w3.org/TR/1999/
  REC-xpath-19991116"
  name="ReceivePayment" bes:appName="Payment"
    bes:queryLanguage="http://www.w3.org/TR/1999/
    REC-xpath-19991116"
  supressJoinFailure="no"
  targetNamespace="http://www.onlinebesservices.com/BPEL/
  ordertocash"
  xmlns="http://docs.oasis-open.org/wsbpel/2.0/process/executable"
  xmlns:bpws="http://docs.oasis-open.org/wsbpel/2.0/process/
executable"
  xmlns:inst="http://www.onlinebesservices.com/BPEL/
extensions/inst"
  xmlns:java="http://www.onlinebesservices.com/java"
  xmlns:bes="http://www.onlinebesservices.com/BPEL/extensions"
  xmlns:wsdl="http://schemas.xmlsoap.org/wsdl/"
  xmlns:xsd="http://www.w3.org/2001/XMLSchema"
xmlns:xsi="http://www.w3.org/2001/XMLSchema-instance">
  <correlationSets/>
    <extensions>
      <extension
namespace="http://www.onlinebesservices.com/BPEL/extensions/
inst" mustUnderstand="yes" />
      <extension
namespace="http://www.onlinebesservices.com/BPEL/extensions"
mustUnderstand="no" />
```

```
    </extensions>
  <variables>
    <variable name="inst:endprocess" type="xsd:boolean"/>
    <variable name="invoiceNumber" type="xsd:string"/>
    <variable messageType="start_ReceivePaymentRequest"
name="ReceivePayment.StartParam"/>
    <variable messageType="start_ReceivePaymentResponse"
name="ReceivePayment.EndParam"/>
  </variables>
  <scope>
    <variables>
      <variable messageType="Receive_PaymentInParams"
name="Receive_Payment.InParam"/>
      <variable messageType="Receive_PaymentOutParams"
name="Receive_Payment.OutParam"/>
      <variable messageType="MakeGLEntriesInParams"
name="MakeGLEntries.InParam"/>
      <variable messageType="UpdateSalesInParams"
name="UpdateSales.InParam"/>
    </variables>
    <correlationSets/>
    <sequence>
      <receive createInstance="yes" name="start_ReceivePayment"
        operation="start_ReceivePayment" portType="ReceivablesPT"
variable="ReceivePayment.StartParam"/>
      <assign>
        <copy>
          <from>false</from>
          <to variable="inst:endprocess"/>
        </copy>
      </assign>
      <assign>
        <copy>
          <from part="invoiceNumber"
variable="ReceivePayment.StartParam"/>
          <to variable="invoiceNumber"/>
        </copy>
      </assign>
      <assign>
        <copy>
          <from variable="invoiceNumber"/>
          <to part="invoiceNumber"
variable="Receive_Payment.InParam"/>
        </copy>
      </assign>
      <invoke inputVariable="Receive_Payment.InParam"
        bes:locate="bes/Receive_Payment" mode="Manual"
        name="Receive_Payment" operation="Receive_Payment"
        outputVariable="Receive_Payment.OutParam"
```

```
            bes:acttype="webUI:Activity"
        bes:userAllocationScheme=""
portType="ReceivePaymentUserActionsPT">
        <bes:roles bes:allocationScheme="default">
          <bes:role>Cashier</bes:role>
        </bes:roles>
      </invoke>
      <assign>
        <copy>
          <from part="paymentNumber"
variable="Receive_Payment.OutParam"/>
          <to part="transactionNumber"
variable="MakeGLEntries.InParam"/>
        </copy>
      </assign>
      <assign>
        <copy>
          <from part="paymentDate"
variable="Receive_Payment.OutParam"/>
          <to part="transactionDate"
variable="MakeGLEntries.InParam"/>
        </copy>
      </assign>
      <assign>
        <copy>
          <from part="totalPymtAmount"
variable="Receive_Payment.OutParam"/>
          <to part="transactionAmount"
variable="MakeGLEntries.InParam"/>
        </copy>
      </assign>
      <assign>
        <copy>
          <from expression="&quot;Payment&quot;"/>
          <to part="transactionType"
variable="MakeGLEntries.InParam"/>
        </copy>
      </assign>
      <assign>
        <copy>
          <from part="customerID"
variable="Receive_Payment.OutParam"/>
          <to part="customerID"
variable="MakeGLEntries.InParam"/>
        </copy>
      </assign>
      <assign>
        <copy>
```

```
        <from variable="invoiceNumber"/>
        <to part="reference"
variable="MakeGLEntries.InParam"/>
      </copy>
    </assign>
    <invoke
      <invoke inputVariable="MakeGLEntries.InParam"
      bes:locate="http://internalbesservices/GL/
      MakeGLEntries"
      name="MakeGLEntries"
      operation="makeGLEntry" bes:portname="GLPort"
      bes:wsdlfilename="MakeGLEntries.wsdl"
      portType="GLPortPT"
      bes:acttype="SOAPHTTPDOC:Activity" />
    <assign>
      <copy>
        <from part="customerID"
variable="Receive_Payment.OutParam"/>
        <to part="customerID" variable="UpdateSales.InParam"/>
      </copy>
    </assign>
    <assign>
      <copy>
        <from part="totalPymtAmount"
variable="Receive_Payment.OutParam"/>
        <to part="salesAmount"
        variable="UpdateSales.InParam"/>
      </copy>
    </assign>
    <assign>
      <copy>
        <from part="shippingOrderDate"
variable="Receive_Payment.OutParam"/>
        <to part="salesDate" variable="UpdateSales.InParam"/>
      </copy>
    </assign>
    <assign>
      <copy>
        <from part="shipmentTrackingNumber"
variable="Receive_Payment.OutParam"/>
        <to part="shipmentNumber"
variable="UpdateSales.InParam"/>
      </copy>
    </assign>
    <assign>
      <copy>
        <from part="paymentDate"
variable="Receive_Payment.OutParam"/>
```

```
        <to part="paymentReceivedDate"
variable="UpdateSales.InParam"/>
      </copy>
    </assign>
    <invoke inputVariable="UpdateSales.InParam"
      bes:locate="http://internalbesservices/Sales/UpdateSales"
      name="UpdateSales"
      operation="enterSalesData" bes:portname="SalesPort"
      bes:wsdlfilename="UpdateSales.wsdl"
      portType="SalesPT"
      bes:acttype="SOAPHTTPDOC:Activity" />
    <assign>
      <copy>
        <from>true</from>
        <to variable="inst:endprocess"/>
      </copy>
    </assign>
    <assign>
      <copy>
        <from>true</from>
        <to part="paymentReceived"
variable="ReceivePayment.EndParam"/>
      </copy>
    </assign>
    <reply name="start_ReceivePayment" operation="
      start_ReceivePayment"
      portType="ReceivablesPT" variable="ReceivePayment.
      EndParam"/>
    </sequence>
  </scope>
</process>
```

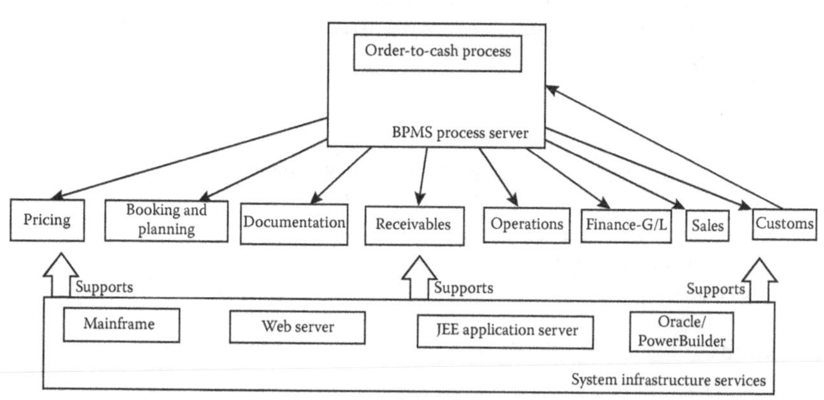

Figure 11.19 Order-to-cash logical view.

11.3.4.6 Embodiment

In this architecture for the order-to-cash system, we use a BPMS process engine for realizing the process layer (run-time), a BPMS process modeler for the design-time, JEE application server for hosting the EJB components, and Java-enabled web servers for the web applications and web service implementations. The services such as POJO services and Send mail services would be automatically provided by the BPMS process engine. Figure 11.19 shows the logical view of the architecture for the new system. The process needs to be deployed into the run-time environment. As part of the deployment, the package containing all the WS-BPEL files, all the WSDL files is deployed onto the BPMS process engine using the deployment mechanism provided by the BPMS. All the EJBs are deployed as beans into the JEE application server. The web services and web applications are deployed on to the web servers with servlet containers.

11.4 Exercise Questions

1. What are the various options you can think of to realize the user activities in a process that you are familiar with?
2. What are the ways in which you would like to service-enable legacy applications in your enterprise?
3. What are the scenarios you have come across where the separation of concerns between the activities associated with different functions/applications become hard to achieve clearly and cleanly?
4. What would be your approach for the scenarios in question 3 and what would be the architectural philosophy behind your decisions?

Chapter 12

Implementation Considerations

12.1 Objectives

- To appreciate the different types of business processes in real life and their infrastructure-related requirements
- To understand which tools and technologies suit different process types
- To be aware of some practical issues/situations faced in process-centric architectural design and some anti-patterns to avoid

12.2 Types of Business Processes

In the real world, different business processes are of different nature. They can be thus grouped into categories (or process types) based on their key nature. Processes within each type exhibit some common characteristics and have automation needs that are a bit different from other types. They have evolved to become so, based on the kind of domain they address, the nature of activities that happen in the process, and legacy needs. The process infrastructure thus required by each type is different. Some process servers are more suited to address certain types of processes better than others.

The BPMS products space is still maturing and there are a plethora of options available today for the architecture implementation. As of now, no BPMS product can be said to be supporting all the process requirements. The products will continue to evolve. Of course, in the future, they will increasingly become more complete capability-wise, for BPM support. Therefore, right now, it is important to keep this in mind while realizing the architecture of the IT system. During the implementation of a process-centric architecture, it makes sense to consider this and choose the appropriate process infrastructure based on the business process being handled.

12.2.1 Rules-Centric

These types of business processes are business rules oriented. Processes belonging to this category are so centered on business rules that other activities in the process become less significant. The common characteristics such processes exhibit are

- They are invariably heavy on business rule-activities. The rule-activities are the most important activities of the process. Results of the rule-activities determine the direction of the process flow.
- Rules appear in the process model as decision points in the process definition and also as rule-activities that are kept separated from the process model.
- Business rules involved in these processes are often complex. Each rule is similar to a program rather than being just a few lines. Reasoning of these rules (inferencing) may involve multiple reasoning approaches such as forward inferencing, backward inferencing, or a combination of inferencing approaches. The specification and reasoning of these rules require better support from the infrastructure.

One example for this type of process is the insurance claims process. In this scenario, when a claim is filed by the customer and processed by the insurance company, complex rules are applied at different stages. Some of them are to check if the claim fulfills all the mandatory criteria for insurance claims and then decide whether the claim is eligible for approval or not. Insurance policies typically have a lot of clauses that need to be satisfied by the filed claim before it is approved. Some of the clauses are exclusive in nature and are conditions that exclude the claim scenario from being covered. Some of them are inclusive; they specify conditions that are covered by the insurance.

Another example is the price calculation in the quote process in the case of a transportation or a shipping company that operates globally under varying taxation regimes, port charges, etc. and not just based on flat per-distance unit rate. The calculated price and quote would typically have a set of line items (such as surcharges) in addition to the basic freight charge.

Rules-centric processes are better handled by a BPMS that is strong in handling business rules, and that too natively. Such a BPMS would provide capabilities that allow business to easily specify the business rules in a business-like language. It manages rules, carries out inferencing of the rules, and executes them upon request from the process engine.

12.2.2 Workflow Oriented

Some business processes are workflow intensive. These processes are mainly about flows involving people and less of systems participating in the flow. The common characteristics are

- The processes mostly consist of manual activities. There is more emphasis on humans performing activities than systems.
- As far as participant involvement is concerned, the processes involve heavy amounts of human interaction. Most of the activities are performed by humans and each such activity is composed of a set of tasks that a person performs on a business entity (or entities).
- They involve a control flow where a work item flows from one user or role to another. As the work item flows through the users, its state changes and there is a progress in the processing of the business entity. The flows in real life are often back and forth. The same person may get the task back for repeated processing or further work.

Account opening process in a typical bank is a good example of this type of processes. The application or request placed by the customer goes through multiple verifications and approvals by various users and roles. Each user may do some work or processing on the request for the account. A higher authority such as the branch manager makes the final call as to whether the account should be opened or not.

Those BPMS that are strongly rooted in managing workflows would suit such processes. This can provide a process server that would let users take part in the process easily, across a number of such workflows. Users get to view the list of work items that they have been assigned to work on along with the step in the workflow that they are to perform. They can manage the order of items, prioritize them, and see all relevant details about the item including its processing stage. Reassigning work and routing the item to other users, are all enabled by workflow-based BPMSs. They excel in providing and supporting such capabilities.

12.2.3 STP Oriented

There are processes that are of straight through process (STP) nature. These processes run in huge volumes and involve a great deal of system participation in the process. From one end to the other end, the work (or the work item) passes straight through with no human intervention.

They share the following traits:

- Processes are short running in duration. They complete quickly. They typically run for seconds, or at the maximum, for a few minutes.
- The process is transaction oriented and involves only synchronous operations. Completion of the process means processing of a business transaction; the unit of work is generally small sized.
- There are only system activities in the process. These system activities together complete the transaction.
- Processes are fully automated. They get triggered and executed automatically without human intervention.
- Volumes of such processes are high. A high number of process instances run at the same time.

An example of STP is the transaction processing of mutual funds in a financial services company. Typically the mutual funds transactions involve short business transactions such as redemption of funds, purchase of funds, and swap of funds. These become system activities in the STP business process and the entire process runs with no user intervention. Per hour, a number of instances of this process runs and complete. Each process instance (mutual funds transaction) completes in seconds.

Another example of a systems-only process is trade processing in an investment bank. This involves the system receiving files with trade data from multiple sources; various operations are performed on the data in sequence such as validation, addition of more data to make it more comprehensive, and routing to a further process. All these operations are individual activities in the process and they are system activities (i.e., automated). Process execution is triggered automatically once the trade files arrive.

STP business processes need a BPMS process engine that strongly supports automation, enables application integration. The process engine also needs to be able to handle transaction processing well and is required to handle large volumes of processes. It would need the process engine to support efficiency qualities of very high performance and scalability. The expected throughput of transactions per unit of time (minute) and time taken for one transaction would be very demanding. An automation-centric or system-centric BPMS fits STP processes well.

12.2.4 EAI Oriented

These processes primarily involve enterprise application integration (EAI). Multiple applications in the enterprise take part in the process and they are often disparate including legacy systems, application packages, and new applications. Such processes are EAI focused and are end-to-end in scope covering multiple departments of the enterprise.

The characteristics of these processes are:

- They contain primarily system activities. The manual activities present in the process are minimal or zero.
- Process spans across multiple applications, with each application performing at least one system activity in it. Application may be running in heterogeneous technologies. They may be a combination of legacy, packages, COTS package, and in house systems.
- Duration-wise, the processes may be either a short-lived or long-running. The long-running processes may run in hours, or even in days. Process may involve some asynchronous activities in it. This means at some steps, waiting would be involved during the process execution.

Sales order processing is an example of a process in this category. Multiple applications such as sales system, order management system, inventory system, and production system work together in the process, supporting the steps in the process such as validating the order details, checking the inventory, and triggering manufacture of the product. They together complete the process. Some of the activities may be asynchronous activities where the process receives messages from external systems and processes. For example, on completion of manufacturing of the goods, the sales order process instance may receive a message from the inventory system indicating that the production is complete and the product is ready.

BPMSs, which natively support EAI and are strong in EAI, suit or support this category of process. They would have the natural capabilities in integrating applications across technologies, and handling required data transformations.

12.3 Process Infrastructure

Process infrastructure is the infrastructure that supports business processes, in the IT system. It realizes the process layer component of the IT system. The software that makes up the process infrastructure is the BPMS. Enabling process management fully through the life cycle of the business processes is the primary concern of a BPMS. There are various BPMS products available in the industry. They can be broadly categorized into two: legacy and pure-play. The sections below explain the types.

12.3.1 Legacy BPMSs

These BPMS products have some legacy in them and they carry that along even as they continue to evolve to address BPM requirements. In some cases, the legacy comes handy, especially to address processes of a certain nature. In other cases, this legacy becomes a burden forcing the implementation to take a circuitous path involving extra effort instead of a simple direct approach. The legacy each product has may be different from the others. The product may have originally been addressing a particular function but would have evolved or moved up to support BPM, and would have later come to be known as a BPMS product. Predominantly, the following legacies are seen in BPMS products and thus they make a categorization for the BPMS products:

12.3.1.1 Application Server Legacy

There are BPMS products that were once application servers, either as J2EE servers providing J2EE containers, or .NET application servers providing services for .NET components. Some examples are IBM Web Sphere, Web Logic Integrator of BEA (now part of ORACLE), and ORACLE application server.

They have evolved into BPMSs and now support business process management in addition to supporting business components of the application in their application containers. Such a BPMS typically supports both A2A and P2P flows. It has adaptors to integrate with various applications; it might use the application server's adaptor capabilities (e.g., JTA). It can connect with identity management systems such as LDAP servers to integrate authentication and authorization functions with that of the BPMS. It provides a solid Integrated Development Environment (IDE) for programming the components of the IT system post their architectural design. Such BPMS products, are good in providing messaging, and asynchronous communication mechanisms (JMS, MQ), since these are already well supported in the application servers.

12.3.1.2 Workflow Legacy

BPMS products with this legacy were once workflow systems (or workflow management systems) or WFMS for short. WFMS have been traditionally used in scenarios where flow of work item among humans was common. An example of such a BPMS product is Staffware (now TIBCO-Staffware).

They support P2P flows naturally and are strong in supporting human interaction. They generate and present work lists to each user according to what the user has to work on. Work assignment, routing, rerouting of work items are natively supported. They are not considered strong in integration of systems. WFMS have been in existence since the early 1990s and thus some of their core components are legacy, having been built in a structured programming language such as C. Due to this baggage, they may be less flexible to changes related to BPM features.

12.3.1.3 EAI Legacy

These systems are BPMS products that have evolved from their EAI tool versions. They were EAI tools used in the domain of application integration in enterprises. Examples are TIBCO, and Biz Talk.

As BPMS products, integrating systems in processes is their native capability and strength. In their previous roles EAI tools used to allow definition of control flows involving various applications, though in a limited way, in association with capabilities to define data mappings between disparate applications—the context was EAI though. A2A flows are well supported. Naturally, integrating human participants in the process is not a strong area for these BPMSs.

12.3.1.4 Rule Engine Legacy

BPMSs with legacy of rule engines belong to this category. Pega is an example. The BPMS would have been once a rule engine and later evolved into a BPMS product with the extension for supporting BPM requirements.

The meta-model such BPMS products use is business rules. This translates into a view of business process where rules dominate the perspective. This is a baggage they carry into their BPMS versions as well. They are very capable of supporting pretty complex business rules in the process and are sophisticated in that. A2A flows are not their strong points. When it comes to BPM related standards, such BPMSs need to grow more in standards-support.

12.3.1.5 DMS Legacy

Some BPMS products come from document management systems (DMS) or content management system (CMS) products background. One example is FileNet (now part of IBM). These products carry the document management legacy and the model.

The processes or works are viewed from a document-centric angle, as the flow of documents through users and also systems to some extent. Strengths of these BPMS products lie in document handling, scanning of paper documents and digitizing them, capabilities of imaging system components, and linking of the documents to the business process. They natively support any flow that involves document flow.

12.3.1.6 Package Legacy

Application packages have also evolved to support BPM and they have become BPMS products by adding those capabilities. They would have been ERP packages or CRM or Sales packages before. Examples are SAP Netweaver, and Chordiant®.

Most of them have enabled business process view and explicit business process support (abstraction) for business processes coming within their application domain (or vertical)—for example, business processes such as customer on-boarding process within CRM, and manufacturing process under ERP. Some of them also have made their products ready-built BPM solutions for specific vertical, such as finance. Such solutions would provide all the business processes in that domain (e.g., finance) and enable the process to be offered at a higher-level of abstraction and allows it to be customized. These BPM products are strong in their specific domain. However, they need to support integration with other processes in the enterprise better. Supporting processes outside their domain is not a strong area for them.

12.3.2 Pure-Play BPMSs

These BPMSs do not have any legacy and therefore no baggage to carry or support. They are purely for BPM. They have been designed and built ground-up, for serving BPM needs alone, and only with the support of business processes in mind. They arrived in the scene only with the arrival of the concepts of BPM. Some examples are Savion, Intalio, and Skelta®.

Pure-play BPMSs support process-centric standards (and BPM standards) the best. These products are also not tied to any particular domain or any industry vertical and thus are flexible to support wide varieties of business processes. The IT systems built with this type of BPMSs for process infrastructure support, can be built as process-centric all through. This is since, any architectural work, design work, or development work done would be guided by process principles and realized fully in terms of that. There would not be a need to use a different meta-model to the process model, for example. Thus, there is a sense of purity (process purity) in the IT system; it can be seen as a clean process-centric IT system.

BPMS products of the pure category do not have application infrastructure services as a strong area. This includes services such as transaction handling, messaging, and security. Some of the products may rely on application servers for this. That is, they may work along with an application server to enable these capabilities. These products would have to keep building more capabilities in supporting human participants in the process better.

12.4 Best Practices

Given below are some best practices for architecting IT systems based on PCA. Many of them are also the critical success factors for PCA in the enterprise. Some of these, especially the ones involving organizational change, would become challenges in the PCA approach.

1. Organization level change—Organizations need to have process thinking embedded within. This plays an important role in the success of process centric architectures. Process-thinking needs to be encouraged and it should become part of the work culture. This will also gradually lead the enterprise to be organized along processes instead of functions. Siloed thinking and business function–oriented thinking needs to be discouraged. Process-oriented roles (such as process owners) need to be created and supported.

2. BPM—The architecture effort and implementation is best done under the overall context of BPM. It should go hand in hand with BPM program for more effectiveness and impact. In the context of BPM, enterprise needs to create an organizational structure to support BPM and process-centric approach. This includes aspects such as skills and training, culture, decision-making, reward systems, creation of teams (cross-functional), collaboration, and governance.
3. Process governance—This is very important to ensure consistency of system architecture efforts. The governance board that is established will direct the vision of the architecture. The specific process-centric architecture will be part of a larger enterprise process architecture vision. The work needs to be driven by business and be actively supported by top management, especially since business processes are cross functional in nature.
4. Responsibilities and roles—Create roles that would take up different responsibilities at the process level. There ideally needs to be a process owner role that owns the overall responsibility for a business process. The process owner owns the process and is accountable for the process throughout its life-cycle and its performance goals. A process manager would be another important operations role. This role would have the responsibility for the day-to-day operation of the business process—this includes monitoring the process executions and taking actions at the process levels such as work assignment.
5. Change in work style and culture—At a business operation level, this means thinking differently about how work should be carried out. Conventional batch mode of work where business operations in a process are always performed in batch might not work well for process performance. For example, a bunch of purchase orders are being processed together, where the orders are piped through each step in the process where a specific action is taken on them (this action could be enrichment of order with more data, evaluation, review, correction of error data, and so on). Each purchase order waits for getting processed along with others at each step, though it could have been processed independently of the others. A complex order, for example, could hold up another order that is simple for no fault of the simple order. Batch-mode work styles like these create (often) unnecessary dependencies between process instances (i.e., trades, orders, requests, applications, etc.) and form avoidable processing bottlenecks. Often batch mode working style is justified by giving scalability and productivity benefits as reasons—It might appear efficient from the specific business operation's (step) perspective, but in the end-to-end process view, the overall process might actually become very inefficient and suboptimal. It is best to optimize the overall process and have the processes run in parallel. It is important to have an end-to-end focus on processes and the relation the specific process has to other processes in the enterprise.

6. Scope—As far as the scope of the work is concerned, it is recommended to not go for a big-bang approach, where the work covers all the lines of business at one go. Going for a big-bang approach would have a bigger impact on the organization and would become very difficult to manage. If PCA is being adopted for the first time in the enterprise, it is best to start small with a single business process that is related to say one product or service or line of business of the enterprise. This can even be a pilot project. Once the IT system for that specific process is architected and implemented, the lessons learnt and the benefits demonstrated can help in further architecting and implementation of iterations, where an increasing number of processes can be covered. PCA need not always be done as a full enterprise level exercise. It can even be applied to a relatively small application in the enterprise such as for example, an aged open items report generation application or intranet publication approval application (e.g., for putting up content on the company's intranet, for knowledge sharing documents produced internally). The small application also gains the benefits of process-centricity and it can integrate with other processes in the enterprise as required in the future without undergoing many changes.
7. Process design—It is very important to get the process design right. That would directly determine how well the business process would perform. Business roles (such as process analyst and business analyst) must drive the process design activity. Business process design principles should be applied during process design for arriving at sound process models. In this context, it often makes sense to consider best practice business process models from industry or other bodies. While looking for reference models, it is important to differentiate between standard process models and best-practice process models. What we want to use are best-practice processes and not necessarily standard processes. Standard process models for industries can get created by extracting common practices from across enterprises within the industry to act as a reference for the industry—they do not really have to be best practices.

   Process definitions should be done based on standards and tools that support process modeling standards should be used. The IT system's architect should also get involved in the process design, however, only in a secondary role—the business role is the primary one in process design.
8. Activities—While designing the business process, much attention must be paid to the granularity of the activities. Activities must be at the right level of granularity for the process. This would give maximum benefits. The design should always be top-down starting from the top level business process.
9. Infrastructure—The system needs to get the right infrastructure in place. That is important to enable other qualities that might be relevant for the system such as efficiency and reliability. As much as possible, known solutions and architectural patterns should be used to meet these quality

requirements. Using a BPMS product along with its own or a separate application server would help in this and is recommended. Throughout the architectural design, detailed design, programming, and testing stages of the IT system, it needs to be confirmed that the quality requirements are being met. Process deployment in production should happen only after thorough testing for this.

If any packaged application is being used in the IT system, it should be loosely coupled by creating an XML based interface on top of the APIs provided by the package to provide a level of abstraction. This interface can also be a web service or an adapter that is available off-the-shelf or even created locally. The interface will act as a wrapper. This same approach can be applied to a legacy application too. In the future, the application (whether legacy or package) can be replaced with another one without impacting the business process.

10. Testing—As part of the implementation of the PCA architecture, system testing needs to be expanded to cover the process level abstraction too. The services corresponding to the individual activities in the process should be tested involving their individual modules. This is to ensure that within the module, the service works as per its specific defined requirements and performs its specific business function. Integration testing should then be done integrating these services. This involves testing the entire process flow, making the process execution go through different paths defined in the process, and covering all the possible paths the process can take at run-time. In the process testing, branching conditions, branches, parallel paths, and joins should be tested for functionality. The overall process should then get tested for the quality attribute requirements such as performance that the system is expected to satisfy.

12.5 Practicalities in Architectural Design

Here, we discuss some of the practical issues faced while designing architecture of IT systems especially based on PCA and the appropriate ways to address them.

12.5.1 Some Common Situations

12.5.1.1 Recurrent Tasks

The design situation may be something like this:

Users require an application that is essentially for scheduling tasks, for work by users, and for tracking the progress of those tasks. The tasks can be iterative too and each iteration is one separate instance.

Approach
Such situations may be relevant in organizations where the nature of work is more human intensive, for example, in a business process outsourcing (BPO) company that provides outsourced services to customers. The effective approach is to go above the task specificity in the requirement and think process support. There is a need to resist the temptation to: design this system specifically as an application for managing tasks, or simply directly use a scheduler product and build the application around it, though that is what it might appear to be.

Architect the system for the processes that those tasks are part of. Use a BPMS for implementation of the system. Implement the entire task scheduling as scheduled activities in the process, implement iteration as iterative activities. These are natively and generically supported by the BPMS. Creating process instances, task instances for user (i.e., activity instances), recurrence of tasks (timed activities or scheduled activities, and iteration), and tracking of the tasks (activities in process instances) are all easily and naturally taken care of by the BPMS.

12.5.1.2 Making Task Nodes Work

The design situation may be something like this:

This new application (NewApp) involves workflow and another existing web application. How do we let a user see his UI from the web application when the time for the user's carrying out of the activity in the workflow comes, that they are responsible to perform?

Approach
Use a BPMS. Architect the application starting with the process component. Specify the process logic and the branch conditions in the process model. Specify the user tasks as user activities in the process. In the process modeler, map the user activities to their respective UI screen identifiers. For example, for a user activity named "approve customer application" the page might be at http://myapplicationdomain/approve.jsp, if we assume a JAVA environment. Mention an identifier to that UI, say approve.jsp, in the user activity in the process model. When the user logs in to the web application, provide the user with a list of tasks the user has to perform. This will be a set of process instances that are currently at the approve activity. NewApp can present this list by querying the BPMS process engine (use BPMS provided API for that) for the process instances having activities (tasks) assigned to this specific user or unassigned to any one but assigned to their role. In this work list, against each item, provide a link to the web application (existing) page for that action, http://myapplicationdomain/approve.jsp here. This can be got from the previous querying for the work list itself. Or, NewApp can also maintain a configuration of mappings between the UI identifier and the full URL (at least the domain part of the URL and the first few levels in it, e.g., http://myapplicationdomain) for the existing

application page corresponding to that UI. Now, when the process instance is at the approval activity, the user's work list will show this in the NewApp screen/page and the user can click on the link shown in the list against this specific instance and that will bring up the web application screen for approval where the user can perform the approval action.

12.5.1.3 Audit Data Capture

The design situation may be something like this:

The business manager wants the transactional details from an existing application be captured in a database that would be later used for audit reporting.

Approach

Instead of changing the code in all the points of the application where the business entity is updated, consider re-architecting the application as a process-centric one using a BPMS for the process layer. It will serve two purposes. One, the audit data would automatically become available from the process repository automatically maintained by the process engine. This will contain all information about each step in each process instance, including when it started and when it completed and who performed the action. This data can easily be queried by the audit reporting application any time. Second, the application becomes now more flexible to business changes in the future. It would be better aligned to the business process.

12.5.1.4 Batch Processing Platform

The design situation may be something like this:

A new platform is required for heavy batch processing of trade data in a brokerage firm. Trade data might come from different sources including external systems, in heavy volumes. Processing is rules-heavy and it involves, receiving the documents (or files) with data, checking the data and validating it, accepting/rejecting for further processing, adding all other relevant data required to do transactions, and sending them to a different system for back-end transaction operations. Validation work and other work are heavily based on rules—some of them are generic, in that the rules apply to all the trade records received in the input file, while some other rules are specific to only some type of records or to only specific data items (e.g., from a type of customer). There are rules that apply before the system decides to accept or reject a trade record. What is the best suitable architectural approach here?

Approach

Looking at the explicit requirements we might be inclined to think in a rules-focused way, since this is a rules-heavy computation. And, it is intuitive to suggest a rules engine centered architecture for the trade platform. However, a process-centric approach suits this scenario better because: There is a clear and well-defined process that the platform is required to perform; there is a strong A2A flow involved; this platform needs to be flexible to accommodate changes to the process in the future depending on new trades introduced or changes in nature of trades; it involves down-the-line processing by other systems in the enterprise and so it needs to direct (route) the trade to the right system based on logic that can be variant; the subsequent systems involved here also take part in the process and thus can be included in the process scope, process flow, and flow management; it needs to be able to handle huge volumes of trades and for that it is more appropriate to have concurrent processing utilized than processing a set of records sequentially in batches, one step at a time; while most of the trade records would get processed automatically, there may be exceptions related to processing of some trades and a brokerage clerk would have to handle those trades manually.

A rule engine is very much recommended here, still consider seeing this from the process perspective first and define the process. This would be a STP type process—it will have only system activities and will be fully automatic. Define exception flows to the process where any particular trade that faces an exception in the execution of the process is routed automatically to an appropriate user for manual handling. Define each step of processing as an activity and associate the activity with the appropriate rule in the rule engine. Define all the rule logic in business friendly notation for each of them (e.g., validation rules, accept/reject rules, data addition) as a separate rule in the rules engine (one rule for each of these steps) and maintain them there. Rule engine gives the flexibility for the rules. Include activities into this process for the transactions to be done by other back-end systems and define the flow including that. Specify the routing logic as process level rules (decision points) in the process to take care of routing the trade being processed to the right back-end system activity for transaction processing. All this makes the process flexible and explicit in the new trade platform. This also enables reuse of the process in some ways for other processing services of the brokerage firm.

Make the process get triggered upon the arrival of each file with trade data from the external system. Use a BPMS for handling the processes. There can be an overall process instance initiated for a batch of trades (one file) and one individual process instance for each trade record in the file—thus the trades can be processed concurrently by running these individual process instances concurrently in the BPMS process engine. This improves the efficiency (performance) of the system, given the volumes to be handled. As an add-on benefit, the system would also support easy monitoring of the process by managers because of the process-centricity and usage of BPMS.

12.5.1.5 Workflow Application

The design situation may be something like this:

A new workflow application needs to be built. Or it may read "build a task approval and/or reject workflow for business users with a dashboard"

Approach
Consider this as a requirement for a process-centric architecture-based system and not just a web application that would support a specific workflow. The difference in philosophy here is, while we are going to use the new system to support the specific workflow at hand, the architecture and the components might come useful for other processes as well. And, this change of philosophy does not mean overheads, or additional effort or trading off any thing. The best approach would be: to pick up a suitable BPMS; understand the workflow and model a business process for it while also considering any P2A or A2P flows that are part of it; design activity services such that thought is also given to the potential reuse (applicability) of them in other processes—some part flows, such as application/document submission and approval could very well be common across multiple workflows; provide the right granularity to the activities so that the process does not reduce to just a taskflow that goes screen by screen; let the process run on the BPMS and allow the BPMS to take care of routing work from one user to another as per the process definition; you can use the BPMS provided user interfaces (user dashboard) for letting the users see their work items and work on those; alerts and notifications related to assigned work items are typically supported by BPMS directly; let the BPMS integrate with the identity management systems (user directories such as LDAP, active directory to name a few) for authentication related to user working on their work items through this system.

12.5.1.6 Third-Party Data Integration

The design situation may be something like this:

To enable business collaboration between your enterprise and its business partners there is a requirement for data sharing.

Approach
One of the options readily thought of is to integrate the data of these two organizations by exchanging data from one to another. For this, data integration approaches such as FTP, EDI, or domain specific standard transfer mechanisms are explored, that primarily focus on batch data transfer. The better approach instead, in this situation is to explore a process-centric solution and through that a real-time integration. We are actually integrating not data but the business processes of two enterprises here. Explore if the partner enterprise can expose (or already exposes) a service (for the partner's process) based on SOA principles that can be invoked by your enterprise for interacting with the partner's business process. The service can be realized by the partner as a web service for interoperability. Then, have the business process of your enterprise supported by systems based on PCA. In that process, have an activity, at the right point in the flow that would invoke the service exposed by the partner. And, if your process demands, have another activity down the line to receive the message from the partner that the partner sends after the partner process is completed.

12.5.1.7 Business Activity Monitoring Application

The design situation may be something like this:

Your enterprise requires a business activity monitoring (BAM) tool (build or buy) that would provide management with snapshot of the business. There are a number of applications (say 20) in the enterprise and the tool would need to be used by all the applications to enable their business activity to be available for management view.

Approach

One way is to build or buy such a tool and then change all the applications to send their business information to the tool following the tool's requirements. This amounts to huge data transfer and could result in redundancy and inconsistency in data. Moreover, the information displayed to the management in the dashboard may not be real time and not correlated properly to processes but rather to functions alone. Another way, which is more effective, is to adopt BPM and move the applications in a phased manner to PCA. Use a BPMS as the process platform for the business processes associated with the applications. As and when applications get migrated to BPM, use BAM capabilities provided by the BPMS for displaying the data to management in the formats they prefer, for those applications too. This would be a more holistic process-based view of the business activities of the enterprise and the BAM component of the BPMS can also send alerts based on events that need attention of the management such as slippages in process deadlines. All the data would not need to be specially sent by the applications to the BAM component—so there is no code change required in them for this purpose. The BPMS automatically would have the required data since it drives the execution of processes.

12.5.1.8 Splitting the Responsibilities between the Specific Application and the Process Layer/BPMS

The design situation may be something like this:

You are using a BPMS and want to realize a process through an application to be architected on PCA. How would you take the design decision of which of the activities in the process are to be performed by the specific application that you are going to build and which ones need to be performed by the BPMS? The process we have at hand is the leave application where an employee applies for leave, their manager logs in and gets the list of leave applications to approve, the manager then approves or rejects the particular leave application, status of the leave application changes to approved or rejected, for an approved leave application appropriate number days get deducted from the leave balance for the employee.

Approach

The best way to split the responsibilities between BPMS and the specific application is to take a process focused view and use the BPMS as a technology enabler of that. Lay out the process concerned with the sequence of activities. From the activities of the process, identify the ones that are manual (i.e., those that are performed by humans with the use of an application provided user interface (GUI)) and ones that system (i.e., those that are performed by system without any manual intervention). In this case, the possible manual activities are: Employee applying for leave, and manager approving leave. The system activities would be: Deduct number of leaves from the employees leave balance. Changing status to approved or rejected with reasons are not system activities or separate activities and they are part of the approve activity of the manager. That activity should update the status and the reason.

Then for each manual activity, one or more GUI screens would need to be designed and an application that would be providing these screens needs to be designed if not already there. We need not have one GUI application for each manual activity. One GUI application for leave that can present the user screen to the employee and the approval screen to the manger is fine in this case as the manual activities still fall within the business functionality scope of the leave application.

For each system activity, consider the activity as supported by a service. For example, deducting from leave balance can be seen by us as one service, provided by a leave service package. In other words, deducting from leave balance would be one operation provided by the leave service package. Design the service interface to take in the leave details like employee number, number of days leave requested, etc. as input and return "OK" as return parameter. Implement the service as a business component (ideally as a web service or EJB or .Net component). Map the values from the previous activities to the input parameters of this service. For example, number of leave days requested parameter value comes from the first manual activity's (apply leave) output. Map this parameter to the input parameter number of days leave requested of the system activity. Specify the service details in the process in the BPMS, and the BPMS would invoke the service automatically at runtime.

The other BPM functionalities, such as assigning to the manager, would be typically performed by the BPMS itself and not our specific application.

12.5.1.9 Existing System with a Process Engine

The design situation is as follows:

For your customer, you are required to design an IT system to support a business process P1. However, there is an existing packaged ERP system (bought off-the-shelf) that has a process engine (BPEL engine) with it. The process P1 has some steps in it that involve business functions provided by this ERP system. What options would you consider for the realization of the process infrastructure?

Approach

First, the process P1 needs to be designed keeping in mind only its own business objectives and key performance indicators. Then for those activities in the process that perform the business functions that the ERP system provides, design the service interface as a wrapper over the APIs provided by the ERP system for those business functions, since the customer has already made investments in the ERP system. It is best to evaluate the process engine that is part of the ERP system to see if it can suit process P1. That is, can it support the process flows defined in P1? Does it suit the needs of the process P1 such as process monitoring, inter-process communication, executing activities that invoke services exposed by other applications in the enterprise that might be in heterogeneous technologies? Will it support the performance and reliability requirements of this process P1? Also ask questions related to the IT strategy and vision—Does the organization have a vision of using a single BPMS product for the entire enterprise (i.e., all the processes)? Does it have a good number of packaged applications in the ecosystem? Do those applications have own BPM engines? Or is the vision one that accommodates the coexistence of multiple BPM engines in the enterprise, given that there might be varying process requirements across the enterprise? What are the cost considerations?

If this evaluation gives right justification, choose to implement the process P1 using the BPEL engine provided by it. Deploy it onto that BPEL engine and let the BPEL engine orchestrate and manage the process. The invocation of the business functions that the ERP system provides would now become native calls in the process.

If the customer's IT strategy mandates the use of the BPEL engine provided in the ERP system, then depending on this evaluation above (suitability for P1), modify the process P1 definition (and design) appropriately to suit the support possible in the BPEL engine provided by ERP system. This might also necessitate changing the service interfaces or creating custom interfaces for other activities in P1 to suit invocation from the ERP system's BPEL engine. All this might involve time, effort, and cost. Selecting this option could also mean slightly reduced agility since there is dependency on the capabilities of this BPEL engine.

Depending on the evaluation, one option could be deciding to go for a separate BPMS product that can generically support the needs of a variety of processes and this can coexist with the BPM engine of the ERP system.

On the other hand, in new enterprises (assuming they would be smaller in size), the best option would be to decide to go with a single BPMS for all the processes in the whole enterprise. This would be beneficial for the future when the organization keeps growing. This option is feasible since everything is being set up from scratch in the organization and the impact of change is less.

12.5.2 Anti-Patterns

Here are some problem situations that are best avoided from getting created.

12.5.2.1 Screen Chaining

Situation

The process is designed and modeled at a wrong level of granularity for the activities. Here process-centric architecture concept is wrongly applied to just achieve chaining of screens from one application or others. Each screen (page) for the user is made a user activity in the business process model. Many of those screens would be just single tasks that are to be performed in combination with other tasks (screens for those tasks) within the same user activity. That is, the screen is a task and it is part of a task flow that is defined for a specific user activity. Task flow being at a level of granularity lower than process activities, should not ideally be made a process itself. Using a BPMS or a process-centric infrastructure for only such a mere screen flow chaining within an application could result in performance overheads, and would provide only minimal benefits related to process-centricity that would not justify the initiative put in.

The right approach here would be to look at a higher level of granularity and model the process with user activities where each user activity is a full logical operation performed by one user in the context of the process. Model the user activity separately as a taskflow. As part of this user activity, the user may be presented with one or more screens that correspond to a task flow. Each screen would correspond to one task in the task flow. The entire activity gets committed in the database only when the user completes action on all the screens for the activity.

12.5.2.2 Huge Data Transfer

Situation

A situation arises when there is a decision taken for creating a new web services application that is to be implemented using JEE. This service is supposed to receive a huge file, as an attachment having a minimum size of 200 MB, from its invokers which could be applications based on any technology platform. This would not be a sound decision and appears to be taken with a very narrow view.

The right approach would be to look beyond the given details. Transferring huge data like this in service calls should ring a bell in the architect's mind. The architect needs to look beyond this specific requirement and ask the question, what is the real motivation for such a mechanism. The answer could most likely be, this application is supposed to be a central place (data store) for all the data belonging to a specific domain or function. And now, that data is spread across other applications and is also redundantly stored in other applications. This service may be meant for transferring this data from the other applications.

Once this is revealed, the architect can design this as a process-centric application by considering the business process involved here. By clear separation of concerns of process logic and application logic, each application would only be expected to own and maintain the business data for its domain. Thus no two applications would end up storing the same business entity's data and there would therefore be no need for huge data transfer between the applications. The process would integrate the application in the context of the process and only the key business data would be used in the process context avoiding any data duplication. For example, in the case of a travel booking process, the booking information can be with the booking application alone and the customer information can be stored and maintained in the customer application (say a CRM package) alone.

12.5.2.3 Batch Integration with Legacy

Situation

In enterprises where there are a good number of legacy systems, especially mainframe-based ones, it is not atypical to find some new applications created for similar (but slightly different) business functions that are otherwise hard to support using legacy systems alone, one of the reasons being the need to use latest technologies to achieve the function. These new systems are built on new technologies but they get all the business data downloaded from the legacy system in batch mode as huge files—either through periodic batch jobs or request-triggered batch jobs running in the mainframe, extracting the data from back-end database managed by the mainframe. This data is read by the new system and stored in its own database, thus resulting in the existence of two parallel systems for the same/similar business function. Other problems with this approach are: applications become redundant; maintenance becomes a major issue—repetitive logic in multiple places; data redundancy and inconsistency, heavy load on the system resources; and time-lag for data visibility in the multiple applications.

Process-driven integration advocated by PCA merits consideration in such situations and helps avoid the problems with batch integration. It would make the business function that needs the data from legacy application get it by invoking a service exposed by the legacy application, as part of an activity in the process. The service can be a service-enabling wrapper over the legacy application, for example. This data will be real-time data, and only that is relevant for the process instance in question—there is no heavy data transfer involved here because this is not batch processing. In the subsequent activity, the associated business component would use the retrieved data and perform the required business logic on it. Also, this retrieved data is not stored in the database separately—it is available just in the process instance. The data remains in only one place—in the legacy system's database.

12.6 Exercise Questions

1. What are some process types that you have come across?
2. Which tools would be best for implementing such processes? And why?
3. Would there be a reason to go with one BPMS for the process layer for the entire enterprise? Identify some of those scenarios.

Bibliography

Abrahams, P. 2004. Business process execution language in brief. IT Analysis. http://www.it-analysis.com/content.php?cid=7086 (accessed August 17, 2008).

Allison, L. Block structured programming languages. Department of Computer Science, University of Western Australia, Western Australia, Australia, and Department of Computer Science, Monash University, Melbourne, Australia. http://www.csse.monash.edu.au/~lloyd/tildeProgLang/PL-Block/ (accessed August 15, 2008).

Arkin, A. 2002. Business process modeling language (BPML). Specification version 1.0. Business Process Management Initiative (BPMI.org). http://www.bpmn.org/Documents/BPML-2003.pdf (accessed August 15, 2008).

Article. 2008. Architectural styles, patterns, and metaphors. Shaping Software. http://shapingsoftware.com/2008/08/10/architectural-styles-patterns-and-metaphors/ (accessed August 15, 2008).

Article. 2009. A quick look at architectural styles and patterns. InfoQ. http://www.infoq.com/news/2009/02/Architectural-Styles-Patterns (accessed August 15, 2008).

Bass, L., Clements, P., and R. Kazman. 2003. *Software Architecture in Practice*. Pearson Education, London, U.K.

Beck, K., Joseph, J., and G. Goldszmidt. 2005. Learn business process modeling basics for the analyst. developerWorks, IBM. https://www.ibm.com/developerworks/library/ws-bpm4analyst/ (accessed August 15, 2008).

BPM. 2007 Conference material. 2007. Accepted papers and material. QUT, BPM 2007. http://bpm07.fit.qut.edu.au/program/index.jsp (accessed August 15, 2008).

BPMI.org, OMG. 2009. BPMN version 1.2. http://www.omg.org/spec/BPMN/1.2/ (accessed March 15, 2009).

Buschmann, F., Meunier, R., Rohnert, H., Sommerlad, P., and M. Stal. 1999. *Pattern-Oriented Software Architecture, Volume 1: A System of Patterns*. Wiley, Chichester, U.K.

Fasbinder, M. 2007. Why model business processes? developerWorks, IBM. http://www.ibm.com/developerworks/websphere/library/techarticles/0705_fasbinder/0705_fasbinder.html (accessed August 15, 2008).

Fielding, R.T. 2000. Architectural styles and the design of network-based software architectures. PhD dissertation, University of California, Irvine, CA. http://www.ics.uci.edu/~fielding/pubs/dissertation/software_arch.htm (accessed August 15, 2008).

Gallagher, B.P. 2000. Using the architecture tradeoff analysis method to evaluate a reference architecture: A case study. Technical Note, SEI, Carnegie Mellon University, Pittsburgh, PA. http://www.sei.cmu.edu/library/abstracts/reports/00tn007.cfm (accessed August 15, 2008).

Green, J. 2008. An implementor's guide to SOA. Westminster Promotions. http://www.soaguidebook.com/chapters.html (accessed December 29, 2008).

Gruchman, G.B. 2009. The process-based view of a company—Principles and applications. Publications, Business Process Trends. http://www.bptrends.com/deliver_file.cfm?fileType=publication&fileName=01-09-ART-Process-BasedViewOfCompany-Guchman.doc-final.pdf (accessed March 3, 2009).

Hall, C. and P. Harmon. 2007. The 2007 enterprise architecture, process modeling and simulation tools report—Version 2.1. A BPT report, Business Process Trends. http://www.bptrends.com/reports_toc_02.cfm (accessed December 17, 2008).

Harmon, P. 2003. *Business Process Change: A Manager's Guide to Improving, Redesigning, and Automating Processes.* Morgan Kaufmann Publishers, Amsterdam, the Netherlands.

Harmon, P. 2003 through 2008. BPTrends Advisors. Publications, Business Process Trends. http://www.bptrends.com/resources_publications.cfm?publicationtypeID=DFFB3CC2-1031-D522-39E0E13C84A1F076 (accessed August 15, 2008).

Havey, M. 2005. *Essential Business Process Modeling.* O'Reilly Media, Sebastopol, CA.

IBM, BEA Systems, Microsoft, SAP AG, Siebel Systems. 2002. Business process execution language (WS-BPEL) specs v 1.1. developerWorks, IBM. http://www.ibm.com/developerworks/library/specification/ws-bpel/ (accessed August 15, 2008).

Information Age Feature. 2006. The assimilation of BPM. Information Age. http://www.information-age.com/channels/business-applications/features/287051/the-assimilation-of-bpm.thtml (accessed December 17, 2008).

Jeston, J. and J. Nelis. 2006. *Business Process Management: Practical Guidelines to Successful Implementations.* Elsevier Limited, Oxford, U.K.

Khan, R.N. 2004. *Business Process Management: A Practical Guide.* Meghan-Kiffer Press, Tampa, FL.

Kopp, O., Martin, D., Wutke, D., and F. Leymann. 2008. On the choice between graph-based and block-structured business process modeling languages. *Lecture Notes in Informatics (LNI), Choice08*:59–72. http://www.iaas.uni-stuttgart.de/institut/mitarbeiter/kopp/INPROC-2008-92%20-%20graph-based-vs-block-structured-modeling–mobis08.pdf (accessed August 15, 2008).

Lublinsky, B. and M. Rosen. 2005. Enterprise integration architecture and web services. *Cutter Consortium Enterprise Architecture Executive Report* 5:11.

Meservy, T.O. and K.D. Fenstermacher. 2005. Transforming software development: An MDA roadmap. *IEEE Computer* 38:52–58.

Miers, D., Harmon, P., and C. Hall. 2007. The 2007 BPM suites report—Version 2.1. A BPT report, Business Process Trends. http://www.bptrends.com/reports_toc_01.cfm (accessed December 17, 2008).

Milner, R. 1999. *Communicating and Mobile Systems: The Pi-Calculus.* Cambridge University Press, Cambridge, U.K.

Muehlen, M.Z. 2007. BPM standards tutorial. BPM Research. http://www.bpm-research.com/2007/09/27/bpm-standards-tutorial/ (accessed August 15, 2008).

Muller, G. 2008. A reference architecture primer. Gaudí project. http://www.gaudisite.nl/ReferenceArchitecturePrimerPaper.pdf (accessed August 15, 2008).

OASIS WSBPEL TC. 2007. Web services business process execution language (WS-BPEL). Version 2.0. http://docs.oasis-open.org/wsbpel/2.0/OS/wsbpel-v2.0-OS.html (accessed August 15, 2008).

OMG. 2006. The OMG and service oriented architecture. Object Management Group. http://www.omg.org/attachments/pdf/OMG-and-the-SOA.pdf (accessed December 17, 2008).

Ould, M.A. 2005. *Business Process Management: A Rigorous Approach.* The British Computer Society, Meghan-Kiffer Press, Tampa, FL.

Pucella, R. 2000. Review of communicating and mobile systems: The π-calculus. Northeastern's College of Computer and Information Science, Boston, MA. http://www.ccs.neu.edu/home/riccardo/papers/milner-pi-calc.pdf (accessed August 15, 2008).

Rosen, M. 2006a. BPM and SOA: What kind of service does a business process need? Business Process Trends. http://www.bptrends.com/deliver_file.cfm?fileType=publication&fileName=07%2D06COL%2DWhatServiceDoesABPNeed%2DRosen%2Epdf (accessed December 17, 2008).

Rosen, M. 2006b. BPM and SOA: Where does one end and the other begin? Business Process Trends. http://www.bptrends.com/deliver_file.cfm?fileType=publication&fileName=01%2D06%20COL%20SOA%20%2DWhere%20Does%20One%20End%20%2D%20Rosen%2Epdf (accessed December 17, 2008).

Russell, N., ter Hofstede, A.H.M., Edmond, D., and W.M.P. van der Aalst. 2004. Workflow resource patterns. Workflow Patterns Site. http://www.workflowpatterns.com/patterns/resource/ (accessed August 15, 2008).

Schmidt, D., Stal, M., Rohnert, H., and F. Buschmann. 2000. *Pattern-Oriented Software Architecture, Volume 2: Patterns for Concurrent and Networked Objects.* Wiley, Chichester, U.K.

Schreiner, W. 1997. Languages with contexts I: A block-structured language. Research Institute for Symbolic Computation, Johannes Kepler University, Linz, Austria. http://www.risc.uni-linz.ac.at/education/courses/ws97/densem/context1/ (accessed August 15, 2008).

Seshan, P. 2006a. SOA and BPM: Complementary concepts for agility. SETLabs Briefings. http://www.infosys.com/research/publications/SETLabs-briefings-SOA.pdf (accessed August 15, 2008).

Seshan, P. 2006b. A generic JMS listener for Apache Axis 1.x. *Java Developer Journal.* http://java.sys-con.com/node/260046 (accessed August 15, 2008).

Seshan, P. and S. Goel. 2006a. Web services integration patterns for Java applications using open source frameworks, Part 1: Implementing invoke patterns. developerWorks, IBM. http://www.ibm.com/developerworks/java/library/ws-pattern-open1.html (accessed August 15, 2008).

Seshan, P. and S. Goel. 2006b. Web services integration patterns for Java applications using open source frameworks, Part 2: Implementing receive patterns. developerWorks, IBM. http://www.ibm.com/developerworks/webservices/library/ws-pattern-open2.html (accessed August 15, 2008).

Silver, B. 2005a. BPMS Watch: BPM and SOA: One technology, two communities. BPM Institute. http://www.bpminstitute.org/articles/article/article/bpms-watch-bpm-and-soa-one-technology-two-communities.html (accessed December 17, 2008).

Silver, B. 2005b. Standards and the process lifecycle. BPM Institute. http://www.bpminstitute.org/articles/article/article/standards-and-the-process-lifecycle (accessed August 15, 2008).

Smith, H. and P. Fingar. 2003. *Business Process Management—The Third Wave.* Meghan-Kiffer Press, Tampa, FL.

Stefansen, C., Rajamani, S.K., and P. Seshan. 2008a. A work allocation language with soft constraints. *CAiSE Forum* 2008: 85–88.

Stefansen, C., Rajamani, S.K., and P. Seshan. 2008b. SoftAlloc: A work allocation language with soft constraints. *ICWS* 2008: 441–448.

Web document. 2008. ISO 9126 Software Quality Characteristics. http://www.sqa.net/iso9126.html (accessed August 15, 2008).

Weske, M. 2007. *Business Process Management: Concepts, Languages, Architectures*. Springer, Berlin, Germany.

White, S.A. 2009. Introduction to BPMN. OMG. http://www.bpmn.org/Documents/Introduction%20to%20BPMN.pdf (accessed March 15, 2009).

Index

Q

R

S

T

U